The Best of
Reader's Digest
Timeless
Favorites

**Reader's
Digest**

New York / Montreal

Contents

Introduction

From the quiet heroism of a widow learning to forgive her husband's killer to the desperate struggles of a family facing down a ferocious storm, the enthralling tales gathered in this volume reflect the universal nature of the human condition. For more than a century, *Reader's Digest* has been sharing stories of small miracles, unlikely friendships, steadfast courage and enduring love—stories that transcend time and place.

Within these pages, you'll find some of our most memorable narratives. You'll thrill to the dramatic account of the pilot who was sucked out the window of an airplane at 17,000 feet—and survived; laugh and cry at the touching story of the parrot who became an old woman's sometimes-inappropriate companion; and chuckle sympathetically at the hilarious high jinks that ensue when a father tries to teach his college-age sons fiscal responsibility.

Running the gamut from dramatic to humorous, poignant to piquant, *The Best of Reader's Digest: Timeless Favorites* will remind you of the essential goodness and incredible gallantry of the human spirit.

Happy reading!

—The Editors of *Reader's Digest*

The Best Investment I Ever Made

The doctor and novelist learns the true value of a second chance.

—

BY **A. J. CRONIN**

Originally published in March 1951

On the second day out from New York, while making the round of the promenade deck, I became aware that one of the other passengers was watching me closely, following me with his gaze every time I passed, his eyes filled with a queer, almost pathetic intensity.

I have crossed the Atlantic many times. And on this occasion, tired after a prolonged piece of work, I wanted to rest, to avoid the tedium of casual and importunate shipboard contacts. I gave no sign of having noticed the man.

Yet there was nothing importunate about him. On the contrary, he seemed affected by a troubled, rather touching diffidence. He was in his early 40s, I judged—out of the corner of my eye—rather short in build, with a fair complexion, a good forehead from which his thin hair had begun to recede, and clear blue eyes. His dark suit, sober tie and rimless spectacles gave evidence of a reserved disposition.

At this point the bugle sounded for dinner and I went below. On the following day, I again observed my fellow voyager watching me earnestly from his deck chair.

Now a lady was with him,

1

obviously his wife. She was about his age, quiet and restrained, with brown eyes and slightly faded brown hair, dressed in a gray skirt and gray woolen cardigan.

The situation by this time had begun to intrigue me and from my steward I discovered that they were Mr. and Mrs. John S., from a small suburb of London. Yet when another day passed without event,

He took a sharp breath and exclaimed, "So you still do not remember me?"

I began to feel certain that Mr. S. would remain too shy to carry out his obvious desire to approach me. However, on our final evening at sea Mrs. S. decided the matter. With a firm pressure on his arm and a whispered word in his ear, she urged her husband toward me as I passed along the deck.

"Excuse me, Doctor. I wonder if I might introduce myself." He spoke almost breathlessly, offering me the visiting card that he held in his hand and studying my face to see if the name meant anything to me. Then, as it plainly did not, he went on with the same awkwardness. "If you could spare a few minutes … my wife and I would so like to have a word with you."

A moment later I was occupying the vacant chair beside them. Haltingly he told me that this had been their first visit to America. It was not entirely a holiday trip. They had been making a tour of the New England states, inspecting many of the summer recreational camps provided for young people there. Afterward, they had visited settlement houses in New York and other cities to study the methods employed in dealing with youth groups, especially backward, maladjusted and delinquent cases.

There was in his voice and manner, indeed in his whole personality, a genuine enthusiasm that was disarming. I found myself liking him instinctively. Questioning him further, I learned that he and his wife had been active for the past 15 years in the field of youth welfare. By profession, he was a solicitor but, in addition to his practice at the courts, found time to act as director of a charitable organization devoted to the care of boys and girls, mostly from city slums, who had fallen under the ban of the law.

As he spoke with real feeling, I got a vivid picture of the work that these two people were doing—how they took derelict adolescents from the juvenile courts and, placing them in a healthy environment, healed them in mind and body, then sent them back into the world, trained in a useful handicraft and fit to take their place as worthy members of the community.

It was a work of redemption that stirred the heart, and I asked what had directed his life into this channel. The question had a strange effect upon him; he took a sharp breath and exclaimed, "So you still do not remember me?"

I shook my head; to the best of my belief I had never in my life seen him before.

"I've wanted to get in touch with you for many years," he went on, under increasing stress. "But I was never able to bring myself to do so." Then, bending near, he spoke a few words, tensely, in my ear. At that, slowly, the veils parted, my thoughts sped back a quarter of a century and, with a start, I remembered the sole occasion when I had seen this man before.

I was a young doctor at the time and had just set up in practice in a working-class district of London. On a foggy November night, toward one o'clock, I was awakened by a loud banging at the door. In those days of economic necessity any call, even at this unearthly hour, was a welcome one. Hurriedly, I threw on some clothes, went downstairs. It was a sergeant of police, in dripping helmet and cape, mistily outlined on the doorstep. A suicide case, he told me abruptly, in the lodgings round the corner— I had better come at once.

Outside it was raw and damp, the traffic stilled, the street deserted, quiet as the tomb. We walked the short distance in silence, even our footsteps muffled by the fog, and turned into the narrow entrance of an old building.

As we mounted the creaking staircase, my nostrils were stung by the sick-sweet odor of illuminating gas. On the upper story the agitated landlady showed us to a bare little attic where, stretched on a narrow bed, lay the body of a young man.

Although apparently lifeless, there remained the barest chance that the youth was not quite beyond recall. With the sergeant's help, I began the work of resuscitation. For an entire hour we labored without success. A further 15 minutes and, despite our most strenuous exertions, it appeared useless. Then, as we were about to give up, completely exhausted, there broke from the patient a shallow, convulsive gasp. It was like a resurrection from the grave, a miracle, this stirring of life under our hands. Half an hour of redoubled efforts and we had the youth sitting up, gazing at us dazedly and, alas, slowly realizing the horror of his situation.

He was a round-cheeked lad, with a simple, countrified air, and the story that he told us as he slowly regained strength in the bleak morning hours was simple, too. His parents were dead. An uncle in the provinces, anxious, no doubt, to be rid of an unwanted responsibility, had found him a position as clerk in a London solicitor's office. He had been in the city only six months. Utterly friendless, he had fallen victim to the loose society of the streets, had made bad companions, and like a young fool, eager to taste pleasures far beyond his means, had begun to bet on horses. Soon he had lost all his small savings, had pledged his belongings and owed the bookmaker a disastrous amount. In an effort to recoup, he had taken a sum of money from the office safe for a final gamble that he was assured was certain to win. But this last resort had failed. Terrified of the prosecution that must follow, sick at heart, sunk in despair, he had shut himself in his room and turned on the gas.

A long bar of silence throbbed in the little attic when he concluded this halting confession. Then, gruffly, the sergeant asked how much he had stolen. Pitifully, almost, the answer came: seven pounds ten shillings. Yes, incredible though it seemed, for this paltry sum this poor misguided lad had almost thrown away his life.

Again there came a pause in which, plainly, the same unspoken thought was uppermost in the minds of the three of us who were the sole witnesses of this near tragedy. Almost of one accord, we voiced our desire to give the youth—whose defenseless nature rather than any vicious tendencies had brought him to this extremity—a fresh start. The sergeant, at considerable risk to his job, resolved to make no report upon the case, so that no court proceedings would result. The landlady offered a month's free board until he should get upon his feet again. While I, making perhaps the least contribution, came forward with seven pounds ten shillings for him to put back in the office safe.

❖   ❖   ❖

The ship moved on through the still darkness of the night. There was no need of speech. With a tender gesture Mrs. S. had taken her husband's hand. And as we sat in silence, hearing the sounding of the sea and the sighing of the breeze, a singular emotion overcame me. I could not but reflect that, against all the bad investments I had made throughout the years—those foolish speculations for material gain, only producing anxiety, disappointment and frustration—here at last was one I need not regret, one that had paid no dividends in worldly goods, yet which might stand, nevertheless, on the profit side, in the final reckoning.

A Mountain of Trouble

A backpacking trip turns disastrous, and a boy must make a heartrending decision: Should he leave his severely injured father to look for help?

—

BY **KENNETH MILLER**

Originally published in October 2016

The Frank Church–River of No Return Wilderness is the broadest sprawl of untamed landscape in the contiguous United States, covering 2.4 million acres of central Idaho. Among the area's most spectacular attractions is the Bighorn Crags, a jagged phalanx of 10,000-foot peaks set amid glittering alpine lakes. Near one of those pools, just after dawn on a cloudless summer day, 13-year-old Charlie Finlayson crouches inside his tent, getting ready for a long hike. He stows a water bottle and some snacks in his day pack, along with a sleeping bag, in case he has to bivouac.

He leaves another water bottle for his father, David; fills the cooking pot to the brim with water from the creek; and also sets out

David Finlayson snapped this photo of his son, Charlie, in the Bighorn Crags shortly before they attempted their most complex climb.

a week's supply of energy bars. Then he takes a GPS reading of the campsite.

He turns to David, who lies pale and gaunt in a bloodstained bedroll, his forehead marked with a gash, his jaw clenched in pain, his leg bandaged. "I'd better get moving," Charlie tells him.

"Good luck, kiddo," David says quietly. "Just take it slow and steady."

Outside the tent, Charlie pauses and mumbles a prayer. "I'm not coming back without a helicopter," he calls over his shoulder as he sets off.

At 52, David Finlayson had already explored many of the world's wild spaces, bagging major summits in Alaska, Europe and South America. David, a respected defense attorney, had split up with Charlie's mom shortly after Charlie was born. The boy lived with his mother in a suburb of Boise, Idaho, but spent most summers with his father. Although Charlie was as calm and contemplative as his dad was voluble and restless—David

called him the Zen master and Good-Time Charlie—both were passionate about nature. When Charlie reached seventh grade, David introduced him to rock climbing.

By the time they set out for the Bighorn Crags in August 2015, Charlie was ready to take on complex climbs. They crammed their packs with enough supplies to last two weeks. After driving six hours from Boise, they hiked for two days to reach Ship Island Lake, a mile-long jewel shadowed by a gallery of pinnacles. In their first week, they did two long climbs.

Their next ascent began on a Monday morning. Around noon, David was inching his way across a granite spire 800 feet above the valley floor, searching for a line of cracks that would lead them to the top. Charlie stood on a ledge a dozen yards to the right, lashed to a tree for safety as he fed rope to his dad. Reaching up, David dislodged a small stone, which tumbled off into the void. In the next moment, he heard a sharp crack from above as something larger broke loose. He barely had time to scream before everything went black.

When Charlie saw his father sailing through the air alongside the massive boulder that had struck him, he yanked on the rope. An instant later, an automatic braking device arrested the fall.

"Dad!" he called. "Are you OK?"

There was no answer.

❖ ❖ ❖

Charlie's destination is the trailhead, 12 miles away, where a couple of volunteers live in a cabin equipped with a two-way radio, which he hopes they'll use to call for help for his dad. The path rises gently at first, but he knows it will grow steeper, reaching 9,400 feet before plunging into a valley and climbing again. It will branch off into poorly marked side trails that can lead a traveler astray. Grizzlies and mountain lions frequent the surrounding woods; as he walks, Charlie blows his emergency whistle to ward them off.

After a mile, the route meets a trail to another lake. Following David's instructions, Charlie takes

"Charlie and I are alike," says David. "We both love to be out there away from everybody."

the detour, hollering to anyone who might be camped there. After a few hundred yards, however, he stops to calculate the odds: It's a weekday, when visitors are sparse. If he continues and encounters no one, he'll have thrown away an hour. He mutters a cussword and hurries back to the main trail.

❖ ❖ ❖

David hung 40 feet below his son, each hidden from the other's view. A minute passed before he managed to

"I had two fears," Charlie says about his hike to get help. "Being alone and facing my fears alone."

call out, "Charlie, are you there?"

"I'm here! Are you hurt?"

Beneath David's dented helmet, his head was throbbing from a concussion. His left arm and foot were shattered, the shinbone protruded through the skin, and blood was dripping onto the rocks below. A vertebra in his upper back was fractured. The pain came from so many places that it nearly knocked him out again.

"I think I've broken some bones," he shouted.

"What do I do? What do I do?" Charlie sounded frantic.

"Can you lower me about 20 feet? There's a ledge there."

Charlie let the rope play out slowly. When David reached the ledge, he yelled for his son to lower his climbing pack, which held a first aid kit. But Charlie was still anchored to a large pine tree, and the pack kept getting stuck in the branches. After readjusting the anchor, Charlie managed to land the pack perfectly.

With his right hand, David slathered his leg wound with antibiotic cream, covered it with gauze compresses and began wrapping it in athletic tape. He felt detached from his own body, as if it belonged to someone else, but he didn't want Charlie to have to see the jutting bone. Once it was covered up, he called for the boy to rappel down and join him, shouting instructions all the way. When Charlie arrived, the two of them added more tape and tightened it as best they could. "Tell me it's going to be OK," Charlie pleaded, struggling to control his fear.

"It's going to be OK," David told him, trying to believe it. "But we need to get off this mountain." He proposed a plan: Charlie would lower David half a rope length at a time, then lower himself to the same level, set a new anchor and begin again.

Although the pulley system enabled the 90-pound child to bear the weight of a 190-pound man, the process proved agonizing for both of them. David was dizzy and nauseated, and whenever his left side touched the cliff face, the pain was almost unendurable. With each pitch, he had to hammer a piton one-handed into the rock, and Charlie had to untangle 50 yards of rope and thread it through the anchor. As the hours passed, David fought to remain conscious. "If I pass out," he said, "don't stick around. Hike back up the trail as fast as you can."

"You won't pass out," Charlie assured his father, and himself. "We're going to make it."

Charlie's hike grows more strenuous as the trail climbs toward the pass. As his heart rate rises, so does his anxiety level. Images flit through his mind: Dad writhing in agony, Dad's eyes rolling back in his head. He focuses instead on the rhythm of his footsteps. Around the three-mile mark, he thinks he hears voices. He gives a blast on the whistle and shouts, "Hello! Can you help me?" Someone yells back, "Sure!"

Sprinting up the switchbacks, the boy encounters two tall, stubble-faced men on their way down— Jon Craig and his 19-year-old son, Jonathan. Choking back tears, Charlie describes his father's plight to the pair. He shows them the campsite marker on his GPS.

The Craigs debate whether to turn around and accompany Charlie or forge on to find his father. "Please go to him," Charlie says, insistent but calm.

"There are three groups camping by Airplane Lake in the next valley," Jon tells Charlie, circling the location on his map. "They can help you get where you need to be." The two men disappear down the trail.

After cresting the pass, Charlie takes the side route toward the lake. His heart sinks as he realizes that none of the groups is there anymore.

It was nearly dusk by the time the excruciating rappelling and belaying finally delivered David and Charlie to the base of the cliff, and the temperature had dropped into the 40s. In his shorts and light Gore-Tex jacket, David was shaking with cold and exhaustion. "That's enough for today," he said. "You'll have to go get our sleeping bags so we don't freeze to death."

Their gear was in their tent, more than a mile down a steep slope covered with scree and boulders. Charlie took off running. He grabbed the sleeping bags and stuffed a backpack with warm clothes and energy bars. Realizing they would need water too, he used his filter pump to fill several bottles from the lake. By the time he found his way back through the boulder field, night had fallen.

David saw a pinpoint of light— his son's headlamp—floating toward him through the blackness. "Good-Time Charlie!" he exclaimed through chattering teeth. After helping David into long pants and a down parka, Charlie zipped him into a sleeping bag. He propped the injured leg on a rock to slow the bleeding. He made sure his father ate some dinner. Then he crawled into his own bag.

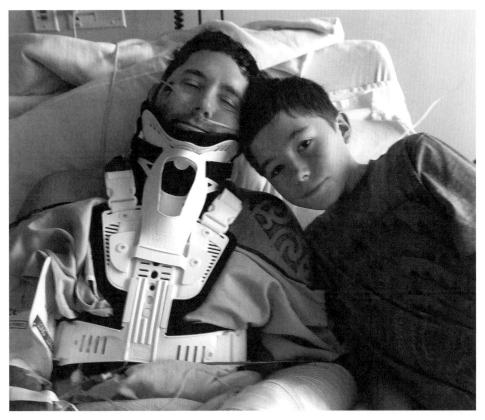

David and Charlie, in the hospital just days after the accident, have plans to go rock climbing together again.

Worried that David would die if he fell asleep, Charlie kept the conversation going; they talked about past travels, the constellations overhead, the accident. Eventually Charlie allowed himself to catnap, checking on his father each time he awoke.

David, however, was in too much pain to drift off. He tried to distract himself by counting breaths. But breathing hurt, so he counted stars.

There was a chance he'd survive, he thought. There was also a good chance he wouldn't. And then what would happen to the kid?

He kept counting.

On the trail, Charlie hears more voices off in the distance. He blows his whistle and calls out, and the voices answer. Following his ears, Charlie gropes his way through the pines to a different pond, half a mile away. There, he stumbles upon a married couple, their three kids, and a family friend, Mike Burt. Hearing the urgency in Charlie's voice, Mike, a former Marine, offers to run the demanding nine miles to the volunteers' cabin, where he hopes to call in medical aid for David. Charlie follows him to make sure help is indeed coming.

When the sun rose on their camp, Charlie was relieved to see that his father was awake and alert. But the mile-wide cordon of boulders, many as big as cars, was a far less welcome sight. The pair huddled in their sleeping bags for an hour or two, until the chill lifted. "Let's go, Dad," Charlie said. "This could take some time."

After wrapping more tape around the blood-soaked bandage on David's leg, they started down the slope. David dragged himself through the obstacle course inch by inch, leaving a trail of red. When he couldn't maneuver between the rocks, he hauled himself over them, crawling up one side and sliding down the other. Sometimes he lost control, landing on one of his shattered limbs and blacking out briefly from the pain. He woke each time with Charlie's tense face looming over him. "I'm fine," David would say, attempting to smile. The boy ran ahead periodically, scouting for the least torturous path, then trotted back to offer guidance. "Just another foot," he coaxed. "Just a few inches."

They reached their campsite around 4 p.m. David plunged his leg into the lake to clean it, and Charlie—unfazed by the gore—covered it with a new dressing.

Toward evening, Charlie cooked dinner on the propane stove. He wolfed down his portions of pepper steak and chicken teriyaki, but his father was too nauseated to eat more than a few bites.

"Charlie," David said, "you're going to have to go look for help in the morning."

Picturing himself separated from his father by vast tracts of wilderness, Charlie burst into tears. "What if I never see you again?" he wailed.

"I'm sorry, kiddo," David said. "We don't have a choice."

That night, Charlie slept with his arms around his dad. David stared out through the tent's mesh window, counting stars.

Just after dawn, Charlie lifted his pack onto his back and headed off on the trail toward the volunteers' cabin 12 miles away, hell-bent on bringing back a helicopter that would carry his father to safety.

Sometime that evening, David Finlayson awakes in traction. He is at Saint Alphonsus Hospital in Boise, where doctors immobilize his arm and leg and stabilize his spine with a brace. Over the coming months, he will undergo several major surgeries and will eventually be able to climb again. But on this night, through the morphine glow, he tries to remember his rescue.

He recalls the Craigs arriving at his campsite. When they told him they'd just spoken with Charlie, he forgot his pain; he wanted to get up and dance. A young ranger named Rachel (dispatched after Mike Burt reached the volunteers' cabin) showed up soon afterward. She kept David company until he was strapped into a harness and lifted by a cable into a hovering helicopter.

The next day, Charlie arrives at David's bedside. Through the tangle of ropes that are IV drips, father and son hug. Good-Time Charlie, the Zen master, had kept his promise. He brought back a helicopter.

"Charlie's as strong as anyone I know," says his father. "People say, 'You must be so proud of him.' They have no idea."

Let Me Explain ...

I know it may seem odd
but, you see, it's like this ...

—

BY **CORNELIA OTIS SKINNER**

Originally published in August 1963

Robert Benchley used to say that there are two kinds of people: those who think there are two kinds of people and those who don't. I'm in the first class. I *know* there are two kinds of people. There are those who do and those who explain. Here I'm in the second class. I am among those who must give elaborate explanations of whatever they do, whether anybody cares or not.

If character traits are inherited, this one must come directly from my mother. Father was a dashing and dramatically brusque non-explainer. Mother was a gentle and completely adorable explainer. Whenever the family traveled, Father conducted our tours in the manner of a benevolent conquering hero, treating all porters, cabdrivers and waiters as vassals whose duty was to serve, not to fraternize. Mother would tread lightly in his magnificent wake, cooing explanations to Father's baffled henchmen.

During World War I, as a voluntary form of food rationing, if you wanted bread with any meal in a restaurant, you had to order it as an extra item. I recall one mortifying moment in a Chicago hotel when the headwaiter, all agog over serving my famous parent, inquired solicitously if we'd care for bread. Father, who at the time was being splendidly patriotic, bellowed an indignant "Certainly not!" I was about to crawl under the table when Mother came blessedly to the rescue. Looking up with her most shimmering smile, she said, "We're not a bread-eating family, you see."

Mother's practice must have set me off on a habit. To this day I not only explain any unusual activity on my part, I also explain the most obvious. If, of a morning, attired in a venerable wrapper, with hair done up in rollers, I slip furtively out into the corridor to drop a letter down the mail chute and run bang into the good-looking young man who lives in the apartment across the way, I say with a nervous giggle as I slip the envelope into the slot, "Oh, I'm just mailing a letter."

If I come home late at night and discover that I haven't got my key and have to send the elevator man for the building passkey, instead of accepting the service with a simple thank-you, I go into an involved sequence on how I'd changed the contents of my daytime bag to an evening one and then decided to switch to this one because the first didn't go with my dress and how usually I am pretty reliable …

I even explain to those trained experts of terseness, telephone operators. Not long ago I had occasion to call friends in Arizona. The head of the household is a former physician. I knew only the address, so I asked the operator to give me Tucson information for the phone number of Dr. X. She inquired if I'd be wanting Dr. X's home or office number. "He won't have an office number because he's not practicing anymore." The operator said nothing in response. "He's retired," I went on. It must have been her continued silence that goaded me into saying, "He's moved out to Arizona for his health," and she mercifully cut me off before I could continue with "He's an asthma sufferer."

Explanations can be awkwardly misleading at times. When I travel overnight on a train that is to arrive at my destination early in the morning, I forfeit no precious sleep by rising before arrival for matutinal ablutions in the washbasin. I wait until I get to my hotel room and spring into a hot tub.

All of which routine I am likely to explain in detail to the Pullman porter, hoping to avert his incredulity when I tell him I require only a 15-minute call. One porter's look changed from disbelief to downright repugnance when I began my explanation with a bright "You see, I never wash …" He walked shudderingly away before I could complete the sentence "… until I reach my hotel."

Some actions would be better left unexplained. A certain friend and I, in a spirit of somewhat distorted humor, have for years exchanged what we call "horror presents"— art objects such as burnt-leather portraits of Hiawatha or bronze Venus de Milos with clocks on their stomachs. It is a childish but harmless whim.

For me the only drawback is the purchase of the present. If I see in a junk-shop window a framed nocturne of Lake Como hand-painted on velvet with the moon of genuine mother-of-pearl, I can't merely walk in and buy it. I have to tell the shopkeeper that my taste doesn't normally manifest itself in this fashion but that I want to send this monstrosity to a friend as a joke. The shopkeeper, who in all likelihood considers the object a rare work of art, is justifiably offended.

Men seldom explain; women, almost always. Yet the most effective non-explainer I know is a woman. Not long ago her daughter phoned her in despair to say that the person she and her husband had engaged to help at a cocktail party that evening had sent notice of inability to show up. My friend told her daughter not to worry, that she herself would be glad to pinch-hit. By way of a lark, she decided to turn up dressed as a maid, and hurried down to buy a uniform.

My friend is blessed with considerable means. She was wearing a sable jacket, a string of genuine pearls encircled her neck, and on the front of her dress sparkled a pair of magnificent diamond clips. She went directly to the domestic-uniform department, and the saleswoman brought out a variety of uniforms in the specified size. My friend selected one and also picked out an apron and that almost-extinct accessory, a wispy maid's cap. The saleswoman asked if it would be a charge-and-send. My friend said no, she wanted to try the things on first. The saleswoman, in stunned disbelief, led the way to a fitting room where the customer shed her sable jacket, put on the uniform, tied the organdy apron about her waist and even studied the effect of the wispy cap. Satisfied, she got back into her street clothes, paid cash and walked out with the box under her arm without a word of explanation, doubtless leaving the salesclerks speculating on how the salaries of domestic servants must have skyrocketed.

I shudder to think of the idiotic amount of explaining I would have tried to do.

The Storybook Barber

*Courtney Holmes offers his young customers
a little something extra with their trim.*

———

BY **ANDY SIMMONS**

Originally published in December 2016

"Hey, how you doin'? What grade are you in? Third? What's your favorite book? *Elephant and Piggy*? Yeah, I got it."

Welcome to the shop of Courtney Holmes, the Storybook Barber.

When Dubuque, Iowa, held its first annual Back to School Bash for needy families, Holmes agreed to participate. Saturday was his busiest haircutting day, but he donated his time and give free haircuts to underprivileged kids so they'd look sharp on that first day of classes. But then he had a lightbulb moment: "The kids should earn their free haircut by having to read a book to me," Holmes said.

The idea was so popular that he continued it once a month for the next two years. Five- to ten-year-old boys would grab a book, settle into the chair and read aloud while Holmes snipped away. After the haircut, they'd review the book, from the characters and vocabulary to the themes—just like in school, only more fun.

"There was this seven-year-old who struggled through his book," said Holmes. He had the boy take the book home and practice. When the child came back, "He read it with no problems. That inspires me."

Our Horse of a Different Color

Everything seemed to be wrong with this filly. Who would want her?

—

BY **PENNY PORTER**

Originally published in September 1995

"**W**ith horses, what you want and what you get are often two different things," my husband, Bill, would tell me.

But foaling season is a time for dreams. We'd just begun breeding Appaloosas on our Arizona ranch, and I was dreaming of blue ribbons and eager buyers. That first year, the blazing coats of nine tiny Appaloosas had transformed our pastures into a landscape of color. Their faces were bright with stars and blazes, their rumps glittering with patches and spots that splashed over them like suds.

As we awaited the birth of our tenth foal, I was sure it would be the most colorful of all. Its father was a white stud with chestnut spots over half his body, and a multicolored tail that touched the ground. The mother was covered with thousands of penny-size dots. I already had a name for their unborn offspring: Starburst.

The night of its foaling, I was monitoring the mother on a closed-circuit TV Bill had installed in our bedroom. I could see the mare glistening with sweat, her

22

white-rimmed eyes full of anxiety. She was within hours of delivering. I dozed off.

Three hours passed, and I awoke with a jolt. A glance at the monitor revealed the mare was flat out on her side. The birth was over. But where was her foal?

"Bill! Wake up!" I shook him hard. "Something stole the baby!" Wild dogs, coyotes and other predators invaded my imagination.

Moments later we were in the dimly lit corral. "Where's your baby?" I called as I got on my knees to stroke the mare's neck.

Suddenly a face popped out of the shadows—thin, dark, ugly. As the creature struggled to stand, I realized why I hadn't seen it on my TV: no colorful spots, no blazing coat. Our foal was brown as dirt.

"I don't believe it!" I said as we crouched for a closer look. "There's not a single white hair on this filly!" We saw more unwanted traits: a bulging forehead, a sloping nose, ears that hung like a jackrabbit's, and a nearly hairless bobtail.

"She's a throwback," Bill said. I knew we were both thinking the same thing. *This filly will never sell. Who wants an Appaloosa without color?*

The next morning when our older son, Scott, arrived for work and saw our newest addition, he minced no words. "What are we going to do with that ugly thing?" he asked. By now, the foal's ears stood straight up. "She looks like a mule," Scott said. "Who's gonna want her?"

We'd begun breeding Appaloosas, and I was dreaming of blue ribbons and eager buyers.

Our younger girls, Becky and Jaymee, ages 15 and 12, had questions too. "How will anyone know she's an Appaloosa?" Becky asked. "Are there spots under the fur?"

"No," I told her, "but she's still an Appy inside."

"That means she's got spots on her heart," said Jaymee. *Who knows*, I wondered. *Maybe she does.*

❖ ❖ ❖

From the beginning, the homely filly seemed to sense she was different. Visitors rarely looked at her, and if they did, we said, "Oh, we're just boarding the mother." We didn't want anyone to know that our beautiful stallion had sired this foal.

> ## "You'd be surprised," I said. "That filly knows more tricks than a short-order cook."

When the filly was two weeks old, we turned her out to pasture with the herd. The other foals' mothers bared their teeth at this strange-looking newcomer. Worse, her own mother seemed to sense that her offspring needed all the protection she could get. So she charged any horse that came within 15 feet of her foal. Little by little, our bobtailed filly learned that the horse world was a place to fear.

But before long, I started noticing that she relished human company. She and her mother were first at the gate at feeding time, and when I scratched her neck and shoulders, her eyelids closed in contentment. Soon, she was nuzzling my jacket, running her lips over my shirt, chewing my buttons off and even opening the gate to follow me so she could rub her head on my hip. This wasn't normal behavior for a filly.

Unfortunately, her appetite was huge. And the bigger she got, the uglier she got. *Where will we ever find a home for her?* I wondered.

One day a man bought one of our best Appaloosas for a circus. Suddenly he spied the brown bobtailed filly. "That's not an Appaloosa, is it?" he asked. "Looks like a donkey."

Since he was looking for circus horses, I snatched at the opportunity. "You'd be surprised," I said. "That filly knows more tricks than a short-order cook. She can take a handkerchief out of my pocket and roll under fences. She can climb into water troughs. Even turn on spigots!"

"Reg'lar little devil, huh?"

"No," I said quickly, then added on the spur of the moment, "as a matter of fact, I named her Angel!"

He chuckled. "Well, it's eye-catchin' color we need," he told me. "Folks like spotted horses best."

I knew he was right. But I pictured our plain brown horse jumping through flaming hoops with white poodles in pink tutus on her back.

As time passed, Angel—as we now called her—invented new tricks. Her favorite was opening gates to get to food on the opposite side. "She's a regular Houdini," Bill marveled.

"She's a regular pain," said Scott, who always had to catch her.

With her huge appetite, I tried giving Angel extra hay before I went to bed each night. Her affection for me grew. Unfortunately, so did her appetite for hay. One morning Scott found her in the hay barn. Her sides bulged. Broken bales littered the floor. Scott was disgusted.

"You've got to give her more attention," I told him. "You spend all your time grooming and training the other yearlings. You never touch Angel except to yell at her."

"Who has time to work with a jughead? Besides, Dad said we're taking her to auction."

"What! And sell her for dog food?"

I corralled Bill. "Let her grow up on the ranch," I begged. "Then Scott can saddle-break her when she's two. With her sweet nature, she'll be worth something to *someone* by then."

"I guess one more horse won't hurt for the time being," he said. "We'll put her down on the east pasture. There's not much grazing there, but …" Angel was safe for now.

Two weeks later, she was at the front door eating the dry food from our watchdog's bowl. She'd slipped the chain off the pasture gate and let herself out—plus ten other horses as well. By the time Scott and Bill had rounded them up, I could see that Bill's patience was wearing thin. He turned to the girls. "You two, give her some attention. Maybe you can even make her pretty."

That summer, the girls groomed Angel, bathed her—and looked

constantly for spots. They rubbed mayonnaise into her coat and fed her packets of gelatin mixed with her grain to encourage hair growth on her stubby mane and tail. This folk remedy was said to work with some Appaloosas, but not with Angel. Still, she loved the attention and, perhaps to show it, she even stopped opening gates.

Then school started and Angel lost her playmates. So she developed new games. When Bill or Scott drove to the field, she'd eat the rubber off the windshield wipers or bend the aerial. If they left a window open, she'd snatch a rag, wrench, glove or notebook off the front seat, then run like the wind.

Surprisingly, Bill began forgiving Angel's pranks. When an Appaloosa buyer would arrive, she'd come running at a gallop, slide to a stop 30 feet away and back up to have her rump scratched. "We have our own circus right here," Bill told buyers. By now, a small smile was even showing through Scott's thick mustache.

The seasons rolled by. Blazing sun turned to rain—and brought flies by the millions. One day, when Angel was 2½, I saw Scott leading her to the barn. Her backside was crawling with maggots, raw from fly bites and the repeated thumping of her ineffective tail. "She gets no protection at all from that stupid tail," he told me as he treated Angel with antibiotics. "I'm gonna make her a new one." That's when I realized Scott's feelings for the horse were starting to change.

The next morning I couldn't help smiling as Scott cut and twisted two dozen strands of bright yellow baling twine into a long string mop and fastened it with tape around Angel's bandaged tail. "There," he said. "She looks almost like a normal horse."

When Angel recovered, Scott decided to try to "break" her for riding. Bill and I sat on the corral fence as he put the saddle on. Angel humped her back. "We're gonna have a real rodeo here!" I whispered. But as Scott tightened the cinch around Angel's plump middle, she didn't buck as many other young horses do. She simply waited.

When Scott climbed aboard and applied gentle pressure with his knees, the willing heart of the Appaloosa showed. He ordered her forward, and she responded as though she'd been ridden for years. I reached up and scratched the bulging forehead. "Someday she's going to make a terrific trail-riding horse," I said.

"With a temperament like this," Scott replied, "someone could play polo off her. Or she could be a great kid's horse." Even Scott was having a few dreams for our plain brown Appaloosa with the funny-colored tail.

Angel was soon helping Scott train young foals to obey. Scott would wrap one end of a rope around Angel's saddle horn and clip the other end to the foal's halter. Angel would pull, sometimes drag, the foal along.

At foaling time, Angel whinnied to the newborns as though each one were her own. "We ought to breed her," I said to Bill. "She's four. With her capacity to love, imagine what a good mother she'd make."

Bill thought this was a good idea. "People often buy bred mares," he said. "Maybe we'd find a home for her." Suddenly I saw Scott frowning. *Could it be he really cares?* I wondered.

During the winter months of her pregnancy, Angel seemed to forget about escaping from her corral. Then in early April, as she

> ## "She gets no protection at all from that stupid tail," Scott said. "I'm gonna make her a new one."

drew closer to her due date, a heavy rain came and our fields burst to life. We knew Angel would once more start slipping through the gates in her quest for greener pastures.

One morning we awoke to an unseasonable cold snap. I was starting breakfast when Scott came through the kitchen door. His hazel eyes loomed dark beneath his broad-brimmed Stetson. "It's Angel," he said softly. "You better come. She got out of the corral last night."

Trying to hold back my fears, I followed Scott to his pickup. "She's had her foal somewhere," he said, "but Dad and I couldn't find it. She's … dying." I could hear the catch in his throat.

When we got to Angel, Bill was crouched beside her. "There's nothing we can do," he said, pointing to the lush green fields, an easy reach for a hungry horse through the barbed wire. "Too much alfalfa is a killer."

I pulled Angel's huge head onto my lap and stroked behind her ears. Tears welled in Scott's eyes. "Best mare we ever had," he murmured.

Angel! I pleaded. *Please don't go!* Choking back my grief, I ran my hand down her fur and listened to her labored breathing. Her legs strained, and her neck arched desperately backward, seeking one last breath. She shuddered. I looked into eyes that could no longer see. Angel was gone.

In a cloud of numbness, I heard Scott call out only a few yards away. "Mom! Dad! Here's the foal!"

Deep in the sweet-smelling grasses lay a tiny colt. A single spot brightened his face, and stars spangled his back and hips. A pure, radiant appaloosa, our horse of many colors. "Starburst," I whispered.

But, somehow, all that color didn't matter anymore. As his mother had taught us so many times, it's not what's on the outside that counts, but what's buried inside the heart.

The Searcher

*James Spring went looking for adventure.
What he found: two little girls caught
in a fractured family saga.*

BY **JOE RHODES**

Originally published in September 2008

The girl in the photo had wide eyes and a princess smile, blond hair, a strand of plastic pearls dangling from her neck. James Spring felt a pang in his heart the moment he saw her on his computer screen. She looked so happy and innocent, so much like his own daughter, Addie, who was tucked in upstairs. When he saw the picture and read what had happened to six-year-old Viana and her infant sister, Faith, he knew what he had to do.

His 40th birthday, on April 29, was just a few weeks away, and Spring was looking to keep a promise to himself. He'd been restless the past few months, distracted by the fear that he'd settled a little too easily into middle age. He was successful and proud of the life he had built: the marketing job in San Diego, the spacious house in the La Mesa suburbs, the loving wife, the two wonderful kids—three-year-old Addie and eight-month-old Caden. But it didn't feel like enough.

When he was younger, he'd been a danger junkie, reporting on civil wars in El Salvador and Guatemala for National Public Radio, getting himself captured by Kuna Indians and being pursued by paramilitary gangs. "I had an inflated sense of my own invulnerability," he says now.

If he hadn't met Kellie, the woman he married six years ago, he'd probably still be coming up against shady characters. But she convinced him—made an ultimatum of it, actually—that if he was going to be her husband and the father of her children, he couldn't go dashing into any more war zones. He fed his need for adventure by scuba diving and racing his motorcycle in the Baja 500. And then, his birthday approaching, he started talking about doing something that would make him feel better about himself.

"Maybe there will be an earthquake and I can dig people out of the rubble," he told Kellie. "Or a helicopter will go down and they'll need people to search." She tried to ignore him, hoping he'd forget about his quest and just have a party in the backyard. But he wouldn't let it go. "I told her, 'I just want to do something that's going to help somebody else.'"

Which is why James Spring was looking up missing-person cases on the Internet in early April, hoping to find someone who needed him. When he saw that photo and started reading about Viana and Faith Carelli, two girls who'd been taken away by their parents—convicts who were suspects in a San Francisco murder, didn't have legal custody of their older daughter and had last been seen by a tourist in the Baja peninsula—it became clear what his birthday gift to himself would be. He was going to load up his Ford Explorer, drive across the border and go looking for those two little girls.

The house in Soquel, California, where Gene and Ellen Pauly have lived for 32 years is overflowing with photos of their family: the five children they raised together, the foster kids they took in, the grand-kids, including Viana and Faith.

Most of the photos of their daughter Michele, Viana and Faith's mother, were taken during her high school years, when everyone called her the golden child. A cheerleader, a ballet and tap dancer, the president of Students Against Drunk Driving, she

Spring near his home in San Diego: "Baja is my backyard."

was the pretty one, the popular one, the daughter every parent hoped to have. She graduated from Aptos High School in 1988, spent six months with a performance group in Japan and earned a dance education degree from Western Kentucky University.

Ellen Pauly, 63, still doesn't understand what happened to that Michele. She doesn't recognize the woman her daughter has become: a meth user, a thief, a con artist, possibly an accessory to murder. "I still love my daughter," she says, "but she's not the Michele we raised. Whether that Michele can ever come back again, it's hard to tell. I'm not counting on it."

Viana, right, and Faith Carelli inspired a stranger's quest to do something meaningful.

Maybe there were problems all along; maybe her parents just didn't know. But there's no question that Michele's life took a turn for the worse after she left Soquel. In 1994 she married Joe Pinkerton, a ski instructor she'd met while working as a dancer in Lake Tahoe. She moved to Los Angeles and started spending time with Pinkerton's friend Richard Carelli. Eight years into the marriage, she left Pinkerton and moved in with Carelli. The two drifted from one dead-end job to another.

The Paulys know little of Carelli's life before he met Michele, other than that he'd had odd jobs, occasionally tending bar or working construction. The Paulys say he could be charming but also frightening. And, they say, he seemed to have an almost hypnotic effect on their daughter.

"Richard was the one who destroyed Michele," says Gene Pauly, sounding more sad than angry. She would disappear from her parents' lives for years at a time. When she surfaced, she was hostile, resentful, usually asking for money.

Ellen is convinced that she might not have seen much of Viana if Michele hadn't been broke in 2004. But Michele needed help taking care of her then-three-year-old daughter, so she moved into her parents' house and told them she'd left Carelli. She got a job. Things looked promising.

And they were—until a few weeks later, when Carelli showed up and took Michele and Viana away. The couple fell into the same patterns as before and soon racked up convictions for drug possession and arrests for petty theft and credit card fraud. The final straw for the Paulys came in December 2006, when police burst into a motel room in nearby Capitola to arrest Carelli and Michele. Meth was scattered on the nightstand; Viana, age four, was found hiding under the bed.

Gene and Ellen Pauly petitioned for custody of their granddaughter and won. But over the Paulys' objections, a judge granted Carelli and Michele the right to unsupervised visits. Viana often spent weekends with her parents and their new baby, Faith, born in October 2007 with Down syndrome.

Michele would disappear from her parents' lives for years at a time. When she surfaced, she was usually asking for money.

At the start of one of those weekends, in January 2008, Ellen noticed that something didn't seem right. Michele appeared more scattered than usual as she scooped up her daughter's overnight bag and went off into the rainy afternoon. Ellen had a bad feeling—but no way of knowing it would be ten weeks before she would see Viana again.

❖　❖　❖

Until that day, Carelli and Michele had been living in San Francisco's Mission Terrace neighborhood, renting a one-bedroom unit in a run-down row house. The previous month, according to a neighbor, Carelli had argued with Leonard Hoskins, another tenant. There was shouting, scuffling, the sounds of a fistfight, and moments later, a

No one was looking for the fugitive parents or the children. If he started searching, he'd be on his own.

bloodied Richard Carelli stumbled from the building, the neighbor says. He thought that Carelli had lost the fight, that the blood was his own, so he didn't call the police. Investigators would later discover that the landlord had been trying to evict Carelli and Michele and that Hoskins had been drawn into the dispute.

Hoskins's sister, Ureena, reported him missing, but the authorities didn't do much more than file a report. Three weeks later, she went to San Francisco and started investigating on her own. She was the one who found the neighbor and persuaded the police—finally, on January 24—to interview Carelli. He denied the fight with Hoskins, but the police brought in cadaver dogs, who seemed to indicate there was a body in Carelli's van. Carelli at first gave authorities permission to search it but then, according to police, changed his mind and demanded his keys back. They impounded it instead and, amazingly, let him go. Eight days passed before police searched the van and found Hoskins's body inside. By then, Carelli and Michele had fled to Mexico, the children in tow.

Though the murder and kidnapping made it onto the *America's Most Wanted* website, the official search never amounted to much. Even after a tourist saw the fugitives in San Quintin, 150 miles south of the border, there was no follow-up. The wait was slow agony for the Pauly family.

"I had pretty much given up," Ellen Pauly says, admonishing herself for the thought. "I was just so angry at everyone, all the screwups, no communication between agencies. I thought no one really cared. And then, when you least expect it, here comes this total stranger. And he proves that there is still decency in the world."

Kellie Spring cried when her husband first told her what he was going to do. But when she saw Viana's picture, she agreed, reluctantly, that yes, he had to go. She asked him only to wait a couple of days before leaving. He needed a plan. He needed supplies. Mostly, he needed to give her a chance to accept what he was about to do.

Spring agreed to wait—and started working the phones. At first he assumed there would be an official search party to join, but after calling law-enforcement officials, it became clear that no one in Mexico was looking for the fugitives or the children. If he went, he'd be on his own.

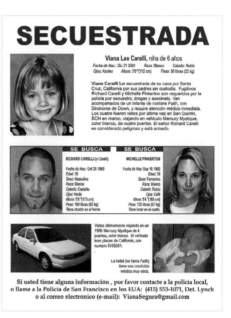

Spring's "kidnapped" poster was crucial to locating the girls.

Next he contacted the Pauly family. Missing-children cases draw attention from all kinds of characters, so he knew he might be seen as some kind of crackpot. Indeed, when he talked to Rob Doubleday, Viana's uncle and the family's spokesman, they'd just heard from self-proclaimed psychics, sure they knew where the children were. Doubleday thanked Spring for his interest but doubted he could help.

Spring made it clear he was going to try anyway. The next day, he had

Faith is doing well in the care of her aunt and uncle, Sherry and Rob Doubleday.

2,500 posters printed up in Spanish, with *secuestrada* ("kidnapped") in bold letters across the top. He included photos of Viana, Faith, Michele and Carelli, along with a shot of a white 1996 Mercury Mystique, the last car they'd been seen in.

He packed a flare gun, a machete and all the food he thought he might need. And then, early Sunday, 36 hours after his initial Internet search, as Kellie watched with Addie at her side and Caden in her arms, James Spring drove away.

"I knew it was important to him and I had to let him go," Kellie says now, recalling how frightened she'd been. "But he was looking for people who were suspected of murder, and neither of us knew what they might do to protect themselves."

As Spring drove across the border that Sunday morning, his plan was to plaster posters at every Pemex gas station and police headquarters between Ensenada and San Quintin.

He never doubted he would find the girls. He'd lived in Baja for four years in his 20s. "I know the whole 1,059 miles of it," he says. "I know every place to look, even the ones the Mexican police don't know about."

Driving through tourist towns and fishing villages, places that weren't much more than a collection of shacks, he thought about what it might be like to confront Carelli: Does he know his way around? Does he speak Spanish? Does he have money? Does he have weapons? That night, in San Quintin, he came across a Mercury Mystique, just like the one Carelli had been driving. *What are the odds?* Spring said to himself, excited that he might have stumbled onto the couple so quickly.

He had the cops check it out, but it wasn't Carelli's car. If the police, skeptical of the American with the posters and the staple gun, had doubted his veracity before, they were really questioning it now. He couldn't afford to cry wolf. "I'm sorry," he told the officers. And then he moved on.

On Monday morning, he headed farther south, to the small village of Santa Marie. A gas station attendant said yes, he'd seen the couple within the past three weeks. An off-duty cop confirmed the sighting. Spring was already closing in. "I can't tell you why, but I woke up that day feeling great," he says. "I felt like something was going to happen."

At a gas station in El Rosario, 36 miles south of San Quintin, he began taping up a poster when an attendant said to him in Spanish, "I have seen this woman."

"When?" Spring asked.

"Three days ago," the man said. "She was asking about a cheap place to eat." Spring walked 100 yards to a motel he knew to be popular with Americans. Sure enough, two men at the front desk told him, the couple had rented a shack a few doors away. Michele was giving dance lessons to local kids to earn a few pesos. "I could feel the goose bumps forming," Spring says. Carelli and Michele were his.

He drove to the police station, a small cinder-block building on the town square, asked for the *comandante*, and informed him that he had a suspected murderer in his village. The comandante requested help from the state attorney general's office, the Baja equivalent of the Texas Rangers, but they wouldn't get to El Rosario before dusk. Until then, Spring and the comandante would have to wait and hope.

Spring kept the Pauly family informed and told Kellie he was safe. He spoke briefly to a U.S. marshal in San Francisco. "This is a tiny village," Spring warned. "Carelli is going to find out I'm here. And when he learns that, he'll leave. And I have him. He's here. Now."

As the sun began to set, Mexican authorities swarmed the house where Carelli, Michele and the kids were staying. Spring was ordered to remain at the police station during the actual arrest. "I was pacing the whole time, literally doing laps around the station," he says. The officers—"big guys in five unmarked trucks, with big mustaches, black leather jackets and AK-17 rifles," according to Spring—made the arrest. Spring listened on the police radio. "I hear the guy kind of giving a play-by-play at the dispatcher desk," he remembers. "'OK, they're at the house. One of the cars is circling around. They got 'em!'"

The officers returned to the station five minutes later, Carelli shackled in the back of one pickup truck, Michele and the kids in another. "They pull right up in front of me on this little patio area and yank Carelli out of the truck," Spring recalls. "He looks at me, and you can just see that whatever he had alive in him is gone. He sees a white face and he knows the jig is up."

Viana looked nervous but unharmed as Spring assured her that everything would be all right. He promised to stay with her and

Viana is back with her grandparents, Ellen and Gene Pauly (background, middle and right).

Faith until they were reunited with the Paulys. "Whenever something bad happened, like seeing her father shackled in a cell, I'd see Viana's eyes get really wide," Spring says. "I'd talk to her and say, 'I have a little daughter myself. And she thinks she's a princess. Just like you.'"

Gene Pauly was waiting on the U.S. side of the border. He hugged his granddaughters, Viana yelling "Grandpa, Grandpa!" He did not speak to Carelli or to his daughter—or even look at them—as they were turned over to federal marshals and escorted back to San Francisco, where Carelli awaits trial for murder and Michele for accessory to murder for helping him avoid capture. Both also face child abduction charges.

By Tuesday evening, Viana Carelli was back in her grandmother's arms. Viana told her that she'd been hungry and dirty in Mexico. And whenever she saw a police officer, in real life or on TV, she seemed frightened.

The family decided that caring for a traumatized six-year-old and an infant with special needs was too much for the Paulys. So Rob Doubleday and his wife, Sherry, Michele's sister, took custody of Faith.

James Spring went back to San Diego, to his coat-and-tie job, no longer feeling so restless. On his birthday, his wife threw a big party that was also a fundraiser for the Polly Klaas Foundation, a missing-children's charity.

The Pauly family has invited Spring to visit the girls in Soquel whenever he wants. They'd like to thank him in person. He appreciates the gesture but has so far declined. "I feel like I've done my bit," Spring says. "In my mind, this was always about the kids. I was never looking for attention or praise. I just wanted to do the right thing."

The Pauly home features new photos of the children, together and happy. Faith is alert and healthy, and although Viana remembers her ordeal and misses her parents, she's full of smiles and hugs most of the time. "That little girl," Gene Pauly says as he watches her skip across the living room floor. "Ten weeks without her was just too long."

"Six Hundred Bucks! And Nothing to It!"

"Earn $$ the Easy Way!" the ad promised. Just the thing, I thought, to teach my college sons something about money. And—they learned. We all did!

———

BY **JOHN G. HUBBELL**

Originally published in May 1982

"Y ou ought to look into this," I suggested to our two college-age sons. "It might be a way to avoid the indignity of having to ask for money all the time." I handed them magazines in a plastic bag hung on our doorknob. A message printed on the bag offered leisurely, lucrative work ("Big Bucks the Easy Way!") delivering more such bags.

"I don't mind the indignity," the older one answered.

"I can live with it," his brother agreed.

"But it pains *me*," I said, "to find that you both have been panhandling so long that it no longer embarrasses you."

The boys said they would look into the magazine-delivery thing. Pleased, I left town on a business trip. By midnight I was comfortably settled in a hotel room far from home. The phone rang. It was my wife. She wanted to know how my day had gone.

"Terrific!" I enthused. I told her of my day's accomplishments, of cocktails and dinner with old pals in the city's foremost eatery. "How was *your* day?" I inquired.

"Super!" she snapped. "Just *super*! And it's only getting started. Another truck just pulled up out front."

"If you've heard of it, mister, we've got it, right here in Advertising City!"

"Another truck?"

"The third one this evening. The first delivered 4,000 Montgomery Wards. The second brought 4,000 Sears, Roebucks. I don't know what this one has, but I'm sure it will be 4,000 of something. Since you are responsible, I thought you might like to know what's happening."

What I was being blamed for, it turned out, was a newspaper strike that made it necessary to hand deliver the advertising inserts that normally are included with the Sunday paper. The company had promised our boys $600 for delivering these inserts to 4,000 houses by Sunday morning.

"Piece of *cake*!" our older college nut had shouted.

"*Six hundred bucks!*" His brother had drooled the syllables. "That's *three hundred clams* apiece! And we can do the job in two hours!"

Then the first truck had arrived. "Both the Sears and Ward ads are four newspaper-size pages," my wife informed me. "There are 32,000 pages of advertising on our porch. Even as we speak, two husky truckers are carrying armloads of paper up the walk. What do we do about all this?"

"Just tell the boys to get busy," I instructed. "They're college men. They'll do what they have to do."

At noon the following day I returned to the hotel and found an urgent message to telephone my wife. Her voice was unnaturally high and quavering. There had been several more truckloads of ad inserts. "They're for department stores, hardware stores, dime stores, drugstores, grocery stores, clothing stores, auto stores and so on. Some are whole magazine sections. If you've heard of it, mister, we've got it, right here in Advertising City! We have *hundreds of thousands*, maybe *millions*, of pages of advertising here!" Her voice kept rising, as if working its way out of the range of the human ear. "All this must be delivered by seven o'clock Sunday morning."

"Listen," I said. "You tell those turkeys that our porch is to be cleared by tomorrow night."

"And what about the living room? And the dining room ? And the kitchen? And the *laundry*?"

"You've got the stuff spread all through the house?"

"It isn't *spread* anywhere. It's *crammed* wall to wall in stacks taller than your oldest son. There's only enough room for people to walk in, take one each of the 11 inserts, roll them together, slip a rubber band around them and slide them into a plastic bag. We have enough plastic bags to supply every takeout restaurant in America!"

"Well, you had better get those guys banding and sliding as fast as they can, and I'll talk to you later. Got a lunch date."

When I returned, there was another urgent call from my wife.

"Did you have a nice lunch?" she asked sweetly. I had had a marvelous steak, but knew better by now than to say so.

"Awful," I reported. "Some sort of sour, stringy fish. Eel, I think."

"Good. We had lunch at McDonald's. We're going to try Burger King for dinner, and Perkins Cake & Steak for break ..."

"You're doing *what*? Why ...?"

"I can't use the kitchen, dear. It's occupied by much of the print advertising in this part of the world. Your college sons have hired their younger siblings and a couple of neighborhood waifs to help for five dollars each. Assembly lines have been set up. In the language of diplomacy, there is 'movement.'"

"That's encouraging."

"No, it's not," she corrected. "It's very *dis*couraging. They've been at it for hours. Plastic bags have been filled and piled to the ceiling, but all this hasn't made a dent, not a *dent*, in the situation! It's almost as if the inserts keep reproducing themselves!

"Another thing," she continued. "Your college sons must learn that one does not get the best out of employees by threatening them with bodily harm."

Obtaining an audience with son No. 1, I snarled, "I'll kill you if you threaten one of those kids again! *Idiot!* You should be offering a bonus of a dollar every hour to the worker who fills the most bags."

"But that would cut into our profit," he suggested.

"There won't *be* any profit unless those kids enable you to make all the deliveries on time. If they don't, you two will have to remove all that paper by yourselves. And there will be no eating or sleeping until it *is* removed."

There was a short, thoughtful silence. Then he said, "Dad, you have just worked a profound change in my personality."

"Do it!"

"Yes, *sir*!"

By the following evening, there was much for my wife to report. The bonus program had worked until someone demanded to see the color of cash. Then some activist on the work force claimed that the workers had no business settling for $5 and a few competitive bonuses while the bosses collected hundreds of dollars each. The organizer had declared that all the workers were entitled to $5 *per hour*! They would not work another minute until the bosses agreed.

The strike lasted less than two hours. In mediation, the parties agreed on $2 per hour. Gradually, the huge stacks began to shrink.

The Saturday-morning bulletin was that saintly neighbors had volunteered station wagons and bodies. Everyone had been driving and delivering into the wee hours and would continue throughout the day. "We'll be at it again until very late tonight," my wife said. "Say, by the way, are you ever coming home? I mean, it *is* Saturday."

"Just finishing things up," I said brightly. "No sense in leaving a lot of loose ends."

"No, of course not. And no sense rushing back here before Hell Week is over, right?"

I ignored her suggestion. "You people have really done a job back there!" I enthused. "Will it be completed by dawn Sunday, as per contract?"

"Easily," she said. "So I suppose we can look forward to seeing you about noon."

"As a matter of fact, my flight should arrive at 12:10."

As it turned out, the job was completed three hours before Sunday's 7 a.m. deadline. By the time I arrived, the boys had already settled their accounts: $150 in labor costs, $40 for gasoline and a like amount for gifts—boxes of candy for saintly neighbors and a dozen roses for their mother. This left them with $185 each—about two-thirds the minimum wage for the 91 hours they worked. Still, it was "enough," as one of them put it, to enable them to "avoid indignity" for quite a while.

All went well for some weeks. Then one Saturday morning my attention was drawn to the odd goings-on of our two youngest sons. They kept carrying carton after carton from various corners of the house out the front door to curbside. I assumed their mother had enlisted them to remove junk for a trash pickup. Then I overheard them discussing finances.

"Geez, we're going to make a *lot* of money!"

"We're going to be rich!"

Investigation revealed that they were offering "for sale or rent" our entire library.

"No! No!" I cried. "You can't sell our books!"

"Geez, Dad, we thought you were done with them!"

"You're never 'done' with books," I tried to explain.

"Sure you are. You read them, and you're done with them. That's it. Then you might as well make a little money from them. We wanted to avoid the indignity of having to ask you for ..."

"Don't worry about indignity!" I shouted, shoving some dollar bills at each of them. "Take the money, and don't give indignity another thought. I can live with it!"

What I Learned at the Shoe Store

Mr. Hill taught more than just selling.

———

BY **WILLIAM M. HENDRYX**

Originally published in November 1993

When our family moved across town in the early 1960s, I lost my boyhood friends and plunged into a lonely period of teenage insecurity. For months, I moped around the house until my dad finally made me get a job sacking groceries at the local supermarket on the southeast side of Dallas. I hated it.

One scorching day, as I carried shoppers' bags out to the parking lot, I looked at the large shoe store across the street. The store had a cool, pristine appearance, with big, awning-shaded windows filled with shiny new shoes. I had always wondered what it would be like to work in air-conditioned comfort, so I decided to find out.

Days later, wearing my best clothes, I summoned all my courage and stepped into that shoe store. A lanky tower of a man greeted me, his gray hair combed straight back and his face glowing with a sincere smile. He wore silver-rimmed glasses, a trim navy blue suit, a conservative tie and a pair of impeccably buffed black wing tips. I was glad I'd dressed up.

"Looking for work?" he asked.

"Yes, sir," I answered, unable

to imagine how he knew that.

"I saw you weren't browsing the displays, so I figured as much," he said, still reading my mind. "I'm John Hill, the store manager. We could use another hand around here. Do you like dealing with people?"

The question caught me flat-footed. I could count on one hand the friends I'd made since we moved to this neighborhood. To me, kids around here seemed cliquish and unreceptive, and I was near the point of saying "who needs 'em" to the entire lot. I dug my toe into the carpet. "I suppose," I answered with little conviction.

"That's not much of an answer," he said, placing a hand on my shoulder. "Half of selling is putting people at ease. If they get the feeling you really care, they'll respond to that. They'll actually become reluctant *not* to buy from you. But if they get the impression you'd rather be doing something else, they'll be out the door before you know it."

He made it sound so simple. Something told me I might learn a great deal from this man who seemed to like everyone.

For whatever reason, Mr. Hill hired me that afternoon. My first days on the job were spent listening to the dos and don'ts. "We don't do things like other shoe stores," Mr. Hill said, pointing toward the busy boulevard outside. "Folks have to go to a little extra trouble to come over here, so we try to give them something extra in return. Think you could do that?"

My self-doubts crept to the surface. "What if you don't have what they want?" I asked, surprised at my own boldness.

Judging by the look on his face, I must have committed sacrilege. "Never tell them that!" he insisted. "Instead, show them what you *do* have."

"But, what if …"

"Show, don't tell," he interrupted. "You can't always offer people what they want. But you can always offer something. Whether they accept it is up to them. But if you show an empty hand, you take away that choice, and they have to look elsewhere.

47

Just remember that you've always got something that will make a person's eyes light up. You just have to figure out what that is."

He then took me on a storewide tour and explained the pay system: hourly wages plus a percentage of sales. The biggest commission was on shoe polish, with purses and accessories close behind.

Next, we pretended I was a customer just arriving. "Welcome to our store," Mr. Hill said, genially shaking my hand. He escorted me to a seat, pulled up a stool and, before I knew it, gently removed my shoes. "Would you mind standing on this?" he asked. Then he measured both feet.

"Aren't you even going to ask what I want?" I said when I sat down again.

"Yes, now that I'm in control," Mr. Hill replied. "See, you're sitting in a comfortable chair with your shoes off. You can't just get up and leave, so this is when I ask people what they have in mind."

"Why don't you just ask my size?" I said.

"Never ask someone's size!" he insisted, shaking a finger at me. "The purpose of measuring is to establish in the customer's mind that you know what you're doing. That gives them confidence in your recommendations."

Confidence. It was hardly my best asset. But Mr. Hill certainly had it, and I was determined to see how it worked. As the days passed, I became his shadow. I watched as he defused the grouchiest of customers by making jokes. Often, they were about his skinniness. "You know," he'd say, patting his bony rear end, "if I don't quit eating so much, I'm going to get too big for this darn stool."

Once, I watched as he worked with two women shopping together. He brought them not only the shoes they had asked for, but several other pairs. While they were trying out the requested shoes in front of the full-length mirror, he handed them the matching purse. "Let's see how this looks," he said, almost innocently. Then he displayed other shoes in a neat semicircle around his stool. Next to each pair he placed a handbag. Who's to say what those customers had in mind when they walked in that day? But when they walked out, each had several pairs of shoes, a couple of handbags and a very satisfied smile.

"If you give people only what they came for," he said during a lull, "then you haven't sold anything. Give them that, then sell them something. It's good for the store's volume, it's good for your commission and it's good for you. Selling gives you a feeling of self-confidence, and once you've discovered it, it's yours for life. You'll use it in more ways than you can imagine, because everything we do involves some form of sales."

Soon after, when it was time to assist my first customer, the butterflies swirled in my stomach. Mr. Hill pulled me aside and offered his assurances. "Just treat them like you'd want to be treated, and the rest will take care of itself," he said.

After seating a woman and her daughter, measuring their feet and showing them matching suede penny loafers, I suggested a water-repellent spray and a wire

> ## You won't always have what people ask for. But you'll always have something *in inventory.*

brush for maintaining the nap. The woman bought everything, and I don't know who was more pleased—me or Mr. Hill.

Though it was hardly an overnight transformation, I became a marginally gifted salesman, thanks to Mr. Hill's example. It was a rare day that I didn't learn some new technique from him.

Once, I even saw him suggest to a rather large woman that the

size-nine shoe she was trying on was actually the size six she had requested. With a puzzled look on his face, he turned the shoe over and showed it to her again. "They must have stamped it upside down," he explained with a silly grin.

Obviously amused, the woman bought the shoes and vowed to come back soon.

As the months lapsed into years, Mr. Hill became more like a wise uncle than a boss. His guidance touched many facets of my life— from career counseling to the torment of teenage romance. "I wish my parents could be more like you," I told him one quiet evening when we had the store to ourselves.

Mr. Hill dropped his chin and peered at me over his glasses. He had met my folks on several occasions and thought highly of them. "And how's that?" he asked.

"You and I can talk about anything and you never get upset. I can't do that with them."

For a long moment his eyes drifted from mine. Finally, he turned back to me and said, "It's difficult to be a good parent and a good friend at the same time, so don't be too hard on your folks. They're fine people."

Mr. Hill was right. I had learned a lot under his tutelage, but I'd taken little of it home with me. Perhaps, if I were to act more like an adult, they'd treat me that way too. I'll never forget the look on their faces a few days later when I volunteered to stay home with my baby sister so they could go out.

I continued working at that shoe store until it was time to leave for college. Never once did I dread going to work—until the day it was time to say goodbye. With the others already gone for the night, I walked up to Mr. Hill and swallowed hard. "You've done an awful lot for me," I said. "I'll always appreciate it."

When he looked at me, his face was flush, his eyes slightly moist. "I didn't do anything," he said, flashing a bright smile. "You did."

"But you showed me how," I countered.

"Anyone could have done that—your folks, your teachers, your pastor. It's just that you were ready to listen when you met me. It was inside you all along."

I thought about that for a moment. Since coming to work at the shoe store, I had taken part in the senior play, gotten involved in some organizations, run for a couple of offices and made many new friends. It turned out my peers had never really closed me out of their lives. It was the other way around, just as it had been with my folks. As soon as I opened up to them, everyone responded.

Have confidence in yourself and others will too. Don't tell, show. Treat people as you would like to be treated. Always offer more than expected.

Those simple rules have since found their way into many corners of my life—from business to family and beyond.

In teaching me about selling shoes, Mr. Hill gave me something far more important—a powerful secret for living. You won't always have what people ask for. But you'll always have *something* in that vast inventory. If not another pair of shoes or a can of polish, try offering a piece of yourself.

Lost in the Pacific Woods

*She set out to scatter her husband's ashes in a national park.
Would she make it out alive?*

—

BY **TOM HALLMAN JR.**

Originally published in November 2018

For 34 years, Jean and Jack Geer doted on each other as they moved from San Francisco to Hawaii to, finally, Port Angeles in Washington state. Then, in December 2016, Jean walked into their bucolic backyard and found Jack crumpled on the ground. Seemingly in perfect health, he had died of a massive heart attack. He was 72.

In the following months, Jean devoured books on grief and loss, hoping she would find the will to go on without him. One task she thought could help: Jack had told Jean that when he died he wanted half of his ashes scattered in Hawaii and half in Olympic National Park, about a 25-minute drive from their home. So in March 2017, Jean dutifully flew to Hawaii to disperse the first part of Jack's remains in the ocean. But she dreaded the thought of parting with Jack forever. She put off spreading the rest of Jack's ashes until she was ready. That day came on July 17.

Jean, 71, took the urn holding Jack's remains, grabbed Yoda, her five-year-old 11-pound Chihuahua mix, and climbed into her 2004 Ford Explorer. It was 4 p.m. A slight woman, just five feet tall, Jean wore capri pants, a Hawaiian shirt and canvas espadrilles. No need for a coat on what should be a 30-minute walk. She planned to be home in time to make dinner.

With its dramatic peaks and old-growth forests, Olympic National Park covers nearly a million sprawling acres. Jean was heading for one special spot off Obstruction Point Road, an eight-mile dirt and gravel byway. She drove in about three miles, pulled her Explorer over on an untamed stretch of road devoid of signs, and got out. She grabbed her cell phone and the urn, stashed her purse in the car and locked the doors. And then Jean and Yoda entered the woods.

The park features one of the world's most diverse populations of wildflowers, and Jean was on a quest for blue alpine forget-me-nots. Their beauty, Jack had once told Jean, moved him. When she didn't see any, she walked deeper into the woods and finally spotted a blanket of blue through a small opening in the trees. Relieved, she walked to the flowers and distributed Jack's ashes. She said a quiet blessing and turned to leave.

Then she paused. Had she come in this way or that? Where was the trail? Jack would have laughed. He'd frequently teased her about her terrible sense of direction. His nickname for her was Wrong-Way Jean.

She saw a hill and headed toward it. If she could make it to the top, she could scan the horizon and spot Obstruction Point Road. Her shoes, which had smooth treads, were ill-suited for the climb. Yoda ran ahead while Jean struggled to maintain her balance. She slipped, dropped the urn, and watched it roll over the edge of the hill and tumble into a gully. Jean crept her way to the slope's side. She spotted the dark plastic urn, barely visible in the underbrush. She hated abandoning anything related to Jack, but the steep hillside was too dangerous to navigate. She eventually made it to the top of the crest, where she saw

Jean Geer, months before she and her dog disappeared in Olympic National Park.

nothing but trees and more hills. She'd been gone from home for a few hours, and it was getting dark.

She reached for her cell phone to call for help. No service. Thirsty, Jean needed water. She randomly picked a route, pushing her way through underbrush and branches that cut and pricked her, until she came upon a small creek. She and Yoda drank deeply. As night fell, Jean was chilled by an awful realization: She would be spending the night in the woods.

She'd heard stories about people who had died in the park, including one who had been mauled by a bear. *Just stay calm*, she thought, forcing herself to focus on the task at hand. First things first—she needed a place to sleep. She spotted a downed tree, about seven feet in diameter, that had fallen onto a big rock next to the creek. The space beneath was large enough to shelter her for the night. She crawled under the log and lay there. Yoda snuggled close, warming her as the temperature dipped into the 40s. An experienced camper, Jean wasn't frightened by

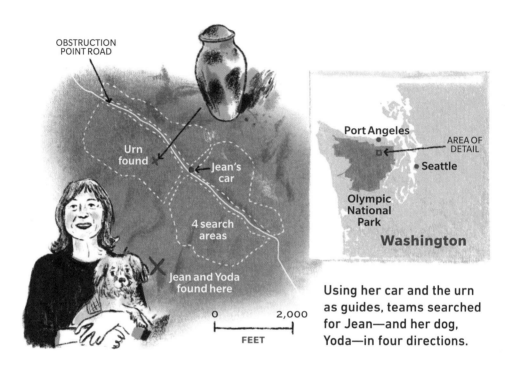

OBSTRUCTION POINT ROAD

Urn found

Jean's car

4 search areas

Jean and Yoda found here

0   2,000

FEET

Port Angeles

AREA OF DETAIL

Seattle

Olympic National Park

Washington

Using her car and the urn as guides, teams searched for Jean—and her dog, Yoda—in four directions.

the forest's strange noises or creepy-crawlies. But her predicament did keep her awake. To distract herself, she thought about the dinner she'd planned but wouldn't get to eat: noodle soup with pork and vegetables, and fresh cherries for dessert.

And she thought of Jack. Jean recalled the first time she'd laid eyes on him. It was 1982. Armed with her MBA, she had applied for a job at a San Francisco bank where Jack served as a vice president. After she

was hired as an assistant vice president, Jack took her to lunch to congratulate her. Mutually attracted, they began to date, fell in love and were soon married. Thinking about Jack made her calmer, allowing her to conclude that if she could make it until daylight, she'd find her way out.

❖   ❖   ❖

At dawn, Jean left the shelter, forging her own trail through underbrush with Yoda now trying to keep up with her. At home, Yoda had the run of nearly five acres, where he chased deer and explored. But this adventure was different. The bushes were high, and he had to tunnel through. With his short legs, he couldn't jump over the logs. Discouraged, he'd yelp for Jean. But Jean couldn't carry him. It taxed her strength, and she might fall. Yoda was on his own.

Jean, meanwhile, was fighting her own battles with panic. So much could go wrong in the wilderness for even a young, able-bodied hiker. But for a septuagenarian, the perils were magnified. Crossing slippery rocks, she worried she'd fall and break a leg. She avoided ravines, knowing that if she plunged into one, she could never climb back up.

Before she knew it, another day had passed. Her chances of being rescued had not improved. As night fell again, Jean and Yoda found another fallen tree to sleep under.

❖ ❖ ❖

The next morning, her third day lost in the park, Jean had given up on finding her own way out. She'd read stories about people who'd endured in the wild, and the rules of survival were simple: Find a water source, don't get injured, and find an open spot to make it easier for rescuers to find you. Then stay put.

By midafternoon, Jean had scouted out the place she'd call home for however long she needed it. She'd found two trees that had fallen next to each other. She used branches to build a roof and to close off one end of the space, leaving an opening for a "doorway." Inside, she stacked branches to use at night to close off the opening. She used moss to make the ground softer.

At the end of day three, Jean and Yoda entered the eight-by-five-foot shelter. As she settled in, so many thoughts, some absurd, ran through her head: She'd bought tickets with a friend to go on an October cruise that would take them to Greece, Italy and Spain. Would she get to go? And then there were those cherries. She couldn't stop thinking about them.

The next day, her fourth lost, Jean settled into her survival routine. Several times over the course of the day, she made her way down a steep hill to drink water. Taking care not to fall, she dug her heels into the ground and clung to the bushes.

She tried building a fire by gathering dry pine needles and then rubbing a small stick against a stone, hoping the stick would get warm enough to ignite. It failed, but she kept trying.

Starving, she ate wild currants, tender pine needles and even ants, which had a lemony taste. Yoda, for his part, impressed Jean with his newfound ability to snatch flies out of the air and dig up grubs for dinner.

By 4 p.m., Jean and Yoda had climbed into her shelter. The hard ground was miserable and the cold was embedded in her bones. But she wasn't giving up. Although Jack had taken care of her for so many years, Jean now harked back to a time when she hadn't been dependent on anyone.

Shortly after World War II, her family had moved to the United States from China. At school, kids would hurl racial slurs and start fights with her. Her father had sat

Jean down and offered this advice: *You are a little person. You won't be strong physically. You must be strong internally.* Somehow, some way, he was saying, Jean had to take care of herself. Hungry, tired and growing weak, Jean drifted off to sleep repeating her father's words.

By now, Jean's brother in Seattle had become concerned. Numerous calls to Jean had not been returned, and when he drove the two hours to her home, there was no sign of her. He contacted the sheriff's office, which sent a missing-person report to all governmental agencies, including an office at Olympic National Park. At 1:30 p.m. on July 22, five days into Jean's odyssey, a park employee spotted the Explorer. He radioed it in, setting in motion a series of alerts that ended with Zachary Gray, of the park's search-and-rescue operations squad, gathering a handful of searchers to look for Jean.

They met at her parked Explorer. Dust and water spots indicated the vehicle had been there for several days. Searchers walked into the woods, calling Jean's name. They

The shelter Jean made. She and her dog, Yoda, ultimately lived in it for three days.

found nothing. At 7 p.m., with nightfall approaching, the search was halted.

The search began again the next day at 6 a.m. Gray now had a team of 37 under his command, which he split into four groups heading out in different directions. Still, he couldn't buck the nagging feeling that this would end poorly. At 71, Jean was likely disoriented and probably injured. Gray had been on ten searches already that year. Nearly all had ended when the team found a body.

At noon, Gray's two-way radio crackled. A searcher had found a plastic urn with Jack Geer's name on the side. Gray had other teams focus on a half-mile radius from where the urn was found. Hours passed. Nothing.

Gray radioed to request a helicopter. Once aboard, he searched below where the urn had been found. Jean, he thought, might have fallen into the gully and dropped the urn. Injured, she likely would have continued walking downhill until she either collapsed or died. Flying 300 feet above tree level, Gray saw nothing but a sea of green. He had another idea. If Jean were somehow alive, she'd need water. He studied the terrain. Far away, he spotted a creek. The pilot made two passes. Nothing. Wait—Gray thought he saw something move. He asked the pilot to circle back.

Then Gray saw a dog. Then a woman with silver hair waving at the chopper. He radioed the team, giving new instructions. From a distance, he watched searchers running to the woman. He saw

revealed that her potassium was low from eating next to nothing for nearly a week. She was released from the hospital that night with a prescription for potassium tablets, which she chased down with a big bowl of cherries.

When rescuers discussed the search, they talked about the small urn. Without it, they would never have found Jean. Gray is convinced that Jack Geer's spirit protected his wife.

Jean doesn't doubt it. But the woman who questioned her will to go on without her husband had found the wherewithal to survive. And with that came a life-affirming conclusion. "It's time to let go and let [my] own light shine, and stand up," she told the *Seattle Times*. "This situation forced me. I realized I had to be on my own and move on to my life."

them hug her. His radio came to life: *We have Jean.*

After six days in the woods, Jean was too weak to walk out on her own. Gray called in a larger Coast Guard helicopter, one that could hoist Jean up into the chopper in a basket, while the ground crew carried Yoda out.

At the hospital, doctors were stunned that Jean's only injuries were scratches on her legs. Tests

"I Can Quit Whenever I Want"

Attorney Jim Heiting's drinking was going to kill him—and possibly others—if he didn't come to terms with his addiction.

———

BY **PER OLA AND EMILY D'AULAIRE**

Originally published in June 1997

Jim Heiting, 17, was a top student at Corona High, 60 miles east of Los Angeles. Bright and athletic, the blue-eyed blond played varsity sports and was president of his senior class.

Then one evening after a football game, Jim and some friends drove to a deserted street amid orange groves. One of the boys produced a quart of mixed beverages. "One inch from every bottle in my parents' liquor cabinet," he boasted.

The youngsters started passing around the bottle. Jim, whose parents sipped wine only on occasion, had never had a drink of alcohol before. But when the bottle reached him, he thought, *Why not? Everyone else is taking slugs.*

The potent mixture burned his throat; the second swallow hurt less. As the bottle continued around, he soon felt a warm sense of abandon.

❖　❖　❖

For many, an occasional drink adds enjoyment to social gatherings. Yet for some, it can eventually lead to

Jim Heiting in his law-office library.

dependency. The process starts slowly and unthreateningly, as it did for Jim.

Ethanol, as potable alcohol is called, irritated the mucous membranes in Jim's throat. Increased mucus secretions gradually diluted this effect and caused the sensation to dwindle, then disappear.

Jim woke up with a queasy stomach and a headache. But he had enjoyed what he could remember of that night.

When the ethanol molecules hit Jim's stomach, about 10 to 15 percent were absorbed through the stomach wall. The rest traveled rapidly to the small intestine, where millions of ethanol molecules entered his bloodstream. Much of the ethanol was detoxified by his liver, but enough reached his brain to produce his feelings of wellbeing.

❖　❖　❖

That evening Jim became roaring drunk. He and his friends headed for downtown Corona at 80 mph, and they eventually parked on a side street. Walking by a church, Jim heaved a metal pole through the sign announcing Sunday worship. Everyone laughed when the glass shattered.

A few minutes later, though, Jim leaned over and vomited. Then he staggered a few paces, fell and passed out. His friends drove him home. Jim's parents were gone for the evening, so his escapades went undiscovered.

❖　❖　❖

Alcohol works like a sedative drug. It affects higher thought processes first, and at greater concentrations begins to affect areas that regulate basic life functions.

The effects of increasing blood alcohol concentration (BAC), the percentage of alcohol in the blood, vary from person to person. But the first consequences are impairment of judgment and, in some cases, a loss of inhibitions. Following this, reaction time slows, after which vision, speech and balance are affected. Stumbling and loss of muscle control occur at an even higher BAC, and eventually death from respiratory arrest can occur.

Jim woke up the next morning with a queasy stomach and a headache, and his mouth felt like dry cotton. But he had enjoyed what he could remember of that night in 1966: the camaraderie and rebelliousness.

Alcohol dilates blood vessels throughout the body. Widened vessels in the skin produced the warm feeling that Jim experienced the night before. Chemical byproducts called congeners, sometimes combined with dilation of blood vessels in the neck and head, led to Jim's headache.

In Jim's stomach the alcohol attacked his mucin, a protective layer that keeps hydrochloric acid from eating away the lining. This caused Jim's nausea and vomiting.

Jim enrolled in Riverside University near his home, where he started guzzling beer at weekend parties. "I've got a hollow leg," he would boast. "I can drink anyone under the table."

Despite his weekend drinking, he got good grades and became the class valedictorian.

Those prone to alcoholism can typically "hold their liquor" better than others. In a study at the University of California at San Diego, male college students who were drinkers but not alcoholics were given the equivalent of three to five drinks. Those who were sons of alcoholics showed a less intense response to all the effects of alcohol compared with the sons of nonalcoholics.

Does this mean that alcoholism always and only runs in families? Not necessarily. There are people with nonalcoholic parents who develop the illness with repeated exposure to alcohol. But it's far more likely to happen to someone with a family history of the disease.

In the fall of 1971, at age 22, Jim married Cindy Hudd, an attractive blonde. In the spring of 1972 he entered Western State University College of Law in Fullerton, California.

To pay for school, Jim worked afternoons in a modular-home factory. After attending evening classes, he tackled a graveyard shift at a wire mill.

By the time he clocked out at 7 a.m., he was too keyed up to sleep. So, sitting in bed, he'd down a 40-ounce bottle of malt liquor. "It's my sleeping medication," he assured Cindy.

Then in the summer of 1973 Jim and Cindy, along with their new son, Jo-Jo, drove to Yosemite. While sipping a beer in a restaurant, Jim noticed a pamphlet that contained ten questions to help the reader recognize a drinking problem.

Jim had checked yes to six questions when he saw the warning at the bottom: "If you answered yes to more than three questions, you're probably an alcoholic." Startled, Jim thought, *I must've misinterpreted them.*

On a second run-through, he answered yes only three times. *I can quit whenever I want*, he told himself.

One weekend soon after, Jim and a friend split a half-pint of whiskey, then hiked into the San Bernardino Mountains. Jim was so drunk he later couldn't remember a thing.

❖ ❖ ❖

One of the foremost psychological consequences of alcoholism is denial of the problem. As for Jim's inability to recall the hike, alcohol interferes with short-term memory. While numerous theories exist, scientists still don't know exactly how alcohol produces such changes in brain function.

❖ ❖ ❖

Jim was now painfully aware that he had a problem, and vowed each morning not to drink that day. To keep that promise, he left all his cash and credit cards on the bedside table. But as the day wore on, he'd start thinking about a drink. At five o'clock he'd casually ask one of his law clerks, "Got ten dollars I can borrow? I could use something to eat." Then he'd buy a bottle of gin and guzzle it on the way home.

On the afternoon of April 6, 1986, Jim was weaving homeward on a motorcycle he'd bought to reward himself for winning a difficult case. He had well over a pint of gin under his belt. Accelerating sharply around a van, Jim passed the vehicle, then cut directly in front of it.

The bike's rear tire suddenly skidded sideways on the rain-slicked road. He overcorrected and the bike flipped, slamming on top of him. The impact broke his collarbone and every rib on his left side. It also punctured a lung and bruised his heart.

Even after Jim's recovery, Cindy worried about his health. His eyes now had a yellow hue, and his belly and ankles were swollen. "You're killing yourself," she told him.

As the liver detoxifies alcohol, it uses part of the alcohol as fuel. This takes the place of the fat that it normally relies on for energy. Fat then accumulates, and some liver cells die. The resulting scars in the liver disrupt normal flow through the blood vessels, which produces varicose veins.

In addition, bile backs up in the bloodstream, causing a yellow hue in the eyes and skin. Fluids also back up beyond what the kidneys can handle, resulting in puffy ankles or a swollen belly. After years of

heavy drinking, the liver can become so scarred that it no longer functions— full-blown cirrhosis—and it shuts down. The patient dies.

Alcohol also increases the levels of triglycerides in the bloodstream, causing narrowing of the arteries. It can cause the pancreas to become severely inflamed. And it can elevate blood pressure and inflame the heart muscle. The most recent available statistics show that alcohol caused an estimated 100,000 preventable deaths in one year alone in the United States, and an additional 17,699 alcohol-related traffic fatalities.

Around 9:30 p.m. on July 17, 1986, almost 20 years after his high-school binge, Jim polished off a pint of bourbon and started driving to a friend's house. Suddenly he blacked out. His Jeep Cherokee barreled across a median strip and rammed into an oncoming car.

Jim suffered only an injured knee and shoulder. But when he saw the small sports car he had hit, his world came crashing in on him. The only person in the Mustang,

Lucinda Wales, a 27-year-old mother of two, had somehow survived. However, both her legs were broken, her left femur was crushed and her right knee was shattered. Her right ankle, right wrist, left arm, jaw and cheek were also in fragments. Her bladder and kidneys had severe damage. Over the next four years she would undergo more than 20 operations.

Police slapped handcuffs on Jim. A test revealed he had more than three times the legal amount of alcohol in his blood. He spent the night in jail before being released on his own recognizance. Meeting with a criminal-defense lawyer, he was told, "I'll represent you on one condition: You enroll in a treatment center."

On September 1, 1986, Jim drove to the Betty Ford Center, an addiction-rehabilitation facility in Rancho Mirage.

Tests showed that Jim's blood pressure was elevated, his liver enlarged. His ability to think was impaired, a sign of alcohol-induced brain damage. The first few days he trembled from head to toe as withdrawal kicked in.

CAT scans of alcoholics' brains show cerebral shrinking, a deterioration that slowly starts to reverse with the absence of alcohol if the condition hasn't progressed too far. In Jim's case it hadn't. He was lucky. Some victims suffer permanent brain damage to the point that they need to be institutionalized for life.

Over the next month, counselors helped Jim understand that only by committing himself totally to the battle would he be able to free himself from the bottle.

When Jim "graduated" from the Betty Ford Center one month later, he feared a relapse. Seeing the "Welcome Home" banner that Cindy and the boys had strung across the garage door, he panicked. *If I go inside, what's to keep me from heading for the liquor cabinet?* "I can't stay," he told Cindy, bolting for his car.

That night Jim attended an Alcoholics Anonymous meeting, where he found the support he needed to go home and try the reunion again.

❖ ❖ ❖

After his sobriety was established, Jim's blood pressure came down and his liver began to revert to normal size. Tests showed that his cognitive functions also began to return toward their former level. The only lingering physical reminder was bone pain from his two accidents.

❖ ❖ ❖

When his day in court came, Jim pleaded guilty to felony drunk driving and served a sentence of over six months. On January 15, 1988, he was released. Later that year he started a local chapter of The Other Bar, an organization of recovering lawyers and judges. "I've taken so much from people," he told Cindy. "I need to give something back."

However, Jim had memories that wouldn't go away. In July 1995 he mustered the courage to phone Lucinda Wales and arranged to meet with her.

"You can't imagine how sorry I've been all these years," Jim told her.

"I needed to hear that," Lucinda answered. "I'm glad you're still sober."

To help Jim recover, Cindy had to quit making excuses for him.

On September 1, 1996, the tenth anniversary of his sobriety, Jim was sworn in as president of the Riverside County Bar Association. His life is now full and contented. Still, the urge for a drink occasionally returns. "The hold that alcohol can get on you is terrible," Jim says. "I thank God every day that I'm sober."

Bear Tracks in the Bathtub

The frolicsome tale of Mister B., a cub who came for dinner—and hasn't left yet.

———

BY **IRVING PETITE**
FROM **THE CHRISTIAN SCIENCE MONITOR**
Originally published in October 1960

All morning we'd heard our dog, Nameless, barking in the woods across the creek, and at intervals her yips were answered by an unearthly screech. Our ranch in the Cascade Mountains southeast of Seattle abounds in wild life, and two months before—in January—we had discovered a black-bear den cross-creek. I assumed now that a cub must have lagged behind its mother as she went through the woods in her search for the first green buds of spring. Since Nameless, a mostly cocker female, wasn't large enough to hurt the screeching infant, I decided that the mother would surely come to the cub's rescue. So I continued my job of splitting cedar shakes.

It was with surprise, then, that I saw a strange twosome emerge from the creek canyon. First came Nameless; then, humping along behind, came a myopic runt bear cub, producing a wailing cacophony. The two had obviously made peace; the cub was simply wailing with hunger and cold.

I stooped down to inspect young Mister B. He was about as big as a pint drinking gourd, with triangular ears for handles. Fur drenched, he was all feet and claws and wide-open mouth with a pink, triangular underlip. My warmth and size probably approximated motherness; at any rate the wailing quieted. He grabbed hold of the arm of my bulky sweater, hoisted himself up and began nuzzling the hollow of my neck, making a moist mumbling sound.

Mister B., who, we figured, was then about nine weeks old, became part of the life of the ranch. As he tried to follow us wherever we worked, he would *whuff*, snuff and whimper in a manner calculated to touch the hardest heart. He was easily affectionate and just as easily outraged. As soon as he was full of warm milk and canned peaches he would climb the nearest human being and nuzzle at an inside-forearm, neck or cheek. But when he was gently dislodged, he would dig into clothes or bare skin with his claw tips and then take a quick bite at neck or arm.

He soon learned to bite and run, in order to miss getting an approximation of a mother-bear swat. Then he would utter an aggressive, high-pitched squall, audible all over the mountain.

Such scenes occurred several times daily for the first two months. Then Mister B. quieted down noticeably, and at the age of five or six months he could easily be talked out of nuzzling; he was beginning to put infancy behind him. His development was somewhat comparable to that of a human infant, for bears continue growing until about the age of five years.

Mister B. loved to help around motor vehicles. If a mechanic was flat on his back under an automobile or truck, Mister B. would happily sit on the man's chest. If the mechanic dislodged him, he would stand stiffly, ears laid back, mouth wide open, and scream.

He early made his favorite hiding place the motor of my car. One frosty morning when I lifted the hood to check the oil, I saw that Mister B. had neatly removed all the rock wool insulation glued to the underside of the hood and had rearranged it to form a nest between the left front fender and the engine

block. There he cuddled, with a warm motor for a mother, his two beady eyes gazing at me innocently.

One evening after supper, I started for the Issaquah Post Office, six miles away. Until the gas pedal gave an unnatural lurch I didn't realize that Mister B. had already retired. In a moment I heard a loud *WAAAAAH*—unmistakably Mister B.'s. I pulled off to the side of the road and raised the hood. There he was, looking worried as all get-out, his mouth oozing a bubble of supper milk.

Mister B. had that persistent curiosity about the universe that is common to all wild creatures, and because, like all baby bears, he was myopic, he was forever sniffing, tonguing and touching things. Bowling down a woods road, he would suddenly stand upright and with one forepaw bend down a vine-maple limb and take the leaves into his mouth. When the wind blew fluff from the cottonwood trees, he examined it critically with tongue and paws.

One June morning I found him

at the top of the Dutch door leading into the garage, hanging on with his right forepaw and leaning far out to peer into a swallow's nest. His object was not to eat the birds—he was not looking for food. Like his relative in the song, he merely "went over the mountain to see what he could see."

Climbing to investigate nearly got him into trouble when, as a tiny cub, he climbed a rear leg of one of my team. The 1,850-pound horse bucked, for the first time in years, and the little bear dropped off— only, in his nervousness, to seek haven up a leg on the mare. After that he was careful to leave horse legs alone.

To Mister B., every tree in the forest sang a siren song: "Embrace Me!" Into the smooth-barked cedars he clopped his fore claws with a quick, wrist-bent gesture, while his back feet dug in like a lineman using heel spikes. He always descended backward, often self-consciously nonchalant, wearing a twig in his mouth like a toothpick. One day he broke off a dead limb high in a fir and came down, head over tail,

through other limbs, crackling and whirling—about 18 feet—*whump!* to the ground. Only seconds later, however, he was heeding another of the siren songs—as many as 200 to an acre, not counting snags, stumps and leaning logs.

Mister B. regarded our house as his, and would climb up the cedar siding and into any window that happened to be open. One night I dreamed I heard the typewriter going, and the next morning awoke to find its keys jammed and my papers scattered over the floor. After that the window to my workroom was kept closed.

On another occasion, friends from California came to visit, and while we adults were conversing in the living room, the children prepared for bed. Whereupon one little girl came back to complain audibly to her mother, "I *would* take a bath, but somebody's been walking around in there with dirty feet."

I went to do a not-unusual chore: mopping bear tracks out of the bathtub. For when Mister B. needed a drink, he would scramble up through the bathroom window from outside, reverse, hang down and drop backward into the tub. Then he would walk along the cool porcelain to slurp from the puddle around the drain. Since he did not wipe his feet after leaving the outside flower beds, tracks did get left in the tub.

Nameless, the dog who had discovered Mister B., was his favorite playtime companion. She would watch with a sort of maternal indulgence while he breaststroked up our sawdust pile, and then, with a *whoof* of joy, went belly-whopping down. On hot summer days she would frequently lead him into the cool shallows of the creek. There she would gambol, round and round, while Mister B. did his best to follow, occasionally rearing to *whap!* the water with his huge forepaws. Then he would whirl and stand up, dripping, as if asking her to box with wet gloves.

Of our five dogs, however, Mister B.'s all-round favorite was a little beagle-cocker puppy. Nighttimes he shared the doghouse or an angle of the front porch with her. She

profited by the association, for Mister B. would nudge a door open and lead her into the house. There he would shinny up the kitchen table or climb by toenail-holds up the drawers to the sink, and whatever cookies, soda crackers or overturned canned peaches fell to the floor were hers to share.

Lately Mister B.'s habits have changed. He goes farther and farther into the hills and stays for longer periods of time, sometimes coming in to *WAAAAH* for milk or canned fruit at the back door at 2 a.m., sometimes not returning at all. It will probably be only a matter of time before he breaks the tenuous ties of dog and human companionship.

In five years, God willing and the woodlands continuing to provide safe hiding places, I expect to be splitting cedar shakes someday when the underbrush will part and out will amble Mister B. I wouldn't be surprised if he put a forepaw over my shoulder, nuzzled reminiscently at my neck and burbled a bar of bear music.

Miracle of the Flower Boxes

It was a block like many others on New York City's Upper West Side: poor, crowded, dirty, teeming with hatred and gang fights. Then the flowers came, and their magic began to spread.

BY **PEGGY MANN**

Originally published in July 1973

Perhaps the two bullet holes in the front window should have warned us off. But when we asked the real estate agent about them, he laughed. "Oh, those are old," he said. "Look at the street now. It's nice and quiet."

It was. It was also a dead-cold snowy afternoon with no signs of life outside. So, lulled by the winter quiet, my husband, Bill, and I bought the rundown brownstone on Manhattan's Upper West Side, moved in and started renovating.

At the first warmth of spring, life spilled out onto the street. The front steps of the brownstone rooming houses were lined with women gossiping in the sunshine and men playing poker and dominoes. Children shouted and shrieked in the street amid a mosaic of trash and car-flattened beer cans, and radios blared Spanish music.

Our neighbors, we discovered, included addicts, pushers and

prostitutes. A mid-block hydrant marked the dividing line between the "turf" of the Young Kings, a Black teenage gang, and that of their rivals, a Puerto Rican gang called the Spanish Angels. Adults walked where they wished, but any communication between Blacks and Spanish was generally ripe with threats and curses.

Since Bill and I are neither Black nor Puerto Rican, our house became a no-man's-land for some younger boys of both groups. The smallest was five-year-old "Little Luis" Gomez, who promptly posed the question asked by many of our friends: "Hey, lady, how come you move onto this crummy street?"

The answer was easy. My husband is English, and he had always lived in a house. I, on the other hand, had grown up in Manhattan, and to me the word *suburb* meant isolation. So, the answer seemed to be: a house in the city. We'd met a real estate agent who had a brownstone in an area scheduled for urban renewal. It was so narrow that it had never been worth turning into a rooming house and had therefore retained its parquet floors, fireplaces and Victorian charm. And the price was only $17,000.

When I explained some of this to Little Luis, he nodded wisely and said, "My big brother, Carlos, he calls you 'The Crazies.'"

Flower Fight

As spring heated into summer, we sometimes agreed with Carlos. The two gangs moved to the backyards at night and shot off small-caliber bullets—to frighten each other, we assured ourselves. Then the dead body of one of the gang boys was discovered on a rooftop across the way. And one evening we came home from work to find a new bullet hole in our front window. It must have been a mistake, we decided, not intended for us.

So we stayed, and continued renovating, living for the most part on hot dogs so that we could turn over our paychecks to our alcoholic man of all work. Now he was building two brick flower boxes for the front areaway. The boys who congregated there made bets as to what the structures were for.

Clarence, leader of the preteen Blacks, thought they might be some kind of garbage can.

The following Friday morning, a gardener's truck drove up, and our boxes were filled with the best topsoil and a blazingly bright array of petunias, geraniums and English ivy. My husband declared that our brownstone was now "a real house."

When I came home that evening, however, only the topsoil and a few trampled flower petals remained. I ran inside, for some reason more shaken by the destruction of the flowers than by the bullet through the window. This *was* aimed at us. The act was as eloquent as a curse: *Get out! You're not wanted here!*

A short while later, the bell rang. Carlos Gomez, the nine-year-old brother of Little Luis and a leader of the preteen Puerto Ricans, stood on the stoop.

"I am sorry," he announced, "about the flowers."

"So am I," I said. "I wonder who did it."

Carlos shrugged and started to leave. Then I heard myself saying, "Wait a minute, Carlos. If … if we planted more flowers, would you be their guardian? We'd pay you 50 cents a week."

Again he shrugged. "*Porqué no?*" And he ran down the steps.

When Bill got home, he exploded. He'd heard what had happened from Pepe Garcia. Carlos had yanked out one of the ivy plants and slung it into Clarence's face. The flower fight that ensued

> ## I was more shaken by the destruction of the flowers than by the bullet through the window. This was *aimed at us.*

had been observed by Carlos's strict grandmother. It was she who sent him to apologize.

The flowers and ivy had cost us $30. "Now," Bill fumed, "you're planning to fork out another $30 for another fight?"

"Well," I said, "this time we'll use flats. They don't cost much."

77

"Worst Block"

When the gardener came again, so did Carlos—armed with a switchblade. He planted the seedlings, ignoring the ridicule of the other boys. Perhaps the new plants were so tiny that it didn't seem worth anyone's while to uproot them. Or perhaps it was Carlos's threat to "get" anyone who touched them. In any case, the flowers grew tall and beautiful, blossoming all through the summer.

By the second summer, we had no fear that our flowers would be uprooted. Or that we would be.

Our daughter Jenny was born, and Fleeta Mae Bostic from North Carolina arrived to help care for her.

One evening, I came home from work to find the block strangely quiet. And police were patrolling. "The peoples been fightin' all afternoon," Fleeta Mae told me. "All Spanish on one side, all colored on the other." As I started putting the baby to bed, there was a crash outside. I ran to the window. A policeman ducked as a brick hurtled past his head. Then more bottles and bricks were hurled through the air.

Squad cars came, sirens wailing. The police commissioner ordered people down from the rooftops. But bricks and bottles continued to crash into the street. As Fleeta Mae and I stared through the louvered shutters, wishing Bill were not working late, we saw a line of helmeted police fire round after round above the rooftops.

Finally, the combatants were driven down. By 11 o'clock the situation was under control, and a curfew was imposed. The next day's newspapers ran headlines about the riot on "the city's worst block."

It was time to do something. If we were to continue to make our home here, we reasoned, we must somehow involve ourselves in the life of our block. But how?

Blooming Pride

"What about those flower boxes?" Bill finally said one night at dinner. "People seem to respond to them." In England, he pointed out, countless dreary row houses are given individual charm and warmth by flamboyant window boxes. Bill decided that we should stop work on our house and use the money to start work on our block.

He ordered dozens of plastic window boxes, and gallons of paint. Carlos, Clarence, Pepe, Little Luis, Bill and I spent that Saturday afternoon painting the boxes, and the following Saturday a nursery delivered several hundred dollars' worth of potted petunias, geraniums and English ivy. When the boys arrived, we spent the afternoon planting the painted boxes. Then we all went out to sell them to our neighbors—for whatever price we could get, but only to people who lived in a room overlooking the street. By evening we'd collected a coffee can full of IOUs, and $204. The money went to buy more flowers and more plastic boxes. In a very short time we had put flowers in—and sold or given away— 12 dozen window boxes. And our block had become a sudden field of color.

It was only a few days before the small miracles began. Bright new curtains appeared, and torn window shades were replaced. Newly polished brass doorknobs gleamed. Landlords provided more outdoor garbage pails, and "airmail"—garbage sailing out of open windows—became a thing of the past. People on back windows, who had not been supplied with window boxes, bought or made their own and planted them.

The fire-hydrant dividing line was forgotten as Blacks and Spanish strolled the evening street, looking upward. Soon people from neighboring streets came to walk down ours, to gaze, to admire. Pride started blooming along with the flowers on West 94th Street. And by the time the cold weather came, the corrosive antagonisms that had caused our "race war" seemed to have submerged.

The following spring, people remembered what had been, and what could be. They planted and tended the tiny seedlings themselves,

> **If we were to continue to make our home here, it was time to involve ourselves in the life of our block.**

and soon the block bloomed again. The magic of it all came home to me one night when I gave a cabdriver my address. "Oh, yeah," he said. "The Street of the Flower Boxes." And so it has remained.

❖   ❖   ❖

The story might have ended right there. It didn't, and how it didn't is a story in itself. Author Mann wrote a children's book called "The Street of the Flower Boxes," *and it inspired an NBC-TV special. But producer-directors David and Suzette Tapper faced a problem when it came to filming. After years under the beneficent influence of the window boxes, West 94th Street had changed; it could no longer be filmed as the story's "before" part. So the Tappers selected a dingy block on Seventh Street between Avenues C and D on Manhattan's Lower East Side.*

As props, the Tappers purchased 400 window boxes and hundreds of pots of geraniums, petunias and English ivy. Actors painted, planted and distributed the boxes just as the author, her husband and their young friends had done a few years before on West 94th Street. When the filming was over, the flower boxes remained where they had been put for the story's last act.

Within a day or two, the miracles began to happen again. Curtains appeared. Doors were painted. Garbage was bagged. And Saturday "block work parties" turned a vacant lot into a beautiful park.

"Suddenly there was something new in the air," the Tappers recall. "The block had become a neighborhood!" It also became a prizewinner. More than 500 blocks throughout New York City entered a contest that summer to determine which city streets had "done the most to improve themselves." Grand Prize winner? Seventh Street between Avenues C and D.

Meanwhile, "flower-box magic" has been at work in other areas. Since 1961, for example, the New York City Housing Authority has sponsored a summer garden contest among its 600,000 public-housing tenants. Wherever contest gardens have been grown, Authority statistics show, vandalism has been reduced. "We've always been aware that plants must be recipients of our care," says horticulturist Charles A. Lewis, a judge in the past nine Housing Authority contests. "But what of the reverse flow of benefits, from

plants to people—particularly city people? Gardening may well be an instrument for great healing in our troubled cities."

Perhaps Little Luis Gomez came closest to the heart of the matter when he said to Peggy Mann: "A flower is sort of like a smile."

The Family That Robbed Banks

Widower Scott Catt had a secret life as a bank robber. But when he wanted accomplices, he turned to the two people he trusted most in the world: his kids.

———

BY **SKIP HOLLANDSWORTH**
FROM **TEXAS MONTHLY**

Originally published in June 2014

Just after sunrise on August 9, 2012, in the Houston suburb of Katy, Scott Catt, a 50-year-old structural engineer, was awakened by his alarm clock in the apartment he shared with his 20-year-old son, Hayden, and his 18-year-old daughter, Abby.

Scott took a shower, dried off, got dressed and walked into the living room. Abby and Hayden were waiting for him on the couch.

"OK, kids," Scott said. "You ready?"

Abby and Hayden nodded. The family headed out the door and walked toward Abby's 1999 green Volkswagen Jetta. Scott was big, six foot four and 240 pounds, and he squeezed himself into the passenger seat. Hayden, six-two and 200 pounds, crammed into the backseat.

Neighbors said the Catts were "regular, everyday people." What happened?

CATT RONALD SCOTT

JID POO179151	Booking No. 1225350	MNI 01228867
Height 6-02	Weight 250	Sex **M**	DOB 6-11-62
Hair BRO	Eye Color. BLU	Facial Hair B	Race W

CATT HAYDEN SCOTT

JID POO179152	Booking No. 1225368	MNI 01228868
Height 6-04	Weight 210	Sex M	DOB 12-7-91
Hair BRO	Eye Color. BRO	Facial Hair	Race W

CATT ABIGAIL NICOLE

JID POO179158	Booking No. 1225382	MNI 01228919
Height 5-07	Weight.135	Sex F	DOB 5-9-94
Hair BLN	Eye Color. HAZ	Facial Hair	Race W

Abby started the car, and five minutes later, she pulled into a shopping center and parked about 50 yards from a Comerica Bank.

Scott grabbed a black garbage bag from the floorboard and took out two pairs of white painter's coveralls, two painter's masks, two pairs of latex gloves and two Airsoft pistols (which look like real guns but shoot plastic pellets). He and Hayden put on their disguises in the Jetta. Scott clipped a walkie-talkie to his coveralls and handed another to Abby.

It was 9:30. They sat for the next 30 minutes, until Scott said it was time to make their move. Abby dropped them off a few stores from the bank and drove to the alley behind it. Minutes later, her dad's voice crackled through her walkie-talkie.

"We're going in," he said.

Robbing a bank is the most traditional of crimes. It's a simple act with an immediate payoff. All sorts of criminals have tried it. "If you're in law enforcement long enough, you'll eventually come across bank robbers of every shape and size," said Troy Nehls, sheriff of Fort Bend County, which includes part of the Katy area. "But I'm not sure there has ever been a bank-robbing family."

The Catts were as unlikely a set of robbers as one could imagine. They had no pressing financial issues and no obvious personal problems. Scott, a widower, worked for an energy company. Abby was a salesclerk at Victoria's Secret, and Hayden was hoping to be a hotel concierge.

Around their apartment complex, the Catts were regarded as "regular, everyday people," one of their neighbors said. Yet when it came to robbing banks, said Nehls, "they were very bold, very daring and very risky. They're lucky they didn't get caught up in a shoot-out."

The Catts pulled off two robberies: the Comerica heist, and the robbery of a credit union two months later. They were getting ready for a third when they were arrested in November 2012.

Reporters tried to find out why a father and his two children would turn to bank robbery, but the Catts weren't talking. Then, late in 2013, the three agreed to plea deals, and they consented to let me interview them.

I was allowed to speak to only one Catt at a time. Abby was the first to be escorted to the visiting room. She sat on a chair, ducked her head, and said after a silence, "Sometimes I feel so embarrassed about what's happened that I just want to disappear."

Hayden came next. "Every night I stare at the ceiling, and I ask myself, 'What were we thinking?'" he said.

Then Scott walked in. He gave me a firm handshake, sat down and pushed his fingertips together. "All I can tell you is that I thought it would help us as a family," he said. He took a breath and blew it out. "I did it for the family," he said. "I swear to you, I would rob banks only for my family."

The story begins in McMinnville, Oregon, southwest of Portland, where Scott was born and raised. His father was a loan officer at First Federal Savings and Loan. At McMinnville High School, Scott played football and fell in love with Beth Worral, a star of the swim team. They married after graduation. After Beth had Hayden and Abby, the Catts built a house in Dundee— "our dream house," Scott told me. But in 1995, Beth was diagnosed with breast cancer, and she died two years later. Hayden was five and Abby was two.

At that point, Scott told me, "life sort of came to a halt." He began drinking heavily. He had a brief second marriage. He went to rehab. He fell behind on house payments, and the family moved in with Scott's mother. He went through a couple of jobs. His car was repossessed.

Between 2000 and 2002, he began thinking about how to make extra money. He remembered that one day his father had come home and said First Federal had been robbed. When Scott asked why no one had stopped the thief, his father replied that the tellers were trained to comply with robbers—because the money was insured, the bank would get it back.

One morning, after dropping off the kids at school, Scott drove to a branch of his dad's old bank. He strode in wearing a ball cap, black sweats, a white painter's mask and sunglasses. He was carrying a trash bag and an antique pistol—unloaded. He went up to a window, demanded the teller's money and ordered her not to add bait bills or dye packs. She dumped around $2,500 into his bag. Scott walked back to his truck, drove around for a while to see if he was being followed, and went home.

A couple of days later, the local paper published a grainy black-and-white frame from a video showing the robber. "My mother said the man looked a little like me, and I just laughed," Scott said. "And that was it."

Scott did his next heist a year later after falling behind on bills, and he got $1,500 from another small bank. Then he landed a full-time job with an engineering company, earning $25 an hour. Still, once a year he'd pull off a robbery, hauling in between $5,000 and $10,000. (Authorities believe he robbed at least five banks in Oregon.)

"I didn't feel like a criminal," he told me. "I didn't load my pistol. I knew I wasn't going to shoot anybody. And I kept telling myself that whatever money I got was insured, so who was really being hurt?"

Meanwhile, Scott was a devoted single father. He cooked dinner for his kids almost every night and took them on vacations. When they got interested in competitive swimming, Scott drove them to practice every day.

Abby and Hayden never once suspected that their father had a secret life. "He'd be up and gone to work by 4:30 or 5 in the morning," Hayden said. "He didn't make great money, but we always appreciated how hard he worked to keep us afloat."

"Dad was a great motivator," Abby told me. "At the beginning of each [swim] season, he pushed me to work hard and set goals. He told me I could be somebody. The night before every swim meet, he would cook us pork chops, noodles, applesauce and a protein shake. I loved it."

One time, Hayden qualified for the state meet, and there was talk about a college scholarship. But by the age of 17, he said, he was drinking too much and quit swimming. Abby lost interest in the sport when she was 15. She started running with what she called "the drinking, partying crowd," and she ended up in an alternative school. After graduation, Hayden found work as a hotel bellman and as a weekend tour guide, and he was still drinking too much. And Scott was again falling behind financially. By 2010, it was time for another robbery.

Scott knew that if he had accomplices, he could get cash from several tellers' drawers and perhaps even get to the bank's vault. But there was no one he could trust to stay quiet—except his children. Maybe he should talk to them about joining him.

He rationalized the idea. As long as they did what he said, they wouldn't get caught. And he would use the money to start a small business they could run. "They were floundering," he told me. "I could see the despair in Hayden, and I thought he could use—I don't know—some inspiration, some excitement. Same with Abby. All I can tell you is that I thought doing it would give us all a little boost in our lives—that it would help us as a family."

Scott approached his son. "We were sitting at the kitchen table," Hayden recalled. "He said he had something important to tell me. He said he had a second job as a

> ## "I didn't feel like a criminal. I didn't load my pistol. Who was really being hurt?"

part-time bank robber. The way he looked at me, I knew he wasn't kidding."

Scott said he would be the "muscle," leading the way in and scaring the employees and customers, and Hayden would be the "bag man," ordering tellers to put money into his bag. They'd wear disguises, go to the bank early in the morning before there were many customers, and be out within three minutes. Scott told his son they could easily grab $40,000 or more.

On the morning of the robbery, Hayden was scared. Scott did the robbery by himself, getting a few thousand dollars, and came home before lunch. "He did it so quickly and so easily that it planted a seed," Hayden told me. "I thought, *My dad really does know what he's doing.*"

Then Scott was laid off. By January 2012, he'd found work in

At home, the family stared wide-eyed at the money, close to $70,000— a stunning haul.

Houston and relocated there. Abby moved in with her grandmother in Oregon, and Hayden went to Hawaii and got a job at a hotel. It seemed like a new era. Scott's job paid well, and he hoped he'd quit thinking about banks. But there were just so many in Texas.

❖   ❖   ❖

By March, Scott had persuaded Abby to move to Texas. She landed a job at Victoria's Secret. (She proudly announced on her Facebook page that she was a Victoria's Secret "Pink Girl.") A few months later, Hayden joined them, and it wasn't long before he began talking to his father about a bank robbery. He wanted money for college.

Scott picked out a nearby Comerica. He began walking past it in the mornings with the family's yellow Lab, Bella, to see when it got busy, and he had his son go in to learn the layout of the lobby. But they needed a getaway driver—and there was only one person who came to mind.

Hayden went into Abby's room. "I need to tell you something," he said. "Dad's a bank robber; I'm going to become one, too, and we want you to join us."

The next day, Scott talked to Abby, promising her that all she'd have to do was drop them off, wait for them to return, and drive home at a normal speed. She agreed to participate. "This was something I felt like I had to do, to protect them, to make sure they got out of the bank and didn't get shot or something," she told me. "I didn't want to let Dad down."

In the apartment, Hayden and Scott practiced bursting into a bank and yelling at everyone to get their hands up. They scheduled the robbery for August 9, when Abby had a day off from Victoria's Secret. The night before, Scott had the kids steal license plates from a car at another complex and put them over the Jetta's plates.

The robbery went off as planned. Outside, Abby gave them time updates over the walkie-talkie. At the three-minute mark, Scott and Hayden ordered the manager to unlock the back door, and they jumped into the Jetta. Abby drove to another neighborhood, and Hayden and Scott threw their disguises, pistols, stolen plates and gloves into a Dumpster. In their apartment, they stared wide-eyed at the money, close to $70,000— a stunning haul from a little branch bank.

They heard sirens and decided to go out. Scott took a ride on his motorcycle, Hayden went shopping and Abby got a manicure. That night Abby was still nervous—"I kept looking at the door, waiting for the police to walk in," she said— but Hayden was overjoyed. "I felt exhilaration, the most intense high I've ever experienced," he said. "It changed my life. I'll be truthful about that."

Scott paid off his bills. He bought a second motorcycle and a $17,000 Tahoe for Hayden and a $12,600 Ford Focus for Abby (the Jetta had engine trouble). He and the kids split the remainder, but by late September, all the money was spent.

He and Hayden decided to rob the First Community Credit Union. Because there was a construction crew working nearby, Scott sent Hayden and Abby to Home Depot to buy two orange safety vests for disguises. Hayden also went to a costume shop to buy a fake mustache.

On October 1, Abby took the day off from work and drove Hayden and Scott to the credit union. The men entered at about 1:50. Their size and guns terrified everyone, and they were in and out so fast that no one got a good look at them. As Abby drove them home, police cars came screaming from the opposite direction. Not one officer gave her a second look. All they heard over the radio was that two tall men had committed a robbery.

The Catts got $29,953, a decent sum. A few days later, Abby told her father she couldn't handle the stress. She wanted to take her cut and move into her own place. Scott promised her an apartment but begged her to remain their wheelman. He had decided to quit his job and make a living as a full-time bank robber, and Hayden would join him.

"The greed had snowballed," recalled Hayden. "I had become consumed with money: spending it, getting more. It was all I thought about, like an addiction."

On November 8, Abby drove them to another bank, but there was too much foot traffic so they called it off. The next morning, as Scott and Hayden prepared to try again, the police came knocking.

❖   ❖   ❖

While studying video of the credit union robbery, veteran detective Jeff Martin had noticed that the safety vests worn by the robbers weren't tattered or dirty at all. He could even see creases from where they'd been folded. He found that Home Depot sold that style of vest and got a subpoena to review purchases at area Home Depots. Just before the robbery, two vests had been purchased in Katy with a debit card belonging to Scott Catt. Security footage showed a young man and a blond teenage girl buying them. After doing a check on Scott, Martin learned he had two children, Hayden and Abby, whose photos matched the customers.

Martin deduced that Scott and Hayden were the robbers and that Abby was the one whom tellers heard counting time over a walkie-talkie. His case was bolstered by video of Abby applying for an account at the credit union a few days before. (Scott had sent her to scope the layout.) He had the Catts arrested and placed in separate interrogation rooms.

Martin decided to first talk to Scott. He assumed that he would declare his innocence, claiming a case of mistaken identity. But Scott confessed all, even talking about his Oregon robberies, which Martin knew nothing about. The detective was dumbfounded, and he was equally dumbfounded when Hayden and Abby confessed.

Although the getaway driver in a bank robbery is liable under Texas law for the same punishment as the bank robbers, the police and prosecutors felt sympathy for Abby and gave her a mild five-year sentence. (She'll be eligible for parole in seven months.) Hayden received a ten-year sentence (his parole will come up in about four years), but Scott was hit with a 24-year sentence.

When I talked to Scott, he'd lost 70 pounds since his arrest, which he attributed mostly to "a lot of remorse" for what he'd done to his children. "When I look back on what I did, what led to this place, I would have been better off—we all would have been better off—if I had gone on welfare and been a stay-at-home dad."

Abby and Hayden didn't seem to know what to think of their father. "He should have been protecting me, instead of the other way around, having me protect him," Abby said. A few minutes later, she mentioned that she had run into her father a day or so earlier in the infirmary. "He told me he loved me, to be strong and to be patient. And then he said he was so sorry. I broke down and started crying. I mean, like I've said, he is my dad."

Abby plans to become a nurse when she's released. Hayden wants to get a degree in advertising, architecture or engineering—"that's right, engineering, like my dad," he said, smiling.

Scott told me his one hope is that his kids will visit him after they're free. He'll be 62 when he's eligible for parole. "If I get out, I want to have a homecoming dinner that night, me and the kids," he said. "We'll go to a good restaurant, tell stories about the old days." He paused. "About the days when we were a family."

High-Wire Act

When a freak accident threatens a skier's life, his friend takes a daring chance.

—

BY **JULIANA LABIANCA**

Originally published in April 2017

Mickey Wilson had been on the mountain only a few seconds when he heard the scream. Wilson, 28 years old and a confirmed ski bum, had just gotten off the chairlift at the Arapahoe Basin Ski Area in Keystone, Colorado, along with his friends Billy Simmons and Hans Mueller. Their friend Richard (not his real name) had been on the chair ahead of them, but when the men reached the top of the lift, he had seemingly vanished. The men walked toward the source of the scream and found skiers stopped on the slope, pointing to the chairlift. And then the friends screamed too.

"My God!" yelled Mueller.

When Richard had tried to jump off the lift, his backpack had become entangled in the chair, which then dragged him back down the hill. In the process, the backpack strap wrapped around his neck, strangling him. Now Richard's body was dangling four feet below the chair, his ski boots ten feet above the snow. The lift operator had quickly stopped the chairlift, and the friends kicked off their skis and ran toward the scene. They made a human pyramid to try to reach Richard, but he was too far

Wilson straddling a slackline, in much the same way he traversed the chairlift cable.

92

Wilson climbs the tower ladder (right) while an unconscious Richard dangles from the lift (center).

off the ground. Wilson ran to the ladder of a nearby lift tower, about 30 feet away. Panicked skiers watched as he scaled the 25 feet. After he reached the top, Wilson's first challenge was to climb onto the two-inch steel cable that held the chairs. As luck would have it, he's a professional slackliner (similar to a tightrope walker). That helped him handle the balance and height, but he knew he couldn't walk on the cable. "I had ski boots on," Wilson says. "And there's no way that would be the fastest thing to do."

The solution: He straddled the chairlift cable, then used his hands to pull himself to Richard. Wilson's greatest fear wasn't that he'd fall, but that he wouldn't reach his friend in time.

"This was life or death," he says.

When he reached Richard's chair, Wilson swung a leg over the cable and attempted to drop down onto it. But as he did that, his jacket caught on the movable footrest, which was in the up position. The footrest began to slide down, with Wilson attached. Before that could happen, he managed to free himself. "We almost had two hanging guys," he says.

Now standing on the chair, he kicked down on the backpack, vainly trying to break the strap. The ski patrol had gathered below, and one of them tossed up a folding knife, which Wilson caught. He leaned over and sliced the strap. Richard plummeted ten feet to the powder below, while Wilson collapsed in the seat. The ski patrol performed CPR on Richard, who had been hanging for about five minutes, then skied him down to an ambulance. Wilson then rode the chairlift back down.

That night, Richard, who had a bruised trachea and a broken rib, called Wilson from the hospital to thank his friend. "No problem, bro," Wilson said. "I always wanted to climb one of those things."

The Lady Who Lived Through Winter

When the house got so cold that toothpaste froze in the tube, it seemed impossible that spring would ever come.

———

BY **JOAN MILLS**

Originally published in April 1974

One of my neighbors sometimes sits for an hour in drizzle and damp, watching what the birds are up to. Then he comes to tell me and, while he's at it, he points out colors in the fire, or shows me a pebble, saying, "Now isn't that pretty!" Musing, he once remarked, "I guess I'm an appreciatin' kind of fella."

And I'm an appreciatin' kind of gal. Only a few weeks ago, I was standing in the middle of a snowbound patch of mud, appreciatin'.

Ooze had seeped into my boots. Ice-melt from the trees was leaking onto my hat. The sun was far away, a bleached circle in the sky. In the whole yard I could see but one bird, a bedraggled winter robin hopping forlornly through slush. But this all seemed beautiful to me! I'd come out my door expecting yet another day of winter; instead, I'd sunk three inches into spring.

The gray and damp were profligate with promises. The thaw meant softening, and warming, and greening; grass where mud was, buttercups where snow was thinning. There'd be buds along these branches! The robin would fall in love and preen his feathers—and there'd be lilacs! And ladybugs, and ten-speed bicycles tick-ticking by, and curtains astir at open windows!

I looked happily down at the mud, and up, and all around. I could have danced right there, in my galoshes! Spring! Oh, my— how I appreciated it!

When the agent said the walls were insulated with chicken feathers, we were entranced.

I'm sure I'd have admired the thaw less had I loved this winter more. A proper winter is 73 inside. It's made of snow sparkles and small adventures, of Christmas lights, Sunday jaunts and the nice ho-hum of roast beef for dinner.

But that's not how it was this year, for me, or for most of us. Wrapped in woollies and uncertainty, I shivered, measuring out the oil; eking out the dollars, making do. And so, when the celestial thermostat was nudged up a notch, I recognized a great occasion! No wonder I stood beamish, appreciatin' the second-most-beautiful mud patch I'd ever been in.

Years ago, you see, I went through a winter worse than this one and therefore experienced an even more extraordinary spring. The ordeal that preceded *that* memorable March glory of mud and melt was no crisis for millions, but it was for five Millses. It was a winter so purely awful that we lost our faith in spring. And we'd no one to blame but ourselves.

On a tender April day earlier that year, we'd fallen fecklessly in love with an old country house in a New England valley. When the agent said he supposed the walls were insulated with chicken feathers, we took it as entrancing news. We enthused over the taped snarl of galvanized pipe in the cellar as if indoor plumbing had just then been invented. We thought our furnace was a marvel—cast iron it was, with a fancy design on the door. So of course we bought the house, and moved in our beds and boxes, three kids and a big dumb dog.

The summer was hot and gorgeous. City friends came admiring. In September, we built fires to sit by on dreamy evenings. October turned the year golden, and then chill. We dialed the thermostat to 70, and waited. Puffs of dust floated up from the floor registers. Bob went down cellar and kicked the furnace. It didn't help. In the morning I called a serviceman. He bit through his cigar when he saw our heating system. The feeble heat we had was the most we'd get, he said, and it was. The furnace wheezed and groaned, and day by day the house grew colder.

I warmed the kids with soup and dressed them in flannel. We moved the supper hour in by the fire. Bob went shopping for supplies and came home walking tall—a man can be happy coping with the elements. Whistling, he stuffed chinks, caulked and storm-sashed the windows, split firewood and insulated the mysteriously windy cellar.

"That'll do it!" he said, proud. I sighed with relief. It was the first week of November, six weeks from official winter. How splendid to know we were prepared!

The very next morning, I found that my underwear, every stitch and strap, had frozen overnight into a ten-gallon ice block lodged in the washer. When I comprehended the disaster, I had to be assisted back to bed.

We tried everything. Space heaters. Boiling water. Rock salt. We called the neighbors and said, *you won't believe this, but*. They came to see, and they didn't believe. I jiggled loosely around the house in despair, feeling breezes I'd never felt before.

Bob approached the washer with an ice pick and returned with two small glassy chunks. He laid them before me on the kitchen counter.

"These any help?" he asked. In one was embedded a garter, attached to a raggedy scrap of rubber. In the other, a single bra cup was preserved.

"Not much," I moaned. I put on a concealing overcoat and sidled into the dime store to buy essentials, including three pairs of pink thermal bloomers. Bob said his grandmother'd worn bloomers like that.

We piled so many quilts on the beds that the littlest child hollered for help when he wanted to turn over. I took to wearing an old fur coat around the house. After a few miserable weeks, I turned it inside out, because it was warmer that way. The kids plucked at my ratty sleeve. "Are we poor now, Mommy?" they asked.

Repairmen came and went. They left us bills, and all their sympathy. Steadily the weather worsened. In January, snow drifted halfway up the windows, and icicles hung halfway to the ground. One after another, the pipes froze and burst.

Bob called a family conference in the upstairs bathroom. "Now listen to me," he said, his breath rising in smoky puffs. Our four blue-tinged faces regarded him solemnly.

"Here is a faucet," he said. "I have managed to thaw a pipe, and this faucet is running. Running water will not freeze. *Nobody is to turn off the faucet!* Do you understand?"

"Yes, Daddy," we all said, blowing on our fingers and nodding earnestly.

Running water does freeze. We made coffee with melted snow. It was terrible. Nothing was easy anymore. The car died in the driveway. Toothpaste froze in the tube.

And yet—the view from every window made me catch my breath. In the parlor and the dining room, two fires burned, lovely all day and in the evening. We'd stand close enough to fry our eyelashes, and then turn to toast our back pockets. Socks and mittens hung on the fire screen, giving off a homey, woolly steam.

But would there be spring? Ever? In my kitchen, I cut the butter with an ice pick. Amazingly, though, we managed. We learned the tricks, and improvised a lot. We laughed, I remember, more than you'd think; and we cherished small amenities.

On a certain March morning, winter tossed down a handful of flakes and then gave way to sun that by the afternoon had spread a humble patch of mud out by the back steps.

All unaware, I picked my cautious way down the steps and over ice. I put my foot on earth that yesterday was iron-hard—and felt it yield. I stopped where I was, astonished, and sensed the brush of suddenly soft air across my cheek.

Was this spring? I turned a full circle to see. Yes! Yes! Gray and wet and beautiful! We'd made it! The thrill was like hearing thousands cheer: "There's the lady who lived through winter!"

I felt that this year too. After a hard winter, the world seems very full of miracles, celebrating survival. There's rain to notice, scudding clouds, sun before breakfast. When the furnace goes off for an hour, a spacious silence falls. Out by the barn's north wall, where snow lingers, crocuses push through. The mouse deserts the pantry to scamper in the fields. One day a first fly bumbles along the windowpane and falls into the butter. All this before the true greening!

> *Repairmen came and went. They left us bills, and all their sympathy.*

Appreciatin' early makes the most there is of spring. It civilizes March and puts a shine on April. I began my appreciatin' this year within a circle of snow. What I've noticed, and been glad for, ought to last me a long time. This I know: If there's another crisis winter—well— I'll make it! Spring will come again, and it will be as sweet as this one.

Blowout at 17,000 Feet

One moment everything was going smoothly on Flight 5390. Then, suddenly, the trip became a nightmare.

———

BY **PETER BROWNE**

Originally published in February 1991

The weather was perfect when British Airways Flight 5390 took off from Birmingham, England, at 8:20 a.m. on June 10, 1990, bound for Malaga, Spain. Most of the 82 passengers were vacationers. Smiles broke out as Captain Tim Lancaster announced, "It's very hot in Malaga. Sit back and enjoy the flight."

With the BAC One-Eleven jet climbing southward, the four cabin staffers began serving breakfast. On the flight deck Captain Lancaster, at 41 a cheerful veteran with 11,000 hours in his logbook, was in the left seat. On his right, flying with Lancaster for the first time, was First Officer Alastair Atchison, 39. He concentrated on radio instructions as Air Traffic Control guided Flight 5390 through the crowded airspace west of London.

At 17,000 feet, 13 minutes after takeoff, the plane was in less air traffic and both pilots could relax. Lancaster unbuckled his shoulder harness, leaving his seat belt loosely fastened. The captain, pointing to the town of Abingdon below, told his co-pilot, "Just beyond, there's my house."

Seconds later, there was a loud explosion. The left windshield vanished in front of Lancaster, and in a flash pressurized air bursting from inside the plane sucked him partway out of the two-by-three-foot hole. Outside, the 320-mph slipstream bent the upper half of his body back against the jet's fuselage.

The door to the cabin smashed in against Atchison's shoulder, then split astraddle the center radio console and the throttles. A blow from one of Lancaster's legs had disengaged the autopilot. The aircraft lurched into a steep bank.

No. 3 steward Nigel Ogden had been standing in the forward galley just beyond the door when he heard what sounded like a clap of thunder. He turned to see Lancaster sliding out of the gap left by the missing windshield. Ogden jumped over the radio console and stood astride the captain's seat to grasp Lancaster around the waist.

So great was the force that it seemed to Ogden his arms were being wrenched out of their sockets, and he could feel himself being pulled after the captain. "Somebody help me!" he shouted. But the rush of air whipped away his voice, and

Atchison was too busy trying to bring the aircraft under control.

Back in the cabin, terrified passengers saw the air fill momentarily with a white mist—condensation caused by the cold outside air colliding with the warmer cabin air. The plane shuddered and seemed to fall. Stephanie Jenkins, on her way to visit her mother in Malaga, thought, *My God, it's a bomb.* Former RAF fighter pilot Michael Lawrence knew at once there had been a decompression and instinctively tightened his seatbelt until it hurt.

Cabin crew chief John Heward, 37, was at Row 5 pouring tea. He sprinted forward to join Ogden on the cramped flight deck. Seeing Atchison groping for throttles covered by the smashed door, Heward flung the splintered panels into the aisle. Then, hooking an arm through the harness on a jump seat behind the captain's, he seized

The left windshield vanished, and pressurized air sucked the captain out of the hole.

Ogden's belt with one hand and Lancaster's trousers with the other.

Atchison quickly realized his predicament. British Airways One-Elevens are not equipped with drop-down oxygen masks for passengers, and his captain was at risk not only of being sucked from the aircraft but also of freezing to death in an outside temperature

of minus seven degrees Fahrenheit. There was only one option: Get down as fast and as safely as possible to 10,000 feet. At that altitude there is enough oxygen so masks aren't needed.

Diving at 370 mph, he was agonizingly aware of the battering Lancaster was suffering. Repeatedly he called on the radio: "Mayday, Mayday. This is 5390. We've got an explosive decompression."

Among the passengers, there was no overt panic as the jet dived, only a shocked silence. *This is the end,* Stephanie Jenkins thought. *And I haven't made a will. I'll never see Gordon and the children again.*

Michael Lawrence was relieved to see the air brakes slide from the wing. He turned to the, passenger next to him: "Everything's working. Stop worrying."

At 10,000 feet, Atchison leveled off. He slowed the craft as much as he dared, hoping it would help Ogden and Heward pull the captain back in. But even with the One-Eleven close to stalling, at 170 mph, they could not budge him. His body was locked in position by the slipstream, arms flailing. It reminded Atchison of a rag doll.

There's no way Tim can be alive. He must have broken his back. When the others on the flight deck looked questioningly at Atchison, he shouted above the wind, "He's dead."

By now, No. 2 steward Simon Rogers, powerfully built and at 29 the youngest of the crew, had come forward from the rear galley to join Ogden and Heward. Crowded into the confined space, the three men tried again to dislodge the captain, but failed.

However, they managed to lift Lancaster's right leg, easing pressure against the plane's left-hand control column, which partly relieved at least one of Atchison's problems. But the left leg remained stuck. The crew was faced with a terrible possibility: Would they have to push their captain out to free the controls? Atchison shook his head. "Hold on if you possibly can."

By now Nigel Ogden was near the end of his tether. A nerve in his right arm had been severed by the sawing motion against the windshield frame. Like all the crew, he was in

shirt sleeves, and his bare arms were numbed by the icy wind that made breathing difficult. *You can't let go,* he told himself. *Think of Tim's family.* But his arms were fast losing all feeling. He yelled at the others, "I can't hold on any longer!"

As Heward and Rogers tightened their grips on the captain's legs, Ogden let go and collapsed on a seat in the galley. Stewardess Susan Prince, 33, joined him. "We think the captain's dead," Ogden gently told her. "But there's a job to do, love. Come on." Prince fought back her tears, and together they went into the cabin to help the passengers. Despite their apparent confidence, neither believed they would survive.

On the flight deck, Rogers strapped himself into the jump seat behind the captain's seat. Reaching forward, he managed to grasp Lancaster's ankle and free his right leg from the controls. But then, to his horror, he suddenly felt the captain slide forward another six inches. Now his torso was entirely outside the aircraft. Moments later, when the jet banked left to alter course, Lancaster's body slid around and down to the side window. For the first time, a shocked Rogers saw the captain's face.

It was streaked with blood, the eyes wide open and black from being bruised, the tongue protruding, the flesh rippling in the slipstream. Sickened, Rogers turned his head away.

At 8:42, nine minutes after decompression, Chris Rundle, the watch manager at Southampton Airport, learned from Air Traffic Control that a BAC One-Eleven was diverting to Southampton with an apparent pressurization problem. Rundle declared a full emergency, bringing in police, ambulances and the fire brigade.

Two minutes later, Atchison came on the radio: "Southampton, this is 5390; do you read?" Rundle gave him a course and altitude to fly, then said, "Is pressurization your only problem?"

"Negative. The cockpit window has blown out. The captain is half sucked out, and I believe he is dead."

About to land an airliner single-handed at an unfamiliar airport, Atchison had only a moment to talk to the passengers. But his voice was reassuringly steady: "Ladies and gentlemen, first officer speaking. Please obey all commands of the cabin crew."

Many passengers were clinging to one another for comfort, still unaware of what had turned a pleasant flight into a nightmare.

Ex-RAF pilot Lawrence, who had offered to help, was called forward and asked to man the main emergency exit. He was appalled by what he saw: the captain's body glistening as though covered by frost. *Suppose the steward loses his grip?* Lawrence thought. *The captain could be blown back into the port engine and destroy it.*

With Prince and Ogden, Heward now began preparing the passengers for an emergency landing, demonstrating how to brace: head between the knees, arms folded on top. One passenger kept repeating, "We're going to crash, aren't we?" Prince managed a smile: "No, no. Look, we've leveled out. Everything's fine."

As Chris Rundle at Southampton Airport guided Atchison in a wide sweep to the south of the city, the passengers in window seats looked down fearfully. Computer sales director David Duncan worried that the plane might break up and crash in the sea. Then he noticed an elderly woman who seemed untroubled. *If she can be calm,* he thought, *then I can too.*

On the flight deck, Simon Rogers, who had been clutching the captain's legs, suddenly felt Lancaster's ankles twitch in his hands, the feet start to kick. Grimly he held on, believing it must be a last muscular spasm from a corpse.

Atchison, easing the throttles back for the final approach, was acutely conscious that a hard landing could shake Lancaster loose; the short runway left little margin for error, and overheated brakes could catch fire. As he looked for the airport ahead, it was impossible to avoid seeing the body flapping outside the window. *Put it out of your mind. Concentrate on flying.*

At three miles out, he reported "runway in sight." Rundle answered, "You're cleared to land," and went to the window to watch. Aboard the plane, Heward saw treetops sliding past and gave the order into his microphone: "Brace! Brace! Get your heads down below the seats!"

David Duncan felt only the slightest jolt. To Stephanie Jenkins, it was the smoothest landing she had ever known. The jet braked to a halt. For a few seconds there was stunned silence. Then the cabin crew

> ### The captain's face was streaked with blood, the eyes wide open, the tongue protruding.

swiftly evacuated the passengers.

It was 8:55, just 35 minutes after Flight 5390 had left Birmingham. "That was a fantastic approach," Rundle radioed to Atchison. In his headset Rundle heard the first officer quietly crying.

As the wheels stopped rolling, fireman John Foskett was astonished to see Tim Lancaster move and lift his head. Scrambling up a ladder to support the captain while eager hands eased him back into the aircraft, Foskett heard him murmur, "Where am I?"

Within minutes Lancaster was on his way to a hospital, where doctors described his condition as "utterly remarkable." Incredibly, he had escaped with frostbite, minor fractures in his right arm and wrist, a broken thumb and extensive bruising.

When the shaken passengers were invited to continue their journey on a Boeing 737 brought from Heathrow, only seven refused.

Investigators discovered that the near catastrophe had been caused by human error. Some 30 hours before the incident, the BAC One-Eleven's windshield had been replaced. All 90 bolts used on the new one were the wrong size, fractionally too small to secure it against the cabin pressure. A blowout was inevitable.

Five months after the incident, after intensive physiotherapy to repair damaged nerves in his arms, Tim Lancaster returned to the flight deck. What he had himself termed "a miraculous piece of flying" earned his first officer, Alastair Atchison, a number of awards, including a gold medal for outstanding airmanship from the British Airline Pilots' Association, which also made special awards to all the cabin crew.

Tim Lancaster still marvels that he survived an ordeal unique in the history of aviation. "I must be the luckiest man alive," he says.

Requiem for a Friendship

"You've got to struggle against disappointment," he told me. "Hang on to personal dignity." In the winter of his life, he showed me how.

BY **DON J. SNYDER**

CONDENSED FROM **YANKEE**

Originally published in October 1982

One afternoon in the spring of 1979, a friend telephoned me at the news office of the Portland (Maine) *Independent*. An author had moved to town whom I might want to interview, he said.

I found Finis Farr in a sunless, sparsely furnished apartment near the waterfront. He was wearing an old Brooks Brothers shirt frayed at the collar, a shapeless necktie and a mud-color tweed jacket. The room had a typewriter set on a card table, a narrow cot in one corner, a director's chair with a sagging seat, and many books—books on loan from the library. "A writer's got to travel light," he told me. "You've got to be perched for flight."

He had a great deal to say that made a lot of sense to me, and over the next three years I kept going back. "Good of you to stop by, old man," he would say. Then we would talk about everything under the sun but mostly about writing books. I was a young writer struggling to get someplace, and he could tell me what it would be like—struggling and maybe getting there.

Finis Farr had written nine books, among them a popular biography of John O'Hara. His most recent, a biography of Eddie Rickenbacker, was soon to come out. Now 74, he had moved to Portland looking for a peaceful place to write. "Oh, this is a grand little city by the sea," he said to me. "I think I'll get a lot of work done here."

His current project was to write a personal history of the 1930s. He figured he could finish this book in two years, and it would be his best. It would say just about everything he ever had to say about life in America, about people following ambitions, holding on to dreams and learning to accept their share of happiness and disappointment.

He knew something about disappointment and spoke about it with a courtly detachment: "You've got to struggle against disappointment. There's so much of it around. I can tell you that the great thing is to hang on

to personal dignity. If you stay impersonal about disappointment you will be very glad you did when enough time has elapsed and your feelings, disarranged as they were, have settled back into calmness and repose."

Finis found calmness in his work. He found repose in books and could quote effortlessly from Wordsworth and Dickens and writers I'd never read. That first year we met several times a week in his apartment, and then one of us suggested we go out for lunch every Thursday. "It's a good idea to get out every once in a while," he said. "Writing is such lonely work."

So every Thursday we would go to the Caffé Domus on Exchange Street. Neither of us had any money, but the proprietors let us take up a table while we drank black coffee. We sat there surrounded by business people and lawyers, marveling at their lunches—towering salads, bottles of wine and rich desserts.

Finis managed to find humor and irony in this: "Maybe it's part of the romance of a writer's life—not being able to buy a respectable lunch. But soon after enough oversized meals these prosperous people you see here will become oversized themselves, and when they deposit their outgrown suits in the Salvation Army bins you will be the beneficiary of their excess."

He liked making me laugh. And he wanted to show a decorous exterior. It wouldn't be long, he said, before he had a contract on his book and with it an advance of enough money to keep him going.

But months went by and there was no contract. The editor at his publishing house wanted to see a detailed outline, and Finis prepared it in a few weeks. Then the editor wanted a lengthy treatment of the book, chapter by chapter, and that took Finis two months. "You have to expect delays," he said. When I asked what the trouble was, he changed the subject to the old, "better" days.

But I knew that those days were far away for Finis ; I had glimpses of the rough edges of his existence. One bleak winter day when there was a vicious wind tearing down State Street, I spotted a man trudging up the hill, his shoulders pitched forward. He looked frail and lonely. It was Finis. He was carrying his bag of books, and one fell onto the ice-covered sidewalk. I watched him bend down slowly three times before he managed to pick it up. On the last try a glove fell from his coat pocket. He didn't notice the glove and walked on toward the library. I waited and then went and got the

> ## "Maybe it's part of the romance of a writer's life—not being able to buy a respectable lunch."

glove, which had holes in two of the fingers. The next morning when I visited him I dropped it on the closet floor while he was in the other room.

By summer there was still no contract. Finally, in the fall, after months of revision and waiting, the publishing house decided it did not want the book. "They sent me packing, old man," he told me when

I called him. "But my agent plans to send the outline to a dozen houses. Soon we'll be in business." By lunchtime that Thursday I had worked out an assignment from the Maine Sunday *Telegram* to do a story on Finis. They agreed to pay $200 for an interview and I planned to split the fee with Finis.

> ## "When I get some cash-money, I'm going to check in here and stay for a whole month."

We had a lot of fun with that interview. We went to the Atlantic House Hotel in nearby Scarborough. As we walked along the beach, I had never seen Finis so animated and hearty. "Ah, that sound—the sea breathing in and out," he said. "It makes you think everything will be all right."

It was late afternoon when we got back to his apartment. When he sat in the director's chair, I suddenly realized how out of character it was

for him to take the seat without first offering it to me. The color had drained from his face, and I saw that something was wrong as he looked up at me. "Say, are we going to go to the shore to do that interview today, old man?"

It took three months for several major publishing houses in New York City to reject his proposal for the 1930s book. He told himself that in the past, before publishers were obsessed with "bestsellers," his *good* book would have been accepted. But that was a cold consolation, and he turned his attention to *my* writing as I began having some modest success.

In early July 1981 an editor at a major publishing house called to say he was recommending my first book for purchase. Finis and I went out to celebrate at the Atlantic House Hotel, where we were now having our weekly lunches. He was on his mettle again that afternoon. "There's a lot to talk about. I want to review the bidding with you. Don't let them try to settle for less than thirty thousand on the advance. You've got to get the ante up high so they have some incentive to promote the book." Three weeks later when we were again at the Atlantic House I had to tell him that the sale of my book had fallen through. Finis set his jaw. "Well, so now you learn to take a blow to the belly, and to get back up on your feet. You've got to come back out swinging."

The rejection had shaken me, and I had almost nothing to say.

"Maybe we ought to get together again tomorrow to see where we go from here," he said.

"I'll give you a call," I told him. But he called me in the early morning. "Would you be able to drive me to the hospital?" he asked. Late that afternoon he was lying in a bed in the cardiac-care unit of Mercy Hospital. I stayed with him

until I thought he had fallen asleep and then stood up to leave.

He called me back to the bed. "You have to write your books," he said. "You must never let them say you gave up." I think he was saying that for both of us, and when I looked into his eyes I saw that he was frightened. In a clumsy, shy way we held hands for the first time. I said, "You're a good friend, Finis." "You're about the best friend I've got, old man," he said.

Finis recovered from that attack, and throughout the fall he worked on his book. "I've decided I ought to finish it. God puts writers on this earth to write books, not worry about selling them. And besides, when I get it done it'll be so damn good they'll have to publish it."

We both felt that 1981 had been the hardest year we'd ever lived through, but of all the things Finis and I did together, the finest was our lunches at the Atlantic House every Thursday that summer. We would eat by the front windows in the dining room, looking at the sea, talking like two privileged passengers on some grand ship.

We did a lot of dreaming out at that hotel.

Finis used to say, "When I get some cash-money I'm going to check in here and stay for a whole month. I'm going to walk down to the water every day for a solid month." I used to tell him that when my first book sold I was going to buy a house near the water and he would have a room there. That was my dream—to get him up close to the sea, to hear him working away in a sun-filled room in a house that would feel like a home to him. But he left too soon. On January 3, Finis died after suffering three massive heart attacks.

On January 8, ten young people, mostly writers and artists, stood together under an empty blue sky on the porch of the Atlantic House Hotel remembering Finis Farr as a fine writer, a humble, gentle man. We came together there to place one of his books in the hotel's library and to show our respect.

Ironically, a publisher, unaware of Finis Farr's death, offered to publish his book just a week after he passed away.

Feathered Friend

*Does a talking bird
mean what he says?*

—

BY **JO COUDERT**

Originally published in May 1991

"I'm going nuts here by myself," Pat Myers confessed to her daughter, Annie. Pat had been virtually confined to her house for a year as she was treated for an inflamed artery in her temple that affected her vision and stamina.

A widow with two married children, she'd been happily running a chain of dress shops. But now that she had to give up her business, her home began to feel oppressively silent and empty. Finally she admitted to Annie how lonely she was.

"Do you think I should advertise for someone to live with me?"

"That's such a gamble," Annie said. "How about a pet?"

"I haven't the strength to walk a dog," Pat said. "I'm allergic to cats, and fish don't have a whole lot to say."

"Birds do," said her daughter. "Why not get a parrot?" And so it began.

Pat and Annie visited a breeder of African Greys and were shown two little featherless creatures huddled together for warmth. Pat was doubtful, but Annie persuaded her to put a deposit down on the bird with the bright eyes. When he was three months old and feathered out, he was delivered to his new owner, who named him Casey.

A few weeks later Pat told Annie, "I didn't realize I talked so much.

The average lifespan of an African Grey parrot like Casey is between 20 and 35 years.

Casey's picking up all kinds of words."

"I told you." Her daughter smiled at the sound of pleasure in Pat's voice.

The first sentence Casey learned was "Where's my glasses?" followed by "Where's my purse?" Whenever Pat began scanning tabletops and opening drawers, Casey chanted, "Where's my glasses? Where's my purse?" When she returned from an errand, he'd greet her with "Holy smokes, it's cold out there," in a perfect imitation of her voice.

Casey disliked being caged, so Pat often let him roam the house. "What fun it is to have him," she told Annie. "It makes the whole place feel better."

"I think *you're* beginning to feel better too," said Annie.

"Well, he gives me four or five laughs a day—they say laughter's good for you."

Once a plumber came to repair a leak under the kitchen sink. In the den, Casey cracked seeds in his cage and eyed the plumber through the open door. Suddenly the parrot broke the silence, reciting, "One potato, two potato, three potato, four ..."

"What?" asked the plumber.

"Don't poo on the rug," Casey ordered, in Pat's voice.

The plumber pushed himself out from under the sink and marched to the living room. "If you're going to play games, lady, you can just get yourself another plumber." Pat looked at him blankly. The plumber hesitated. "That was you, wasn't it?"

Pat smiled. "What was me?"

"One potato, two potato—and don't poo on the rug."

"Oh, dear," said Pat. "Let me introduce you to Casey."

Casey saw them coming. "What's going on around here?" he said.

At that moment Pat sneezed. Casey immediately mimicked the sneeze, added a couple of Pat's coughs at her allergic worst and finished with Pat's version of "Wow!" The plumber shook his head slowly and crawled back under the sink.

One morning while Pat was reading the paper, the phone rang. She picked it up and got a dial tone. The next morning it rang again, and again she got a dial tone. The third morning she realized what was going on: Casey had learned to mimic the phone faultlessly.

Once, as Pat opened a soda can at the kitchen table, Casey waddled over and snatched at the can. It toppled, sending a cascade of cola onto her lap and the floor.

"*#@!"Pat said. Casey eyed her. "Forget you heard that," she ordered. "I didn't say it. I never say it. And I wouldn't have now if I hadn't just mopped the floor." Casey kept his beak shut.

Later a real estate agent arrived to go over some business. She and Pat were deep in discussion when Casey screamed from the den, "*#@!"

Both women acted as though they'd heard nothing.

Liking the sibilance, Casey tried it again. "*#@!" he said. And again. "*#@! *#@! *#@!"

Caught between humiliation and amusement, Pat put her hand on her guest's arm. "Helen, it's sweet of you to pretend, but I know you haven't suddenly gone deaf." They both broke up laughing.

"Oh, you bad bird," Pat scolded after the agent left. "She's going to think I go around all day saying four-letter words."

"What a mess," Casey said.

"You're darned right," Pat told him.

Casey's favorite perch in the kitchen was the faucet in the sink; his favorite occupation, trying to remove the washer at the end of it. Once, to tease him, Pat sprinkled a handful of water over him. Casey ceased his attack on the washer and swiveled his head to look at her sharply. "What's the matter with you?" he demanded.

If he left the kitchen and Pat heard him say "Oh, you bad bird!" she knew to come running. Casey was either pecking at her dining-room chairs or the wallpaper in the foyer.

"Is it worth it?" asked her son, Bill, looking at the damaged front hall.

"Give me a choice between a perfect, lonely house and a tacky, happy one," said Pat, "and I'll take the tacky one any day."

But Pat did decide to have Casey's sharp claws clipped. To trim them without getting bitten, the vet wrapped Casey tightly in a towel, turned him on his back and handed him to an assistant to hold while he went to work. A helpless Casey looked at Pat and said piteously, "Oh, the poor baby."

Pat often wondered if Casey knew what he was saying. Sometimes the statements were so appropriate she couldn't be sure. Like the time a guest

had lingered on and on talking in the doorway and Casey finally called out impatiently, "Night, night."

Yet, whenever Pat wanted to teach him something, Casey could be maddening. Once she carried him to the living room and settled in an easy chair as Casey sidled up her arm and nestled his head against her chest. Pat dusted the tips of her fingers over his velvet gray feathers and scarlet tail. "I love you," she said. "Can you say, 'I love you, Pat Myers'?"

Casey cocked an eye at her. "I live on Mallard View," he said.

"I know where you live, funny bird. Tell me you love me."

"Funny bird."

Another time Pat was trying to teach Casey "Jingle Bell Rock" before her children and grand-children arrived for Christmas dinner. "It'll be your contribution," she told him.

"Where's my glasses?"

"Never mind that. Just listen to me sing." But as Pat sang "Jingle bell, jingle bell, jingle bell rock" and danced around the kitchen, Casey simply looked at her.

Finally Pat gave up. And all through Christmas dinner Casey was silent. When it came time for dessert, Pat extinguished the lights and touched a match to the plum pudding. As the brandy blazed up, with impeccable timing Casey burst into "Jingle bell, jingle bell, jingle bell rock!"

Pat's health improved so much she decided to go on a three-week vacation. "You'll be all right," she told Casey. "You can stay with Annie and the kids."

The day her mother was due back, Annie returned Casey to the apartment so he'd be there when Pat got home from the airport.

"Hi, Casey!" Pat called as she unlocked the door. There was no answer. "Holy smokes, it's cold out there!" she said. More silence. Pat dropped her coat and hurried into the den. Casey glared at her.

"Hey, aren't you glad to see me?" The bird moved to the far side of the cage. "Come on, don't be angry," Pat said. She opened the door of the cage and held out her hand. Casey dropped to the bottom of the cage and huddled there.

In the morning Pat tried again. Casey refused to speak. Later that day he consented to climb on her wrist and be carried to the living room. When she sat down, he shifted uneasily and seemed about to fly away. "Please, Casey," Pat pleaded, "I know I was away a long time, but you've got to forgive me."

Casey took a few tentative steps up her arm, then moved back to her knee. "Were you afraid I was never going to come back?" she said softly. "I would never do that."

Casey cocked his head and slowly moved up her arm. Pat crooked her elbow, and Casey nestled against her. Pat stroked his head, smoothing his feathers with her forefinger. Finally Casey spoke.

"I love you, Pat Myers," he said.

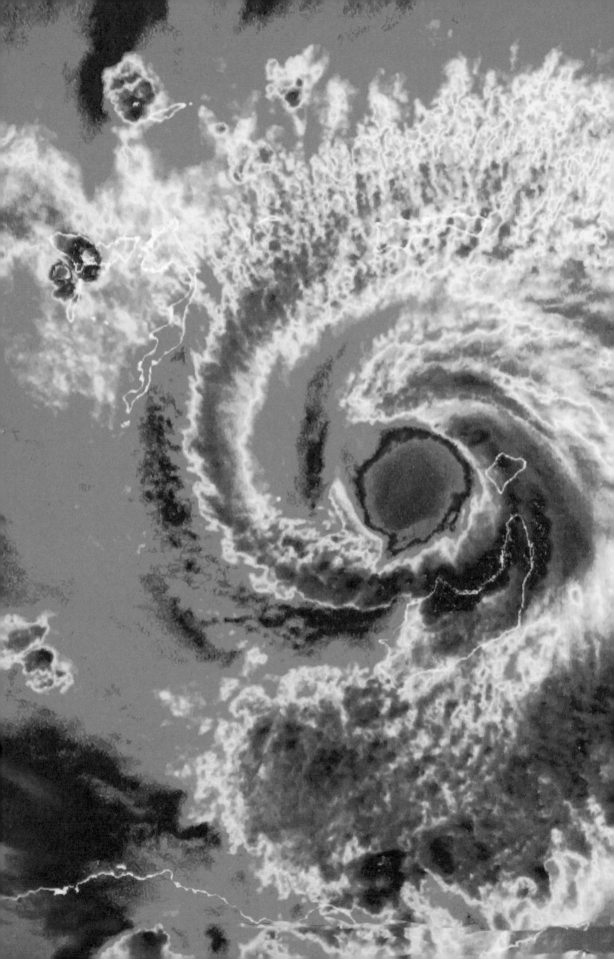

Face to Face with Hurricane Camille

The Koshak family braved "the greatest recorded storm ever to hit a populated area in the Western Hemisphere."

—

BY **JOSEPH P. BLANK**

Originally published in March 1970

John Koshak Jr. knew that Hurricane Camille would be bad. Radio and television warnings had sounded throughout that Sunday, August 17, 1969, as Camille lashed northwestward across the Gulf of Mexico. It was certain to pummel Gulfport, Mississippi, where the Koshaks lived. Along the coasts of Louisiana, Mississippi and Alabama, nearly 150,000 people fled inland to safer ground. But, like thousands of others in the coastal communities, John was reluctant to abandon his home unless the family—his wife, Janis, and their seven children, ages 3 to 11—was clearly endangered.

Trying to reason out the best course of action, he talked with his father and mother, who had moved into the ten-room house a month earlier from California. He also consulted Charles Hill, a longtime friend, who had driven from Las Vegas for a visit.

John, 37, was familiar with the power of a hurricane. Four years earlier, Hurricane Betsy had demolished his former home a few miles west of Gulfport. But that house had stood only a few feet above sea level. "We're elevated 23 feet," he told his father, "and we're a good 250 yards from the sea. The place has been here since 1915, and no hurricane has ever bothered it. We'll probably be as safe here as anyplace else."

The elder Koshak, a gruff, warm-hearted machinist of 67, agreed. "We can batten down and ride it out," he said. "If we see signs of danger, we can get out before dark."

The men methodically prepared for the hurricane. Since water mains might be damaged, they filled bath-tubs and pails. A power failure was likely, so they checked out batteries for the portable radio and flashlights, and fuel for the lantern. John's father moved a small generator into the downstairs hallway, wired several light bulbs to it and prepared a connection to the refrigerator.

Rain fell steadily that afternoon; gray clouds scudded in from the Gulf on the rising wind. The family had an early supper. A neighbor, whose husband was in Vietnam, asked if she and her two children could sit out the storm with the Koshaks. Another neighbor came by on his way inland—

would the Koshaks mind taking care of his dog?

It grew dark before seven o'clock. Wind and rain now whipped the house. John sent his oldest son and daughter upstairs to bring down mattresses and pillows for the younger children. He wanted to keep the group together on one floor. "Stay away from the windows," he warned, concerned about glass flying from storm-shattered panes. As the wind mounted to a roar, the house began leaking—the rain seemingly driven right through the walls. With mops, towels, pots and buckets, the Koshaks began a struggle against the rapidly spreading water. At 8:30, power failed, and Pop Koshak turned on the generator.

The roar of the hurricane now was overwhelming. The house shook, and the ceiling in the living room was falling piece by piece. The French doors in an upstairs room blew in with an explosive sound, and the group heard gunlike reports as other upstairs windows disintegrated. Water rose above their ankles.

Then the front door started to break away from its frame. John and

Charlie put their shoulders against it, but a blast of water hit the house, flinging open the door and shoving them down the hall. The generator was doused, and the lights went out. Charlie licked his lips and shouted to John, "I think we're in real trouble. That water tasted salty." The sea had reached the house.

"Everybody out the back door to the cars!" John yelled. "We'll pass the children along between us. Count them! Nine!"

The children went from adult to adult like buckets in a fire brigade. But the cars wouldn't start; the electrical systems had been killed by water. The wind was too strong and the water too deep to flee on foot. "Back to the house!" John yelled. "Count the children! Count nine!"

As they scrambled back, John ordered, "Everybody on the stairs!" Frightened, breathless and wet, the group settled on the stairs, which were protected by two interior walls. The children put the cat, Spooky, and a box with her four kittens on the landing. She peered nervously at her litter. The neighbor's dog curled up and went to sleep.

The wind sounded like the roar of a train passing a few yards away. The house shuddered and shifted on its foundations. Water inched its way up the steps as first-floor outside walls collapsed. No one spoke. Everyone knew there was no escape; they would live or die in the house.

Charlie Hill had more or less taken responsibility for the neighbor and her two children. The mother was on the verge of panic. She clutched his arm and kept repeating, "I can't swim, I can't swim."

"You won't have to," he told her, with outward calm. "It's bound to end soon."

Grandmother Koshak reached an arm around her husband's shoulder and put her mouth close to his ear. "Pop," she said, "I love you." He answered, "I love you"—and his voice lacked its usual gruffness.

John watched the water lap at the steps, and felt a crushing guilt. He had underestimated the ferocity of Camille. He held his head between his hands and silently prayed: "Get us through this mess, will you?"

A moment later, the hurricane lifted the entire roof off the house and skimmed it 40 feet through the air. The bottom steps of the staircase broke apart. One wall began crumbling on the marooned group.

❖   ❖   ❖

Dr. Robert H. Simpson, director of the National Hurricane Center in Miami, Florida, graded Hurricane Camille as "the greatest recorded storm ever to hit a populated area in the Western Hemisphere." It shot out winds of nearly 200 mph and raised tides as much as 30 feet. Along the Gulf Coast it devastated everything in its swath: 19,467 homes and 709 small businesses were demolished or severely damaged. It seized a 600,000-gallon Gulfport oil tank and dumped it 3½ miles away. It tore three large cargo ships from their moorings and beached them. Telephone poles and 20-inch-thick pines cracked like guns as the winds snapped them.

To the west of Gulfport, the town of Pass Christian was virtually wiped out. Several vacationers at the luxurious Richelieu Apartments there held a hurricane party to watch the storm. The Richelieu Apartments were smashed apart as if by a gigantic fist, and 26 people perished.

Seconds after the roof blew off the Koshak house, John yelled, "Up the stairs—into our bedroom! Count the kids." The children huddled in the slashing rain within the circle of adults. Grandmother Koshak implored, "Children, let's sing!" The children were too frightened to respond. She carried on alone for a few bars; then her voice trailed away.

Debris flew as the living-room fireplace and its chimney collapsed. With two walls in their bedroom sanctuary beginning to disintegrate, John ordered, "Into the television room!" This was the room farthest from the direction of the storm.

John put his arm around his wife. Janis understood. Shivering from the wind and rain and fear, clutching two children to her, she thought, *Dear Lord, give me the strength to endure what I have to.* She felt anger against the hurricane. *We won't let it win.*

Pop Koshak dragged a cedar chest and a double mattress into the room. At that moment, the wind tore out one wall and extinguished the lantern. A second wall wavered. Charlie Hill tried to support it, but it toppled on him, injuring his back. The house, shuddering and rocking, had moved 25 feet from its foundations. The world seemed to be breaking apart.

"Let's get that mattress up!" John shouted. "Make it a lean-to against the wind. Get the kids under it."

The larger children sprawled on the floor, with the smaller ones in a layer on top of them, and the adults bent over all nine. The floor tilted. The box containing the litter of kittens slid off a shelf and vanished in the wind. Spooky flew off the top of a sliding bookcase and disappeared. The dog cowered with eyes closed. A third wall gave way. Water lapped across the slanting floor. John grabbed a door that was still hinged to one closet wall. "If the floor goes," he yelled at his father, "let's get the kids on this."

In that moment, the wind slightly diminished, and the water stopped rising. Then the water began receding. The main thrust of Camille had passed. The Koshaks and their friends had survived.

With the dawn, Gulfport people started coming back to their homes.

They saw human bodies—more than 130 men, women and children died along the Mississippi coast—along with dead dogs, cats, cattle. Strips of clothing festooned the standing trees, and blown-down power lines coiled like black spaghetti over the roads.

Before dawn, the Mississippi National Guard and civil defense units were moving in to guard property, set up communications centers, help clear the debris and take the homeless to refugee centers. By 10 a.m., the Salvation Army's canteen trucks and Red Cross volunteers and staffers were going wherever possible to distribute hot drinks, food, clothing and bedding.

From across the country came several million dollars in donations; household and medical supplies streamed in by plane, train, truck and car. The federal government shipped 4,400,000 pounds of food, moved in mobile homes, set up portable class-rooms and opened offices to provide low-interest, long-term business loans.

Camille, meanwhile, had raked its way northward across Mississippi, dropping more than 28 inches of rain into West Virginia and southern

Virginia, causing rampaging floods, huge mountain slides and 111 additional deaths before breaking up over the Atlantic Ocean.

Like other Gulfport families, the Koshaks began reorganizing their lives. John divided his family in the homes of two friends. The neighbor with her two children went to a refugee center. Charlie Hill found a room for rent. By Tuesday, Charlie's back had improved, and he pitched in with Seabees searching for bodies. Three days after the storm, he decided not to return to Las Vegas, but to "remain in Gulfport and help rebuild the community."

Near the end of the first week, a friend offered the Koshaks his apartment, and the family was reunited. The children appeared to suffer no psychological damage; they were awed by the power of the hurricane, but enjoyed describing what they had seen and heard on that frightful night.

Meanwhile, John, Pop and Charlie were picking through the wreckage of the home. It could have been depressing, but it wasn't: Each salvaged item represented a little victory over the wrath of the storm. The dog and cat suddenly appeared at the scene, alive and hungry.

Once, in a low mood, John said to his parents, "I wanted you here so that we would all be together, so you could enjoy the children, and look what happened."

His father, who had made up his mind to start a welding shop when living was normal again, said, "Let's not cry about what's gone. We'll just start all over."

"You're great," John said. "And this town has a lot of great people in it. It's going to be better here than it ever was before."

Later, Grandmother Koshak reflected: "We lost practically all our possessions, but the family came through it. When I think of that, I realize we lost nothing important."

The Message
of the Pond

*Both families knew the searing loss
of senseless death. Together,
in a desperate struggle to save another life,
they found renewal.*

——

BY **PETER MICHELMORE**

Originally published in December 1989

After their 17-year-old son, Randy, died suddenly from a heart abnormality in 1978, Steve and Mary Shivers moved from the city of Richmond, Virginia, to a small farm nearby. They kept their jobs—Mary as a high-school attendance counselor, Steve as a filling-station manager—and in their spare hours turned the property into boarding stables for horses.

"The outside of a horse is good for the inside of a man," Mary had said. So it proved. In riding and roping, her husband and their older son, Stevie, found release from sorrow. And their robust companionship was healing for Mary too. She took comfort in Steve's belief that God had taken Randy for a special reason.

But all was shattered on December 10, 1984, when Stevie, 24, collapsed in the driveway. Mary watched in horror from the kitchen window while her husband tried to resuscitate their son. "Please, God," he cried, "don't take this boy. I need him."

Death was attributed to acute cardiac arrhythmia, as in Randy's case, but doctors could not explain why the disorder had twice struck strapping boys in the same family.

After months of torment, Steve finally began to recognize that God had not taken his boys to punish him. The world was imperfect, its suffering indiscriminate. Crushed though he was, Steve was only 47 and felt he had to go on with his life and his work.

For Mary, however, there was no relief. "It will change, honey," Steve told her. "One day it will." But Mary could find no solace.

She attended meetings of The Compassionate Friends, Inc., a self-help organization for bereaved parents. Yet she still slipped back into a consuming misery that isolated her from Steve's own determined struggle. To her, he seemed stiff and uncaring.

One year passed, then another. On January 28, 1987, a heavy snowfall had closed school, but Mary took scant pleasure in the sparkle of sunshine on the meadow outside. "My feelings have gone dead," she told Sherri Tolley Arden, 37, leader of the Richmond chapter of Compassionate Friends. With her two daughters, Sherri was visiting Mary that afternoon. "I'll never care for anyone again," Mary told her.

Suddenly Sherri's daughter Brett, 11, bounded up from the pasture and burst into the house. "Lance has fallen into the pond!" Lance was a boarder's 23-year-old Appaloosa gelding.

The two women and blacksmith Jim Roberts, 36, who had joined them for coffee, were up and outside in an instant. Slogging through the snow, they reached the frozen pond at the center of the meadow. Forty feet out, Lance's white head bobbed in a patch of dark water. Snorting in fright, he was twisting and straining to find a footing. But the pond was 20 feet deep at that point.

"Get ropes from the barn," Mary told the others. "I'll phone Steve."

Steve's instruction was crisp: keep the horse's head above water until he arrived—in 15 or 20 minutes. Mary hung up, then dialed Lance's owner, Patti McFarland.

The rescuers assembled at the pond with ropes and a plywood sheet to distribute weight on the ice. Inching out, Jim tried to lasso the horse's neck, but the panicked animal turned away. The only way to save him would be to go onto the ice and fasten the line to the muzzle ring on Lance's halter.

"Brett will go," Sherri announced. "She's the lightest."

> *Forty feet out, the horse's white head bobbed in a patch of dark water. He strained to find a footing.*

"Yes," Brett insisted, "I can do that."

Mary looked at them in amazement. Six years earlier, Sherri's ten-year-old son, Jason, had drowned. Both mother and daughter had witnessed it. How could they take this risk? "No," Mary said emphatically. "Let the horse die."

Sherri's gaze was locked on the stricken animal. In her mind she saw Jason at Virginia Beach, his surfboard shooting up from a wave behind him, his face contorting as the board cracked the back of his head and sent him under. She had run to him, plunging into water

Fervently now, Mary wanted the horse to live.

———

made soupy with swirling sand. But Jason had disappeared, and his body had never been recovered.

"Brett will go," Sherri repeated as she tied a lifeline to her daughter's belt. The courageous youngster lay on the plywood, and Jim slid her out to the brink. Sherri gripped the lifeline, with daughter Wesley, eight, at her side.

"Here Lance, c'mon Lance," Brett cooed. She saw that his lips were blue from cold and bloodied from ice cuts. She felt a tremor of fear. Fumbling with numb fingers, she needed several attempts to

secure latch to halter.

Hauled back safely, she lined up with the others on the rope. Lance was big—1,200 pounds—and the ice was three inches thick. By pulling, they hoped to forge a channel through the ice to the shallows. They were heaving when the catch on the halter snapped and they went sprawling in the snow.

Sherri swiftly grabbed another rope, lay on the plywood and told Jim, "Shoot *me* out this time."

Why, Mary wondered, *is she doing this?*

The ice creaked under Sherri's weight, and she pictured herself falling in under Lance's thrashing hooves. She groped for the halter in the numbing water, made the attachment and signaled to be pulled back.

The horse was weakening now, his breath coming in gasps. The people holding the rope were barely keeping Lance's head above water when Steve arrived.

He backed a tractor to the edge of the pond, attached the rope and began pulling. Lance reared, but his big shoulders hit the ice, and he fell back in the water as the rope broke.

Steve gunned the tractor back to the barn. Returning with a thin, steel cable, he fashioned a loop and sent it whizzing over the ice in an expert lariat throw. Snared at the neck, Lance made another effort to move forward. But he was too exhausted. His shoulders became wedged into a V-shaped gap in the ice, his head sagged and his ears drooped. "This will kill him," Steve said, switching off the tractor.

Looking to the huddle of people, he saw Patti McFarland. She had owned Lance since childhood. More than a pet, he was her best friend. Now the 25-year-old legal secretary had her head on Sherri's shoulder, sobbing.

Watching, Mary felt an outpouring of compassion. An inner voice counseled that they had already put themselves at risk and that Steve would be justified in calling off further rescue attempts. But, fervently now, she wanted the horse to live.

Caution was the last thought in Steve's mind. Twirling a new rope, he looped it over Lance's head and moved to the far side of the hole. With boot heels braced in the ice, he pulled hard to free Lance's shoulders. Suddenly the ice cracked. Steve pitched forward. He felt leaden weights on his legs as his boots filled. *That's all she wrote*, he thought as the water closed over his head.

In one instant, though, his certainty of drowning was replaced by a will to fight. Instinctively he lunged for the horse's tail. Seizing it with both hands, he hauled himself up and around to Lance's neck. Hand-over-hand he pulled himself to firm ice along the cable strung between horse and tractor.

Water spilled from his boot tops, and he was soaked to the skin, yet when he stood, the chill left him. *You're no quitter, man*, he thought.

"I'm getting the mauls!" he yelled. "We'll chop him out."

After Steve returned, he and Jim began hacking at the ice. A big chunk gave way, and Lance struggled forward.

The sight of her husband filled Mary with pride. Aghast when he went into the water, deathly afraid his heart would not take the shock, she had marveled at his run through the snow in water-soaked clothing. *No matter what,* she thought, *he'll keep trying. And I thought this man had no feelings!*

Piece by piece, the ice broke, opening a channel. Steve put more tension on the cable until Lance's hooves finally touched bottom.

When the horse was knee-deep, Steve laid down his maul. "Come, Lance," he called warmly. Raising his head, the old horse stumbled onto the hard ice and into Patti's tearful embrace.

After covering Lance with blankets and walking him for three hours to restore body warmth, Steve and Patti dosed the horse with cough syrup and put him in his stall. He would soon recover.

The rescue had been a grueling hour-long ordeal, yet everyone trooped back to the house feeling that they had shared a wondrous experience. "We sure gave it our best shot," Sherri said. Rarely since Jason's death had she felt such exaltation. As for Steve, he couldn't remember when he last felt so good about himself.

Mary had a sense of being tuned in to a dimension of life that she had forgotten. Warming by the fireplace later, she could contain it no longer. "Did you see what we did?" she said. "Is there a message here?"

That night Mary went over and over the events, and the next morning told Steve, "I know what it meant yesterday. It meant that we *do* care."

And in Mary's gleaming eyes, Steve read the message of the pond. To him, it was the affirmation of a loving God. By giving so profoundly of themselves to save a life, they had discovered a way to renew their own. "Yes, honey, we do care," said Steve. "We always did."

He kissed her, then clamped a Stetson on his graying hair and went out to feed Lance his oats. *It's the breakthrough,* he thought. *Mary's going to make it.*

And at that moment, Steve Shivers felt like singing.

Free to Kill

They were two lives converging on a deadly course. Once they intersected, the result was a vicious crime made more tragic by the fact that it could have been prevented.

—

BY **HENRY HURT**

Originally published in February 1998

Short tail swishing, the day-old black-and-white calf nuzzled its wet nose into Amy Jackson's hands as she reached over the wooden railing to rub its head. Prancing on the fresh straw, the wobbly calf again pressed toward Amy, licking the girl's hands and fingers. She laughed with delight and rubbed the calf's ears.

Amy was 11, a happy child with brown hair and brown eyes. She lived with her brother, Bobby, 13, and their father, Robert (known as Bob), in the rural North Carolina town of Yanceyville. Home was an old house trailer at the Shumaker Dairy, where their dad worked as herd manager.

This summer of 1995 had been a fairly happy time for both Jackson children. Amy's softball team, the Ace Hardware Bullets, was having a great summer, with an 11-1 record. Six kittens had been born to Amy's gray cat. And newborn calves arrived almost every day.

Six months earlier, the children's mother, Shana, had walked out on her 14-year marriage. Shana said she loved the children but was sick of the daily grind. Bob left home each day at 2 a.m., worked six hours, then went out again at 2 p.m. for another six hours.

These days Jackson and the children rarely heard from Shana, even though she was living only about an hour away. The Jacksons did not have a phone in their trailer.

Hazel-eyed with a ruddy face, high cheekbones and a prominent nose, Jackson did not mind his brutal work schedule. He took care of medicating the 150 cows, scheduling the breeding and making sure the milk met the dairy's prizewinning standards.

Amy: a young girl with big dreams.

Bob Jackson wanted Amy and Bobby to have better lives than his 365-day-a-year regimen. The only dairy work he let his children engage in was the part that was fun: occasionally feeding the new calves. He found spots for his son and daughter on the local ball teams. Though he had to get up at 1:30 each morning for work, he still spent his evenings at the games.

"When I was a kid, I never got to do anything like that," Jackson says. "All I did was work. I wanted Amy and Bobby to have something more."

Shy and a little awkward, Bobby seemed to depend upon his more purposeful little sister to take charge of things. "Amy would set the alarm clock on school days and get me up," Bobby says. "She'd fix break-fast and make sure we were on time for school."

Amy loved school and nurtured ambitious dreams. In a school essay she wrote of her hopes for the future: "I plan to go to college to be a nurse and [hope to have] a handsome husband who's a Christian and has a lot of money. And I hope I can have a car and a two-story house and two children. And when I die I want to go to heaven."

That summer Amy was excited about turning 12 in August and buying a purse-style book bag, like the other girls had. Amy took her savings to Wal-Mart and bought the burgundy book bag of her dreams.

Bob Jackson says with a little smile, "Sometimes I think the main reason she was looking forward to the school year was so that she could get on the bus with that bag."

Night Traveler

A help-wanted ad for a dairy worker in the Statesville *Record & Landmark* caught the eye of Archie Lee Billings, 21, as he sat in his mother's living room near the small town of Harmony in western North Carolina.

Squatly built with a moon face sprouting a scraggly beard, Billings had powerful hands and forearms from years of manual labor. His black hair and dark eyes were in sharp contrast to his dough-white skin.

He liked to work at dairies because the job was outside and involved tasks he enjoyed. He even liked the working hours because they gave him

time to roam rural neighborhoods in the middle of the night, traveling noiselessly by foot or on a bicycle.

It was John Shumaker, the owner of Shumaker Dairy, who had placed the newspaper ad in February 1995. The new man's job would be to assist his herd manager, Bob Jackson.

Archie Billings picked up his mother's phone and called the number. He spoke with Shumaker, a direct, businesslike man who reviewed Billings's work experience and wrote down the young man's references. With his wife and four daughters living on the farm, Shumaker made sure to check out all the men he hired.

When Billings finished talking, he told his mother he was glad the Shumaker Dairy was so far away—about 120 miles—from his home in Iredell County, where his troubles with the police made it hard to find work. If he could just get this job, Billings told his mother, no one would know of his past.

Archie Billings was an illegitimate son of a notorious mountain bootlegger named Harvey Cass, who was nearly 70 when Archie was born. Cass never saw fit to give his name to Archie and the two other boys that he fathered with Archie's mother, Ozell. Billings was her maiden name.

The log house on Brushy Creek where Archie was born had a kitchen, two rooms and no plumbing. When Archie was six, Ozell moved her family to slightly better quarters in Union Grove.

At age 13, Archie used a needle and some blue ink to inflict a small tattoo on his left hand. After that, he swore off needles—even for the drugs that he soon used. "I just couldn't stand the pain," he said.

Archie quit school after ninth grade. By then he was drinking and smoking marijuana, occasionally with his mother, and getting into trouble.

Soon Archie moved in with his brother Keith and Keith's girlfriend. One night in June 1991, Keith was awakened by her screaming. He jumped up, flicked on the light and saw that Archie had crawled into her side of the bed. "I beat the hell out of him," Keith recalls, "and threw him out of the house." Some months later Keith gave Archie a second chance and invited him back.

In February 1992, less than a month after his 18th birthday, Archie Billings refused to stop for a police officer, and by the time police caught him, he faced eight charges, including reckless driving and possession of marijuana. Billings had no driver's license for the court to suspend, but he was fined $200 and given a six-month jail sentence. That was suspended for two years on the condition of good behavior; the term of his two-year unsupervised probation began on April 9, 1992.

Late on the night of April 19, 1992, Keith heard a noise outside his bedroom. As he walked down the hallway, there was a loud blast, and he felt a sudden force that slammed him against the wall. He turned on the light. Before him stood his brother holding a sawed-off shotgun.

Without a word, Archie had fired one shot into Keith's chest. "Archie then threw down the shotgun and picked up a .22 rifle and shot again," Keith recalls.

Even as a .22-caliber slug tore through Keith's left wrist, he lunged for the rifle and wrenched it away from his brother. Keith's girlfriend got him to the hospital where, after extensive surgery and a long recuperation, he survived.

Since the brothers had not been arguing that night, Keith speculates that Archie intended to kill him so he could rape the young woman.

Davie County Deputy Sheriff John Coley investigated the shooting. Arrested and jailed overnight, Billings was charged with "assault with a deadly weapon with intent to kill and inflicting serious injury." He was released the next day on an unsecured bond of $500. Eight months later the charges were dropped after Keith and his girlfriend did not testify.

Even though the assault was committed just ten days after Billings's probation began, records show no attempt by the court to revoke probation and put him in jail.

In May 1993, after a fight at a convenience store, Billings was charged with beating a man in the head several times with a hammer. In a plea-bargain agreement reached five months later, Billings pleaded no contest to a misdemeanor charge of simple assault. His only punishment: He had to pay court costs.

Meanwhile, Billings got into more trouble with his car: no driver's license, no registration and no insurance. The judge fined him $25 and gave him a 30-day jail term, which was suspended. Instead, Billings was placed on a year's unsupervised probation without so much as a mention of his ongoing probation.

He was "riding high and laughing loud," according to his brother Keith. "No matter what he did, he'd go to court and they just let him go."

Billings's infractions continued, and so did his luck. By the time a jail sentence was finally handed down in January 1995, Billings had turned an ominous page in his life. Finally, he was up to something even the careless legal system could no longer overlook.

Crossing the Line

In the 34-month period between February 1992 and November 1994, Archie Billings was employed by at least two local dairies. In his off hours, he prowled country roads terrorizing a local family.

Near one dairy where Billings worked was a farm and nursery operated by Carolyn and Daniel

Allen. They had two daughters, ages 12 and 17. In November 1994, while the family was at church one Sunday night, someone broke into their home by smashing open a basement door. The Allens called the police.

An investigation revealed that things had been disturbed in both daughters' bedrooms. Even more distressing was the discovery of marks indicating someone had placed a ladder against the side of the house under the girls' second-story bedrooms.

This was chilling. For months the two girls had been hearing suspicious noises outside their windows. In their innocence they had dismissed these as normal night sounds.

Daniel Allen and the county sheriff's office would ultimately learn that more than a half-dozen families in the area had complained about a particularly aggressive peeping Tom.

Though deputy sheriffs investigated, Allen was not happy with what he felt was the scant attention they gave the matter. "It may have been a little thing for them," he says, "but it was a pretty big thing for us. I decided I had to protect my family."

Two nights after the burglary, Allen walked around in the dark, armed with a shotgun, watching his house. When he saw and heard someone lurking in the shrubbery beneath his daughters' bedroom windows, he called out, then fired three shotgun blasts at the fleeing intruder.

Later that night the family found a jacket in the yard, obviously dropped by the person who had fled. Inside the collar were inked six letters: ARCHIE.

But even being shot at did not seem to discourage the interloper. The next night the Allens heard strange sounds again.

This guy wasn't going to stop until somebody killed him or caught him, Allen recalls thinking. So he began his own investigation. He was able to track the jacket to a nearby dairy and was soon talking with Iredell County Detective Sergeant Ronald Wyatt. When Wyatt heard the story, he suspected this Archie just might be the young man he'd been having run-ins with for years: Archie Billings.

Wyatt questioned him. Billings told the detective: "If I was there, that ain't against the law. Look, we both know what I did, but it's stupid for me to tell on myself."

Billings ultimately pleaded guilty to two counts of secret peeping and was given 45 days in jail.

Soon after Billings was released, he appeared in court to plead guilty to the separate charges of breaking and entering and larceny at the Allen house. Superior Court Judge Catherine C. Eagles imposed "a community punishment." This meant that he would serve no time on the charges of breaking into the Allens' house and stealing items. The judge gave him a sentence of eight to ten months, suspended for 36 months.

Eagles also placed Billings on supervised probation and ordered him to pay $137 in court costs and $928 in restitution to the Allen family.

Moreover, Billings was ordered to report to a state mental-health agency for evaluation, which he did on March 7, 1995. He was interviewed by primary therapist Loy W. Devine, who concluded that Billings was not a danger to others and that no follow-up sessions were necessary.

On the night in March 1995 when Archie Billings called John Shumaker to answer the newspaper ad, the dairyman knew none of this. He was impressed by Billings's experience and was interested in hiring him.

While one of Billings's references checked out satisfactorily, that was not the case with Barry Myers, who runs a 650-cow dairy where Billings had also worked. Myers declined to comment to Shumaker on anything about Billings, saying his lawyer had warned him against providing any

This guy wasn't going to stop until somebody killed him or caught him, *Allen thought.*

———

references. (In fact, Myers had fired Billings; his son had spotted Billings looking through a bedroom window, and other employees also suspected the young man had been loitering around their homes.)

Shumaker did not like the non-committal response from Myers, but he remained interested in Billings. Shumaker asked him to come for an interview with him and Bob Jackson.

Confident that he would land the job, Billings packed and got one of his brothers to drive him to Caswell County. Among the few possessions he took was a rusty ten-speed bicycle.

After the interview with Shumaker and Jackson, Billings got the job. With the post, he was given a place to live, a house trailer Shumaker owned about a mile from the dairy. It was a pleasant bicycle ride along Yanceyville's County Home Road.

Welcome to Caswell County

Billings established himself as an excellent worker and quickly fit into his new surroundings. He soon got to know the people in the neighborhood, including the four Shumaker girls and Bobby and Amy Jackson. He often had candy in his pockets for the children.

"He'd stop by the house now and then," recalls Bob Jackson. "We tried to be neighborly. I remember when he needed to get some things at Wal-Mart. I drove him there, and Archie bought us lunch. Amy was with us."

Sarah Shumaker, John's wife, remembers once having all the dairy employees to the house for a cookout. "Archie fit right in," she says. "He was friendly and playful with the kids and an excellent employee."

Sarah's daughter, Lucia, 15, was often working alone on a remote part of the farm when Archie would come by. "I never once felt uncomfortable around him," Lucia says.

Amy Jackson, however, seemed to sense something amiss. Her Little League coach, Garry Chandler, remembers a night when he drove her home after a game: "She asked me to wait while she went in to be sure Bobby was home. She said there was a new man working on the farm and that he'd been hanging around the house."

By most people's accounts, Archie Billings did all right in Caswell County. He regularly checked in with his local probation officer as required by the court. Says Shumaker: "Archie told us he'd gotten in trouble over racing cars and that's why he was on probation."

On June 23, 1995, Billings and a woman he knew were at a Yanceyville bar. Billings became provoked over something. He quarreled with the woman's father and her boyfriend and then hit her in the face.

"Yes, I heard about it," recalls Bob Jackson. "Archie might have even told me himself. But we never once smelled alcohol on him. Besides, by then we thought we knew him."

Night of the Knife

On the late afternoon of Thursday, July 6, Billings mentioned to Jackson that he wanted to hear a band that night at Country's Place, a Yanceyville beer joint. Jackson offered to drop him and his bike off there.

Country's Place is owned and operated by a middle-aged, pony-tailed man named Brodie "Country" King. He remembers Billings as a quiet guy who stopped by now and then for a beer.

King also remembers Billings on that particular Thursday night: "He sat at the bar and ordered a draft beer. Drank it and left. He didn't say anything. I remember thinking he had one of them 'ain't nobody home' looks on his face."

Billings finished his beer, then hit another joint in Yanceyville. Accounts of what he did next conflict. Some say he drank a little moonshine whiskey and may have smoked some drugs. But no one thought he was drunk or out of control.

What is known for sure is that in the dead of night, Billings headed east along County Home Road. The night was steamy and the ground wet from days of rain. He was going toward the Shumaker Dairy and the trailer where Amy and Bobby Jackson slept. Billings knew that at that time their father was at work in the barn.

Billings also knew the noise made in the barn by the milking machines would make it impossible for the father to hear any sounds from the trailer. Moreover, from his visits to the Jackson home, Billings knew the family did not have a telephone.

Not only would the two children be asleep—they would also be alone and have no way to call for help.

Usually, Bobby Jackson slept in his own room, but he had neglected to clean out his rabbit cage, and his room smelled. So he asked Amy if he could sleep on the lower half of her bunk bed. She agreed and took the top. They turned in after their father went to bed around 9 p.m.

Jackson checked his children about

Bobby Jackson, at work on the farm, idolized his sister.

1:40 a.m. before leaving for work. Bobby remembers his father coming into the room before he drifted back to sleep. As always, Bob Jackson left the hall light on and locked the door to the trailer behind him.

It was sometime after Jackson had begun milking that Archie Billings crept up to the Jackson trailer. He hoisted himself up through one of the windows and slipped inside.

Bobby Jackson was awakened by a violent movement on top of him. Then he felt a knife blade being thrust into him. Confused, terrified, hurting terribly, he opened his eyes and saw, just above him, the face of Archie Billings, the friendly farmhand who had often given him and his sister candy.

Billings drove the knife into the boy again and again until, finally, Bobby slumped onto the floor by the bunk bed. In excruciating pain, he began to drag himself toward the door. He was trying to reach his room, where he kept his BB gun.

Seeing movement, Billings pounced on the boy again, stabbing him repeatedly. Remaining still for a moment, Bobby waited until Billings had turned away. Then the boy once more pulled himself toward his room. Blood poured from his wounds.

In a final burst of savagery, Billings leapt upon the boy one more time and slashed him across the neck, inflicting a gash nearly one foot long and one inch deep.

As he lay there motionless and nearly unconscious, Bobby heard Amy protesting as Billings dragged her from her bed. "No, Archie! No! No! No! Archie!" she screamed.

Amy broke away and, perhaps not realizing her father had gone to work, fled to his bedroom. Billings charged after her, then paused.

"Archie came and turned me over," Bobby recalls. "I acted like I was dead. Then he went after Amy."

Billings cornered the 11-year-old in her father's room, where he raped her on her parents' bed. After that, he went back into the next room,

where he kicked Bobby, turning him over one more time to make sure that the only eyewitness was dead.

Moments later Bobby's eyes peeped open. He saw Amy, partially clad in pajamas, running from the trailer with Billings running after her. They vanished into the darkness.

Stabbed 23 times, Bobby Jackson lay bleeding to death. In addition to the horrendous, gaping slash across his neck, there was a six-inch-long gash across his back. Some wounds were so deep that his stomach was punctured, as was one lung.

Outside, Billings caught up with Amy. He dragged her across the road and through a soybean field. The little girl fought Billings as best she could, scratching him as he dug his fingers into her upper arm.

About 1,000 yards from her home, a few feet into a grove of pine trees, Billings hurled Amy Jackson to the ground. There, he raped the child once more and stabbed her in the throat, severing her jugular vein.

For the last 45 seconds of her life, Amy Jackson was likely conscious, according to doctors. She bled to death on the wet, muddy ground at the edge of the soybean field.

Afterward, Archie Billings hustled through the hot night toward the dairy. He hid his bloody clothes in one of the buildings and put on fresh ones that he found there.

Then, like the reliable employee he was considered to be, Billings got ready to show up for work early.

Grisly Discovery

At 5:20 that morning John Shumaker was awakened by a phone call from the 911 dispatcher. The officer said that Amy Jackson was missing and that her brother, who was dying from a knife attack, had called 911 and mentioned a man named Archie.

Shumaker said there was an Archie who worked at his dairy, but he wasn't due at work until seven. Then Shumaker went to the milking parlor, where he found Bob Jackson.

Shumaker explained that something was terribly wrong with Amy and Bobby. Once outside, they could see dozens of blue and red lights flashing on the hillside by the trailer.

Jackson pleaded with police to let him into the trailer. They gently refused. Minutes later Jackson was on his way to the hospital to stand vigil by his son. Before leaving, he asked Shumaker to get word to Shana.

Around 6:20 a.m. Shumaker found Billings in the milking parlor. "What in the world are you doing here so early?" the owner asked.

"I'm surprised to see you too," Billings replied cheerfully. Shumaker was rarely in the barn this early in the morning. At that moment the dairy owner noticed that Billings was wearing a pair of pants left in the barn long ago.

Shumaker told his employee that something had happened over at Bob Jackson's trailer and that he would like to drive Billings there. The police needed to talk to him. Billings calmly went along.

Even as Amy Jackson's body lay in the woods a thousand yards away, Billings insisted he knew nothing. He said that he had been out drinking and had simply come to work early. After a few minutes of questioning, Billings was taken into custody.

What he did not know was that two things had gone very wrong with his plans. First, Bobby Jackson, despite 23 stab wounds, had refused to die. Second, Bob Jackson had installed a phone in his trailer a few days before the attack. Moments after Billings disappeared into the night, Bobby had crawled to the phone and dialed 911.

Four minutes later, Sarah Clayton and other EMS technicians entered the Jackson trailer. The scene, the medics later said, was horrible—blood was smeared on walls, all over the floors, the furniture, the beds. Sarah Clayton put Bobby on oxygen and gingerly covered the slash across his neck so that doctors could repair it. By 5:19 a.m. they were on their way to the hospital, 12 miles away. They got there in 11 minutes.

"He was fighting with everything he had," says Jackson, who reached the emergency room before 7 a.m.

Jackson stood there, convinced his son could not survive. Suddenly, from a few feet away, Jackson saw Bobby's eyes open. Then he heard the most wonderful words of his life.

"Hi, Dad," said a very small voice.

Twelve hours later, after a massive search effort, a bloodhound located Amy's body. As a lead for her scent, the tracker had given the dog Amy's new burgundy book bag.

The Trial

By May 22, 1996, nearly a year had passed since the murder of Amy Jackson and the brutal attack on her brother. On this day, coincidentally Bobby Jackson's 14th birthday, opening arguments began at the jury trial.

The next day District Attorney Joel H. Brewer's steady voice rang through the Caswell County courtroom: "The state of North Carolina calls Bobby Jackson." This was the prosecutor's star witness, left for dead by the man who murdered his sister. Bobby's savage neck scars were visible as he shyly took the oath.

Less than 20 feet away sat Archie Billings. He was represented by two defense lawyers, assisted by a jury consultant and others, all paid for by the state of North Carolina.

The defendant sat at the defense table wearing a blue blazer, gray slacks and a striped, clip-on necktie. Cocky, he twiddled his thumbs and flicked at bits of lint on his tie.

Brewer, 45, a prosecutor for 15 years, sat alone. With dark eyes and close-cropped salt-and-pepper hair, Brewer calmly and softly reassured his witness. Behind him sat Bob Jackson and his wife, Shana, now reconciled. Beside them were the Shumakers and other neighbors from County Home Road.

The prosecution's case was straightforward: that Billings had devised a carefully laid plan to

> ## *The district attorney asked the jury, "Do we accept that when your father dies, it's OK to rape and murder little children?"*

rape and murder Amy Jackson while she and her brother were alone, asleep and defenseless, and to murder the only eyewitness, Bobby—now in court to point out his sister's killer.

A powerful part of the evidence against Billings had been introduced the day before: the recording of

Bobby's 911 call. It was logged at 4:51 a.m. The boy's voice was calm but barely audible. "A man came in here ... he had a knife ... his name was Archie." At this point the breathing became so heavy, the voice so weak, that it was unclear whether the boy would live long enough to finish.

Dispatcher David Vernon is heard calming Bobby.

"He took my sister. My dad. He's in the barn ..."

The courtroom was cloaked in silence, broken only by the sobbing of Shana Jackson. Others wiped away tears. The playing of the 911 tape was one of the only times any color came to Billings's face. Slightly flushed, he looked down and flicked at his tie.

Now, sitting in the witness chair, Bobby Jackson calmly pointed to Archie Billings as the man who had stabbed him and abducted his sister.

Billings briefly met Bobby's gaze and then looked away. He showed no emotion at all.

He became animated only when the jury was shown the autopsy photographs of Amy Jackson, for which Brewer apologized. When Brewer flung the pictures on the defense table to be inspected by the defense team, Billings hunched forward for a look.

Later, as Brewer made his powerful argument for the death sentence, his voice grew softer. He sat on the defense table, less than three feet from Billings, took off his watch and asked the jury to think about the last 45 seconds of Amy's life. The courtroom was utterly silent while the seconds slowly ticked by.

Then Brewer closed, saying that by his actions Archie Billings had shown the world that he believed in capital punishment and that now the jury should give him the same.

In response, the defense did not deny that Billings committed the crime. They argued instead that Billings's mental capacity was diminished by drugs and alcohol. and that he had been exposed to a variety of abusive sexual activity. Billings lacked strong role models had grown up in an "impoverished environment," his lawyers claimed, that was aggravated by the death of his father when he was 11.

Brewer asked the jury: "Do we [accept] ... that when your father dies, it's OK to go out and rape and murder little children?"

Then his voice dropped: "Amy Jackson didn't even get to be more than 11."

The jury found Billings guilty of every charge and recommended the death penalty.

At sentencing, Judge J. B. Allen Jr. looked down at Archie Billings as he said: "I sentence you to death. And may God have mercy on your soul."

Death Row

Central Prison in Raleigh is where those sentenced to die in North Carolina are taken for their appointment with the death chamber. Death's menu here offers inmates execution by either gas or lethal injection.

Wearing a red jumpsuit, Billings is polite but wary; his handshake is firm. Sitting at a conference table, Billings looks down as he twists a pencil stub between his powerful fingers. "I was always lucky nobody did much to me," he says. Then he looks up. "But maybe I'd be better off if they'd made me go in [prison] sooner."

When it's suggested that the Jackson family might have been better off too, Billings rubs the little pencil nub back and forth and says nothing.

When he's asked about the Jackson children, Billings says, "I liked them. Bobby, he was quiet and happy. I could tell he liked his family. Amy, she was a good kid. She was happy, too, and liked her daddy and brother. All of 'em was nice to me."

Asked about the oddness of his comments in light of what he did to Amy and Bobby, Billings smirks. "Now you're talking about my case. And we ain't gonna talk about my case for legal reasons. But I'll tell you I don't blame what happened on nobody but me."

With good appeals lawyers, Billings knows he may not be executed for 10 or 15 years. But he says he will not drag out his fate. After one appeal he' ll be ready to die. He says he'd rather be dead than cooped up like this.

Asked about his death sentence, Billings says, "I think about it all the time." His eyes becoming more intent, he adds, "Much as I hate needles, I'll probably have to go with that. The guys here say the gas takes 18 minutes, and I couldn't stand that."

Then, without prompting, Billings observes: "This will be an easy out for me. What happened to Amy was a lot more painful. If I should die, I guess I should be tortured the way the evidence shows Amy and Bobby were."

Then his eyes dart up wildly from the table top, his voice edged with fury: "But I ain't scared of nothin' or nobody, and I sure ain't scared of dying."

Peace at Last

Today life goes on in Yanceyville. More than two years have passed since death cast its shadow upon this gentle neighborhood. Crops are planted and harvested. The cows "freshen," bearing the calves that keep the milk cycle going.

Bobby Jackson carries milk and feed to the 14 new calves. He enjoys caring for them, but he doesn't want to be a dairyman. "I'd like to be a police officer," he says with his shy smile. Bobby has a lasting impression of the warm professionalism of the police officers who worked so carefully with him to develop the case against Billings.

The Jackson family reunited in grief, hope and love.

Bobby's parents, reunited by the tragedy, are living in a house in town and have a new baby girl. "I feel like God just sent her to us," Bob Jackson says, his voice breaking.

In the wake of Amy's murder, the North Carolina legislature enacted a sex-offender registration provision called the Amy Jackson Law. It makes available the records of certain sex offenders to prospective employers. Ironically, peeping Tom crimes are not included, so the law still would not have done any good in the case of Archie Billings.

"But it's a step in the right direction," says Bob Jackson.

Many people look back with their private regrets. John Shumaker still grimaces when he thinks that he's the one who hired Archie Billings, but he isn't sure what he might have done differently. "We never saw any sign that we had such a monster among us."

Keith Billings wishes that he had pressed charges against his brother. "May God drop me dead," he says. "I wish Archie had killed me if that meant he wouldn't have killed that little girl," he says

Shana Jackson also fights the demons of recrimination. "I'll never get over it," she says, weeping, as she holds pictures of her children as babies. "If I'd been there where I was supposed to be, it never would have happened."

And Barry Myers, who refused to discuss Billings when John Shumaker called him, says he'll always wonder whether he did the right thing in sticking by his lawyer's advice.

One of the cruelest ironies to emerge from the entire case concerns probation. The fact is Billings got away with flouting the law and never had any of his probations revoked. By the time the state of North Carolina finally terminated Billings's last probation, he had been on death row nearly six months.

Bob Jackson is proud of his son. Bobby showed an extraordinary will in surviving and doing his best to protect his sister. His physical scars will be visible for the rest of his life. But the unseen scars are the ones that most concern his parents. About those, only time will tell.

A Fallen Soldier's Final Salute

At the airport, a group stops to honor an American hero.

—

BY **CHERYL MACDONALD**

Originally published in June 2016

t's a Saturday morning, and I am eager to fly away. My husband and I will meet up with our son on the other side of the country to learn and explore together. At the airport gate, my husband wanders away to stretch his legs. Moments later, he returns and whispers in my ear. I rise and follow him around the corner toward a large window facing the landing area. A crowd, solemn and still, gathers at the window.

Now I am one of those peering in silence. On the tarmac, Marines stand straight and tall in formation, the plane door open, a ramp waiting.

A white hearse is parked nearby. A man and a soldier stand on either side of a woman, supporting her, waiting for a sight she must surely have hoped and prayed never to see.

The ramp begins to move, and a flag-draped casket starts its descent. Airport personnel stand in reverent stillness. A few place their hands over their hearts, as I have done. We're joined in witness, sending love to an honorable soldier whose name we'll never know.

The woman's face is contorted in pain as she wails in the way only a mother can, though her cries are unheard by those of us on the other

side of the window. She collapses, knowing she will never again hear "Mom" from her son's lips. She'll never feel his loving arms encircle her shoulders or relish his sweet peck on her cheeks.

A square-jawed man grimaces in pain, weakened by grief. The father holds his head in his hands and turns it back and forth, a refusal to accept this new reality. His son, the tiny boy he no doubt wrestled playfully, the teen he probably taught to drive, the son he stood so proudly by as he donned his Marine uniform, now lives only in his memory.

Those behind the glass stay silent, reflecting on this life, this loss, as the family and soldiers depart. A dozen of us women, with red-rimmed eyes and tear-stained cheeks, move slowly, sharing a mother's profound grief.

Soon, each of us will fly off and return to an ordinary life made extra-ordinary by this soldier's courage, by this family's sacrifice and by this love shared by all who look out the window and know.

The Car in the River

*The machine was in 15 feet of black water,
and time was running out
for the trapped girl inside.*

BY **E. D. FALES JR.**
FROM **POPULAR MECHANICS**

Originally published in August 1970

Toward four o'clock on Saturday, February 21, 1970, in Miami, Florida, Mark Smith, 17, drove a friend's Mustang to the edge of a seawall on the Miami River to wash it. The car was a sleek fastback. Its huge rear wind-shield sloped so that it was more skylight than window. In the right-hand bucket seat was Mark's girl, Nancy Burns, pretty, blond and also 17. She wanted to help, but Mark didn't want her to get dirty. "All right, then I'll sit in the car and watch you," Nancy said.

Mark parked the Mustang at a 45-degree angle to the river. Its left front wheel, nearest the water, was resting on the three-foot-wide concrete seawall that fronts the river, six feet below. The river was 15 feet deep. The car's other wheels were on the grass of the Sky Harbor Marina, owned by Mark's father, John Smith.

It took Mark a half hour to wash the Mustang. At 4:30 he began to coil the hose. He noticed that Nancy had all the windows shut. A few yards beyond the car, he saw his father working on his yacht, *Pocahontas*.

Inside the car Nancy reached to turn the ignition key to the accessory position so she could use the radio. By mistake she turned it to "ignition."

Mark saw the Mustang lurch forward. A stick-shift model, it had been left in low gear and was being propelled by its starter motor. He got the left door open and tried to get his foot on the brake. The car began to go over the edge.

Standing on *Pocahontas*, Mark's father saw the rear wheels come off the ground, and the rear section begin to lift. For seconds it teetered. Stunned, he saw his son wrestling with the car, half in, half out, trying to hold it back. Then, as the car's nose tilted down more steeply, a river piling squeezed the door shut, shoving Mark outside.

Thrown back, Mark attacked like a terrier. He hurled himself headfirst over the top of the car, smashing a huge dent in the roof as he went, to get at the door on Nancy's side. He had the door open and was reaching into the cockpit for Nancy and shouting "Get out! Get out!" when the car tilted up almost on end and slipped slowly into the river. As it hit the water, the pressure slammed the door on Mark's right foot, trapping him on the outside, dragging him down.

It was approximately 4:32 p.m. Mark's father was running for his bungalow. Clawing at the telephone, he dialed "0" and pleaded, "Operator, call help—quick."

In seconds, an "EM" alarm— one long bell, an emergency rescue call—clanged in Miami's West Side Station 16, and in Station 12 two miles to the north. Ladder 16, noted officially as Lad 16, siren hooting, roared out at 4:33, following Eng 16. On the left footboard of Lad 16 rode Fireman Larry Norton, a former lifeguard. *Someone may die,* Norton was thinking. Realizing that he might have to go in the water, he removed his watch.

Underwater, Mark, choking, managed to pull his right foot away from the car door. When he surfaced, he screamed, "Nancy's down there. Somebody's *got* to get her!" He gulped a few breaths, then dived, hunting the car. He failed to find it. With his lungs nearly bursting, he kicked to the surface, shaking like a leaf.

Among those now on the dock was a British yachtsman, David

Harley. In his hands was a coil of half-inch nylon line. Tying his rope to the piling, the Englishman threw the coil, then dived in. He found the Mustang 15 feet down. By feel, he knew one door faced up. He pulled, but it wouldn't budge. He tied the rope to the door handle and came up.

Mark was struggling to dive in again, but he was in such obvious shock and exhaustion that friends held him back. He saw firemen and police coming on the run.

Fireman Bob Lane, still in trousers and shirt, dived in first. Fireman Dan Green almost landed on him. Lane descended along the rope, found the latch and tried to open the door. It wouldn't open. Dan Green, too, found the door jammed. He could tell by feel that it was the driver's door. The car appeared to be lying on its right side. Firemen Sam Givens and Paul Dammann also were in the water now. They took turns going up and down the rope, but the door wouldn't open. The rescue squad now was passing out wet suits, fins and masks.

When the car went over the wall, Nancy Burns had no real sensation of falling until she saw waves coming up the windshield. In her Red Cross lifesaving course she'd been taught that a bubble of air remains trapped in some cars. "I can't blow my cool," she told herself. It got very dark. Water rose around her legs, waist and chest. When it got over her head, the bubble of air suddenly began to seem very theoretical. It dawned on her that she had only a short time to live.

Mark was reaching for Nancy and shouting "Get out!" when the car slipped into the river.

In the blackness she lost her sense of up. She tried to swim to the rear of the car but found her way blocked by the headrests. Holding her breath, she squeezed between them. Her head was underwater , but suddenly she rose to a clear place and could take a deep breath. She was in the backseat, against the left side and, relieved, she knew she'd found the air bubble.

The next few moments she lay against the back seat, floating and thinking. By feel, she learned more about the air bubble: it began down near her waist over the middle of the back eat, stretched back into the "greenhouse" behind the seat, and seemed about six feet long, two feet wide and 18 inches deep. Lying in the bubble, she could touch the submerged front seat with her feet.

> **Thirteen seconds gone, he desperately needed to refill his lungs. But could he leave the girl, when she was so close?**

Another minute passed and she began to wonder, *Will Mark come?* Then an awful thought struck her: *Maybe Mark has drowned.*

This is the time when trapped victims go wild. They beat frantically at the car. In their efforts they use up what little air they have. Nancy kept her cool. Again she began to plan: "If I get excited I'll use up oxygen. But I've got to let them know I'm alive, or they'll give up and leave me."

She began to rap at the rear windshield. After a few moments she lay quiet, looking up. "Those are mud clouds," she thought. And then, for an instant, the clouds took form. She saw two dark legs. Mark had come! In frantic haste, she rapped the glass. But after a few seconds the legs went away. Mark had been unable to find the car.

Breathing now came harder. The car had been under water perhaps five minutes. The bubble, diminished by small leaks, kept shrinking. Once she felt the car rock. Water came in faster. She could hear it. She felt herself swept higher. Frightened, she huddled far back under the rear window, her head tilted to raise her mouth and nose into the air pocket. The water was up to her chin.

And the air in the bubble was slowly turning to suffocating carbon dioxide. Nancy slapped her face with her left hand, saying, "Stay awake, Nancy." Then she blacked out.

Nancy had now been in the water for about ten minutes. She did not know that Fireman Larry Norton, the former lifeguard from Lad 16, was at this moment outside, still in his uniform, trying to peer in.

On his first trip down, Norton, like the others, tried the driver's door. But he noticed a difference. Although the others had reported *standing* on it, he found himself floating beside it. The car, then, must have shifted with the tide. It now lay half upright, at 45 degrees.

On his first dives Norton could hold his breath for 60 seconds. But now it was shortening. On his fourth dive he began tapping the window, hoping for a response. He heard nothing. "Whoever is in there is dead," he thought.

On his next dive he couldn't find the car. He had to come up after 15 seconds, exhausted.

He gulped air for a few seconds, then did two more quick dives. He kept finding only the unopenable driver's door. Never had he known how confusing water and mud could be. He realized that another 15-second dive was the most he could manage. He dived for the eighth time. It took three seconds to dive and find

the driver's door. He struggled briefly with it.

Eight seconds gone. He dived over the hood and came out under the passenger side; if the car rolled now it would crush him. Carefully, he felt for the door; this one was open the width of two hands. He tugged cautiously. It opened two feet more, digging down into the mud and sending a swirl of slime inside. In the murk he saw nothing. Then he started to enter the car.

Thirteen seconds gone, he desperately needed to refill his lungs. He had no energy left. But could he leave the girl, when she was so close?

Once Norton had saved three children in a pool. He learned then that in crisis a diver sometimes can "double-extend" his time down. He began working his chest muscles, to squeeze out any pockets of air that might remain unused in the lungs. It may have worked, for suddenly he was able to thrust his head and shoulders up inside the tilted car. Next, he was inside up to his waist.

Holding the doorpost with his left hand, he groped with the right up the driver's seat back to the tall headrest. High against the ceiling, his hand touched an object: a small, sandaled foot.

Twenty seconds had passed. Fighting exhaustion, Norton worked with furious speed. He got a firm grip on Nancy's right ankle, and began to pull hard. The girl came down floating into the front seat. He circled her slim waist with his right arm. And suddenly he knew he was through. His lungs could take no more. He hesitated. And in that moment he felt a hand ever so slowly wrapping itself around his right arm.

The touch of life electrified him. New energy surged through him. He began to fight to get her out of the car and to the surface in time. He braced his feet against the hard steel of the half-opened door and gave the girl a powerful shove. She shot upward. A second or two later she surfaced, her blond hair streaming on the water; the next moment Norton shot up beside her. He pulled her toward the seawall. Her face was gray, her eyes closed. Was he, then, too late? At that moment the girl threw back her head in a long, shuddering gasp

for air. She cried, "Help me!"

Nancy Burns does not remember being pulled from the car. She does remember crying out, and being dragged across the marina lawn. The men of Station 12 knew that seconds counted. They dragged her, hips up, face down, to get out all the water that she might have swallowed. Only drops came out. Even unconscious, Nancy Burns refused to surrender and inhale water.

Nor had Fireman Norton surrendered. On his eighth dive he had "double-extended" his time to 40, perhaps even 45 seconds—to Red Cross experts a marvel of endurance.

Nancy's next awareness was the rich, warm smell of green grass, the smell of life. She couldn't get enough, and she gulped deep, sweet breaths. She heard Mark's worried voice: "Her eyes won't open." And she realized, "I'm *afraid* to open them. If I look now, I'll still be under water." Then she was in the ambulance, getting oxygen, and a fireman's hand was ever so gently parting her eyelids. After being submerged for close to 15 minutes, Nancy Burns was seeing life again.

Notes from Gary's Mom

*Helicopter parents can't hold a candle
to this mother.*

—

BY **COURTNEY ZOFFNESS**
FROM **THERUMPUS.NET**

Originally published in June 2015

From: <MommaGlo@aol.com>
Date: Sun, May 31, 2015, at 12:31 AM
Subject: Gary's internship
To: Tuck Lanson, CEO <Tuck@LansonCorp.com>

Dear Tuck,
Gary is excited to start his weeklong internship at Lanson Corp. tomorrow! It occurs to me that there are a few small issues that may (or may not!) arise during his time there. I'm sure everything will be fine, but I'm his mom. And moms worry.

1. Gary's really concerned about doing a good job. If you could request that your employees furnish him with compliments and positive feedback—which I have no doubt he'd earn, so it wouldn't be insincere— that would be so great.

2. Gary is weak in the math department and thus has apprehensions about tasks related but not limited to numbers, sequences, patterns, proportions, and quantification. I've given him $15 for lunch, which should cover a sandwich and chips (no soda, please), but he may get worked up when a cashier prompts

him for money or he attempts to count his change. Perhaps you can assign someone to negotiate these dealings with/for him?

3. Gary has inflammatory acne. He's taking doxycycline, which seems to be helping, but it's giving him diarrhea, which has led to dehydration, which has led to halitosis. Please don't take it as a sign of disrespect if he's popping mints while chatting with you. Trust me: It's actually a sign of respect!

(Pee-eww!) Also, I read that his medication can be deactivated if he's too close to a microwave, so if you could seat him in a cubicle far from the kitchen, that would be ideal.

4. My son has a history of orthodontic issues that I may as well address. Gary has exceptionally large teeth and a small jaw, and when he was 12, the dentist pulled four of his molars to prevent overcrowding. Though Gary wore headgear for years, his teeth never moved to fill in the gaps. Now he wears a retainer garnished with four fake teeth, which he has to remove to eat. Doing so makes him extremely self-conscious. Is there somewhere he can dine by himself (your office?) so no one will catch sight of his situation?

5. While Gary is of perfectly average height for his age, he feels short. This prompts him to misjudge where his head and feet are relative to the ceiling and floor. If Gary requests help fetching something off a shelf within his reach, please comply. As his therapist says, we all have our own realities, and his is as valid as yours or mine.

6. Oh, and for what it's worth, Gary is allergic to pinecones, pistachios, lime-flavored Life Savers, mite excretion, mouse excretion and double-sided sticky tape.

And that's all! (Phew!) Thanks again, Tuck. We can hardly wait.

All best,
  Gloria

P.S. Due to Gary's anxiety over starting this position, he may get there a little early. Would it be possible to have someone there to let him in around 6 a.m.?

P.P.S. Alternatively, there's a chance that, due to his anxiety, he'll be up all night and will crash around 6 a.m., in which case we'll need to let him sleep in for a bit. Cool?

Face to Face with Her Husband's Killer

A drunk driver took the life of Patty O'Reilly's husband. Here's how she turned her rage and despair into forgiveness.

—

BY **KENNETH MILLER**

Originally published in June 2016

On the day Patty O'Reilly met the man who had killed her husband, Danny, his wedding band hung next to a small crucifix on a gold chain around her neck. Patty clutched a family photo album as guards ushered her into a windowless room at California State Prison, Sacramento. She sat at a wooden table and leafed through the pages, her chest tight as she recalled the moment each picture was taken: Danny dancing. Danny getting married. Danny playing with their daughters.

When Dave Mancini* shuffled in, accompanied by a correctional officer, Patty was struck by how frail he looked. His uniform hung from his skinny frame, and his face, accented by a graying mustache, was drawn. He seemed as anxious as she was—and far less powerful than he'd appeared from across a courtroom two years earlier. Fidgeting, Dave took the seat across from her. The mediator who'd arranged the meeting

After Danny's death, "my faith sustained me," says Patty, right, with her daughter Siobhan.

*Names have been changed.

161

led a silent meditation. Then Patty and Dave exchanged stories about the day that united them. It was the worst one of their lives.

On April 19, 2004, Danny had risen at 6 a.m. to make a pot of coffee. As usual, he and Patty had taken their mugs to the sofa and read each other a passage from a spiritual writer—a private communion ritual for these devout Catholics. Then Patty fixed breakfast for their girls, Erin, 12, and Siobhan, seven, while Danny cut roses from the garden to send off to school with Erin.

Danny was a former ballet dancer who worked as a marketing analyst for a winery in Sonoma County. He and Patty had met in ballet class in their 20s, and they still shared a passion for jetés and pliés. At 43, Danny was as lean and muscular as ever. Patty, 39, now ran a ballet school of her own.

Patty's car was in the shop, so Danny biked to work that morning and let Patty use his car. She ran errands while the girls were in school, then picked them up and took them to her studio, where they did homework while she rehearsed her students for an upcoming show.

Home around 9:30 p.m., they came in through the back door, and the girls went straight to bed, but there was no sign of Danny. The dog whined to go out, and when Patty opened the front door, a card with the sheriff's number fluttered to the floor.

She called the number and told the operator she'd be waiting in the garage. If the news was bad, she didn't want the girls to hear her wailing.

Ten minutes later, the sheriff arrived. The news was very bad.

On the worst day of his life, Dave woke up with a pounding hangover from yet another drinking binge. After popping a couple of Percodans and smoking a joint, he called his girlfriend, Alyce Malone*, for a ride to the doctor's office to refill his oxycodone prescription. Dave, who was 46, had become addicted to the powerful opioid analgesics he'd been taking since breaking his back a few years earlier. "I'm a mess," he told her. "If I don't get those pills, I'm gonna go off the deep end."

But Alyce passed on giving him

a lift. "A DUI would serve you right," she said.

Furious, Dave climbed into his pickup and drove to see his doctor, who took one look at him—gaunt, unshaven, almost incoherent—and referred him to a detox program at a nearby hospital. On the way to the clinic, he bought two quarts of beer and drank them in the hospital parking lot. After waiting an hour for his name to be called, Dave ran out of patience and took off across town to a neighborhood where he knew he could find heroin. He'd never used the stuff, but he felt desperate. The dealer he was looking for wasn't around, so Dave found another liquor store, drank two canned cocktails and passed out in his truck. When he awoke, he called Alyce, but she again refused to pick him up. He drove back toward the clinic.

En route, as he weaved through Santa Rosa, Dave rear-ended a car. Afraid of losing his license, he sped away. Swerving around a bend, he spotted a man on a bicycle. He had a flash of Alyce's ex-boyfriend, an avid cyclist, and a jolt of jealous rage electrified him. By the time he slammed on the brakes, it was too late. He'd hit Danny O'Reilly with a force that sent his body flying over the guardrail.

When a patrol car appeared, Dave staggered out of the truck and cursed at the officer, reaching for his waist-

> ## Dave and Patty exchanged stories about the thing that united them: the worst day of their lives.

band as if he had a gun. He hoped the cop would shoot him. Instead, he was pepper-sprayed, handcuffed and taken to jail.

❖ ❖ ❖

As the weeks after Danny's death passed, Patty's grief curdled into bitterness. One evening, when the girls were supposed to be showering, Patty heard giggling instead of running water. "I don't need this!" she screamed. Patty immediately felt ashamed. Her hatred for Dave, she realized, was hurting those she loved.

my Name is ☆ to Jail For Eighteen
Siobhan (shavon), i'm teen years, me
eight years old. and my Sister
you Might be Erin thought it
suprised but i'm Should have been
not Mad at 13 and a 1/2. but it's
you! but i am very only 6 month's
Sorry. I would away Now! ☆
like to come and best wish's, ☆
See you. When i heard Siobhan
you were going

"When I heard you were going to jail for [14] years, me and my sister Erin thought it should have been 13 and a half," wrote eight-year-old Siobhan.

Soon afterward, Patty received court papers outlining Dave's background. She read that Dave had been raised Catholic. She also learned that as a small boy, he had been sexually abused by his father. When she read this, Patty welled up with empathy.

Four months later, Dave pleaded guilty to vehicular manslaughter, hit-and-run and driving under the influence. At his sentencing hearing, he apologized tearfully. "I pray one day one of you will find a hint of forgiveness," he said. Patty rose and spoke about the damage he'd done. "I've had to tell our daughters that their father would never be coming home again," she said. "I have lost my best friend … my companion."

She paused, then added, "I do have the capacity to forgive."

That was as much as she could

say. She asked the judge that Dave be held fully accountable for his crime, and a 14-year sentence was imposed.

With Dave locked up at San Quentin State Prison, Patty believed it was over. But one day her youngest daughter, Siobhan—now a pensive second grader—asked her mother if she could visit Dave in prison. Patty said no. A week or two later, Siobhan asked again. Patty searched the girl's dark brown eyes. She and Danny had raised their daughters to forgive anyone who sincerely apologized. Patty saw Siobhan's request as a sign that Patty had more forgiving to do. "We can try," she told Siobhan.

"Good," the girl said. "I made him a card." Decorated with stars, a panda sticker and a drawing of a crying face, it read: *My name is Siobhan. I'm eight years old. You might be surprised, but I'm not mad at you! But I am very sorry.*

"I wanted to see him, and I wanted him to see me as well," Siobhan says now. "I wanted to tell him in person, 'I'm sad, but I'm OK, and I forgive you.' It wasn't a conscious thought process. It just seemed like the thing to do."

Patty was touched by Siobhan's generous spirit, but she wanted to meet Dave herself before deciding whether to bring her little girl. Researching her visitation options, she read about Rochelle Edwards, a mediator with the nonprofit Insight Prison Project who was starting a program based on the concept of "restorative justice," which encourages structured dialogues between inmates and victims. Increasingly influential in correctional systems across America, this face-to-face communication has been shown to help repair harm caused by the crime.

Patty called Edwards. "The process isn't easy," Edwards told her. "But it can be a powerful experience for everyone involved." Edwards explained that both parties would spend at least six months preparing for the meeting. For practice, she suggested, Patty could volunteer as a surrogate victim for groups of inmates at San Quentin.

Although Siobhan was too young to participate then (the minimum age is 18), Patty seized the opportunity. She hoped to find a deeper forgiveness— one that didn't feel like surrender.

❖ ❖ ❖

Patty and Dave met on September 28, 2006, at the prison near Sacramento to which Dave had recently been transferred. Before they exchanged stories, Patty slid her daughter's well-worn card across the table to him, along with a new one from Siobhan: *I just want to make sure you know that I forgive you. I do still miss my dad; I think that's a lifelong thing. I hope you're feeling OK.*

Dave winced. "The resiliency of a child is incredible," he said quietly.

Patty told him about Danny: devoted husband and dad, skilled cook, and biking buff. She listed family milestones her husband had missed in the two years he'd been gone and those he would miss in the future: graduations, weddings, grandchildren. As she wept, she recounted Danny's last day and the days that followed. She shared the details of her daily struggle to raise her daughters and how she still nearly broke down whenever a cyclist rode past. She told Dave how she'd hated him. Then she revealed that she'd given up her anger.

"Forgiveness doesn't mean you're off the hook," she said. "I want you to deal with what you've done—to confront the pain and let it change you."

Dave then spoke of his father's abuse, of how the old man had given him his first drink at age seven and how the whiskey had seemed to transport him to a better world. He told how he'd started businesses and lost them, found love and squandered it, how he'd tried rehab again and again and managed to stay sober for 14 years—until, in 1996, a piece of stage equipment he was installing fell and cracked his spine. He explained how he'd hoarded extra pain pills and plunged back into drinking.

"My rage at my father was at the root of it all," he said. "Does this give me an excuse to do what I did? No."

Patty shared the photo album, showing scene after scene of Danny basking in his family's love. "It was such a wonderful life," Dave said. "I'm so sorry."

In keeping with the guidelines of restorative justice, Patty asked Dave to make specific commitments: to stay active in Alcoholics Anonymous, to continue in psychotherapy and to share his story as a cautionary tale.

She requested that he send letters updating her on his progress. He promised he would do it all.

After four hours, Patty walked out of the prison. For the first time since she had seen the sheriff's card fall from her door, she felt free.

❖ ❖ ❖

In March 2015, Siobhan turned 18—finally old enough to meet Dave face to face. He had been transferred to a prison in San Luis Obispo and would be paroled in May. Five days before Dave's scheduled release, Patty drove Siobhan to the prison. Patty cried in the car as her daughter, who still seemed so young and vulnerable, disappeared inside.

Siobhan joined Rochelle Edwards in a boardroom with barred windows. When Dave entered, Siobhan was relieved to see that he appeared fit and calm; he was no longer the haggard scarecrow her mother had described. He offered his hand, and she shook it.

Siobhan read Kahlil Gibran's poem "The Coming of the Ship": *How shall I go in peace and without sorrow? Who can depart from his pain and his aloneness without regret?* Dave

repeated his story, up to the day that had changed them all. Then he described his life since.

Dave said that after meeting her mother, he'd resolved to get sober and pull himself together. He'd struggled with depression and medical troubles

> ## As a little girl, Siobhan asked if she could visit Dave in prison. "I wanted him to see me," says Siobhan now.

and had occasionally resorted to using marijuana or pills smuggled into prison. Eventually, he was diagnosed with bipolar disorder and prescribed mood stabilizers. Dave told Siobhan that he hadn't touched alcohol or illicit drugs for five years. He'd gone through intensive psychotherapy and attended AA meetings daily, mentoring 20 inmates in the program. "Your family's forgiveness saved my life," he said. "Now I'm trying to do the same for other people."

Siobhan discussed her own depression and struggle to stay focused on schoolwork. She was thriving now, she said, ready to graduate and head to college. She asked him to make a list of at least five people he could count on for support when he left prison. He told her he would.

Thanks to restorative justice and her journey toward forgiveness, "I feel less like a victim," says Patty.

The meeting lasted an hour and a half, and Siobhan walked out smiling.

Patty visited Dave that afternoon. She read him the passage that she and Danny had shared on his last morning, from the medieval mystic Hildegard of Bingen: *I saw a woman bowed to the ground under the assault of many whirlwinds. And I saw her regain her strength, pulling herself up, resisting the winds with great courage.*

"Those words have always comforted me," she said, handing him the book. "I hope they'll do the same for you."

Dave was released the following Friday. He's living in a halfway house, volunteering as a crisis counselor for survivors of rape and domestic violence, and searching for paid work that will make use of his hard-won experience.

"I've been given an incredible gift," he says. "I want to do something magnificent to honor it."

Patty, who continues to work with inmates, cherishes the gifts she has unearthed during her long journey of forgiveness. "My best qualities—things like patience and gratitude—have been nurtured," she says. "I feel less like a victim and more like a person who makes things happen."

Perhaps most important, she feels that justice has been served. Helping her husband's killer transform himself, Patty explains, "was my form of vengeance. I got a life for a life."

The Man Who Trapped Bonnie and Clyde

The story of the trigger-happy outlaw pair who terrorized the Midwest and Southwest in the early 1930s and of the Texas-sized lawman who finally brought their murderous odyssey to a bloody end.

BY **JOHN REDDY**

Originally published in May 1968

On a foggy January morning in 1934, a work detail of prisoners plodded stolidly out of the Eastern Texas State Prison Farm to work in the adjoining fields. Suddenly, ahead of them, a man and woman materialized from the mists and opened fire. A guard crumpled, mortally wounded. Five of the convicts scrambled after the pair through the wet underbrush to a car hidden in a nearby river bottom. There, all seven piled into the car and disappeared in the fog.

The daring prison break was engineered by the notorious Clyde Barrow and Bonnie Parker to free a friend, Raymond Hamilton. For over two years, Bonnie and Clyde had been on a spectacular crime

spree across the Midwest and Southwest, defying the efforts of the FBI, state and local police and even the National Guard to trap them. The killing of the prison guard brought their murder score to at least 12, most of them law officers, and led to mounting clamor for their capture. It also brought into the hunt a remarkable lawman: retired Texas Rangers Captain Frank Hamer.

Loner on the Trail

Tough and independent as a longhorn, Hamer stood six feet three inches tall and weighed over 200 pounds. He had oaklike arms and fists, developed by work in his father's blacksmith shop. As a youngster, he lived like the Indians he had read about, hunting and riding through the San Saba hill country, cultivating keen powers of sight, smell and hearing, and often staying out for days at a time, sleeping on the ground. When he joined the Rangers at 22, he was a superb horseman, could throw a knife

Bonnie Parker playfully points a shotgun at her partner, Clyde Barrow, in 1932.

with deadly accuracy and soon won the reputation of being one of the best shots in Texas. But, despite this skill, he rarely resorted to his gun. His usual means of dealing with unruly customers was to clout them with one swipe of his open palm.

A dedicated officer, he nevertheless was a loner who preferred to track down criminals by himself rather than as part of a team. He retired from the Rangers in 1932. But when the superintendent of the Texas prison system asked 50-year-old Hamer two years later if he would undertake to track down Bonnie and Clyde, he agreed. He was appointed a member of the Texas highway patrol and on February 10, 1934, embarked on a solitary search.

Hamer had never seen either one of the pair, so he set out to learn as much as he could about them. It became apparent that their trail had been marked by violence almost from the day their paths crossed.

Odyssey of Crime

When they first met in Dallas in 1930, Bonnie was 20 and Clyde was 22. Married at 16, Bonnie had been deserted by her husband and was working as a waitress. The son of an illiterate tenant farmer, Clyde had left school in sixth grade and thereafter displayed an allergy to hard work. Not long after their meeting, Clyde was jailed in Waco, confessing to two burglaries and five auto thefts. On a visit to the jail, Bonnie slipped him a revolver that she had concealed in her brassiere. Clyde escaped, was recaptured and served two years in the Texas state prison at Huntsville.

Reunited with Bonnie back in Dallas, Clyde (minus two toes that he had chopped off to escape prison work detail) discovered that 90-pound Bonnie shared his fondness for firearms, fast cars and excitement. Equally adept with shotgun, pistol or machine gun, he coached her until she could shoot like Annie Oakley. A week after teaming up with her, Clyde and two companions were accused of killing a man in a holdup in Hillsboro. Shortly after, Clyde and Hamilton killed two officers at a dance in Atoka, Oklahoma.

So had begun the bloody odyssey of Bonnie and Clyde that eventually drew Hamer onto their trail. They had embellished the growing aura of legend around them with a flair for self-dramatization. Bonnie wrote doggerel about their lurid exploits. They delighted in photographing each other clowning with guns or smoking big cigars, and sent the snapshots to the newspapers.

Hamer studied these pictures and interviewed people who knew the pair and their habits—how they dressed, what kind of whiskey they drank, their tattoos. He learned of Clyde's ability to drive hundreds of miles in a night, over bumpy country roads, sticking up a bank in Texas one day and a store in Kansas the next. They often joshed amiably with their holdup victims, as if it were all a lark. Bonnie sometimes even kissed them. Yet Hamer never forgot that they were both dead shots who came out with guns blazing at the sight of an officer.

Hamer learned, too, that Clyde seemed to have an uncanny, animal-like sixth sense of impending danger. Once they were holed up in Joplin, Missouri, with Clyde's older brother Buck, recently paroled from prison; his wife, Blanche; and W. D. Jones, a 17-year-old punk whom

Clyde had known in Dallas. Scouting a holdup job with Jones, Clyde suddenly had one of his premonitions. "It's in the air," he said to W. D. "I can smell it."

Clyde drove back to the hideout and put the car in the garage. Upstairs, Bonnie was writing a bit of doggerel, "The Story of Suicide Sal," while a pot of beans bubbled on the stove. Suddenly, police bullets began shattering the windows. Barrow and Jones fired back from the garage, while Bonnie blasted away from upstairs. "Get to the car!" Clyde screamed. Blanche, terrified, ran away. The others leaped into the car and burst from the garage in a hail of fire, yanking Blanche in with them two blocks away. Two officers lay dead behind them.

Deadly Strike

Despite this almost miraculous ability to shoot their way out of traps, luck was beginning to run out for Bonnie and Clyde. While they were speeding along a Texas road, their car overturned and caught fire. Bonnie was hideously burned. But even this didn't halt their depredations. They held up a dozen more banks, while Bonnie, a gun cradled in her bandaged arms, lay in the backseat of the car; Clyde had to lift her in whenever they set out to stage another stickup. They slipped from crime to crime, from state to state, swapping stolen cars and switching license plates as they went.

By this time, law officers were swarming over several states in pursuit. In July 1933, Bonnie and Clyde made incredible getaways from police traps near Platte City,

Former Texas Rangers Captain Frank Hamer, pictured on the day after the ambush.

Missouri, and Dexter, Iowa, but Buck and Blanche were captured—Buck to die from wounds a few days later. Young Jones, his nerves frayed, fled to Texas, where he, too, was captured. Alone now, Bonnie and Clyde lived in their car, parking by back-country roads at night.

Just when their fortunes seemed at their nadir, they executed the Texas prison break. Two of the escapees—Hamilton and Henry Methvin—joined them in a new spree of stickups. Then began the pursuit that would take Frank Hamer thousands of miles through nine states. Like Bonnie and Clyde, Hamer virtually lived in his car, roaming remote rural roads. He first picked up their trail in Texarkana; then, just as he felt he was getting close, on Easter Sunday 1934, they struck again in their deadly fashion.

Parked on a lonely road near Grapevine, Texas, Clyde was napping in the rear seat and Methvin was standing guard when two motorcycle officers pulled up. "It's the law," Bonnie whispered, shaking Clyde awake. "Let's take 'em!" he shouted to Methvin, and the escaped convict opened fire, killing the two instantly. On April 6, near Commerce, Oklahoma, the gang (minus Hamilton, who had defected after a dispute over the division of loot from a bank holdup) added what was believed to be a 15th victim to their toll.

On a Lonely Road

Then came the break Hamer had been waiting for. He learned that the gang occasionally visited Methvin's father in Louisiana. Hamer also learned that the elder Methvin was frightened of Bonnie and Clyde and would agree to help trap them in return for leniency for his son.

Henry had told his father that if the gang ever got separated, they were to meet on a lonely stretch of road near Arcadia, Louisiana. So, the next time the trio visited Methvin, the father got his son aside and told him of the plan to capture Bonnie and Clyde. Henry agreed to trigger the ambush by slipping away at the first chance.

The chance came the next morning. Bonnie, Clyde and Henry drove to Shreveport, and Henry went into a store for supplies. When he didn't reappear, Bonnie and Clyde, assuming that he had been frightened away by something, drove off. They returned to the elder Methvin and told him to be on the lookout for Henry, and to meet them the next day at the Arcadia rendezvous point. Methvin passed the word to Hamer.

That night, Hamer, local sheriff Henderson Jordan and four other armed officers hid themselves under some pine branches at a point where the couple were to meet Henry. They decided to try to take the two alive unless Bonnie and Clyde went for their guns.

Dawn broke with no sign of the outlaws. A few cars and logging trucks passed in the morning stillness. The posse, crouched in the dewy pines, was chilled to the bone. Then a truck driven by the elder Methvin rumbled up. Methvin was told to remove a wheel as though he were repairing a flat tire. Shortly after nine o'clock, just as Hamer had begun to wonder if Barrow had once again sensed a trap, a car was heard approaching at high speed. Behind the wheel was Clyde, wearing dark glasses. Bonnie, in a red dress, was beside him. They skidded to a halt.

"Got a flat?" Clyde asked.

"Yeah," Methvin said. "Did you find Henry?"

Then the officers moved in. At the command "Put 'em up! We've got you covered," Clyde tromped on the gas, and he and Bonnie went for their guns. A shattering volley rang out from the posse.

The car—riddled with 107 bullet holes—rolled down an incline and came to rest against an embankment. Hamer and the others rushed up, guns leveled, but both Bonnie and Clyde were dead. The car contained an awesome arsenal: three Browning automatic rifles, two sawed-off shotguns, nine Colt automatic pistols, one Colt revolver, 100 machine-gun clips of 20 cartridges each, and over 3,000 rounds of other ammunition. A shotgun, seven notches carved in the stock, was between Clyde's knees; Bonnie had a pistol with three notches.

This was the only tangible legacy that remained of Bonnie and Clyde for their dreadful years of bloodshed, terror and flight.

Could Anyone Be Alive?

For the men trying to save three kids in a burning house, timing would be everything.

—

BY **ANITA BARTHOLOMEW**

Originally published in April 2002

Tom Konchesky was tired after a long shift in the production department at Mylan Pharmaceuticals. It was a crisp November afternoon. Gusts of wind blew leaves across neat suburban lawns into the intersection where he slowed his Chevy S-10 for a stop sign. All he wanted to do was get home, clean up, play with his two little boys and spend a quiet evening with his wife.

Taking a shortcut to the polls to vote in the presidential election, federal coal-mining inspector Bill Brown headed toward the same intersection of Killarney and Colonial drives in Morgantown, West Virginia. As he slowed to stop, there was an explosion so strong it shook the ground and rocked his truck.

❖ ❖ ❖

A block away, auto mechanic Allen Fortney was standing outside the garage where he worked, shooting the breeze with his boss, enjoying the pleasant weather, when a burst of hellish thunder pounded his ears.

A spark was all it took to set off a gas explosion that leveled the Halbritter home.

The stunned men watched as 200 feet past the intersection an entire house blasted from its foundation as if launched by a rocket. Seconds later the roof, walls, windows, floors and furniture came crashing down.

Shingles and drywall rained on the roadway. Shattered glass covered neighboring yards. Bricks and pipes tore through tree branches.

A spark, drawn to a leak in the house's natural-gas line, had detonated it like a bomb. Flames sprouted in the mound of rubble that had fallen where the house once stood.

It took Konchesky a moment to grasp that his truck hadn't exploded. Then, realizing that someone could be trapped under the mangled remains of the house, he rushed to help. Right behind him were two other guys from the Mylan plant, Gene Tritchler and Camille Mikalik, who were headed home along this same route.

To their amazement, a frail-looking young woman stood shakily on top of the ruins, her hair singed and shriveled, her face burned red, her clothes torn and smoldering. She turned in a circle, dazed, looking everywhere but appearing to see nothing and screaming hysterically, "My babies are in there!"

"Where did you last see them?" Konchesky asked. Through her sobs, the woman managed to tell the men that her children had been on their way up from the basement toward the back of the house.

Taking her gently by the hand, Konchesky guided her to safety off the smoking pile. "Stay here," he told her. "We'll get them." He and the two other Mylan workers clambered across the steaming debris.

Running from the opposite direction, Allen Fortney leapt over a fence and reached the back of the house just as the three others did. Without a word, without being fully aware of one another, they began working as a team, hauling aside chunks of roof, wall and siding—looking for any space where someone might be trapped.

Right time, right place, right stuff—the five who stopped to help. From left, Mikalik, Tritchler, Fortney, Konchesky and Brown.

Right behind the others, Bill Brown also ran toward the explosion. In his 30 years working in coal mines, he had seen dynamite tear mountains apart, but he had never seen anything like this. *No one could have survived that*, Brown thought. Still, he had to be sure.

Fire poked through the tangled mass, climbing about as high as his knees and spreading fast. He tried to orient himself. This must be where the garage had been—a minivan sat in the driveway in front of a burning mound. At the back of the house, Brown could hear other men throwing debris out of the way. He moved a few feet down the drive, peering across the flattened remains of the garage. For a moment, through the smoke, he thought he saw a child's head. Was it a trick of the light? Was it a little girl? Was she alive?

Picking his way carefully across the ruins, in danger of falling through, Brown started toward the spot. Flames shot higher, burned hotter.

❖ ❖ ❖

Around the rear of the house, the impromptu team of four hefted a huge section of what might have been part of the roof. It was too heavy for them to throw off the pile. So Mikalik, a burly six-foot-one former coal miner, braced his back to hold the slab while the others kept digging. "C'mon, guys," he shouted. "We gotta hurry. This is heating up."

They uncovered the top of a refrigerator. At its base were a boy and a girl, wedged between it and a wall.

Then all of a sudden they heard children's voices below. They were screaming for help.

Ignoring the flames, Konchesky and Fortney reached deeper into the small opening they had made, breaking through wood, drywall, siding and shingles to get to the source of the terrified cries. With Fortney on one side of the small space and Konchesky on the other, there was no room for Tritchler. He called to his friend Mikalik, "I'm going to go around front." Maybe he could find another way under the rubble.

As Fortney and Konchesky grabbed, pried and kicked their way through the heaped debris, they uncovered the top of a refrigerator. And there, several feet below, huddled at its base were a boy and a girl. They were wedged between the appliance and a section of wall that had fallen onto it to create a perilously unsteady lean-to.

Electrical wiring twisted through the framing. It knitted the crumbling wall together, making it impossible to completely break it apart. But the men kept punching and tearing at it, until they had an opening maybe 14 inches across—just enough for a child to crawl through.

While Mikalik kept his weight braced against the slab, Konchesky stuck his head and arms down into the opening and yelled to the boy, "Crawl to me so I can pull you out."

"No," the child cried. "I'm not leaving without my sister."

The boy had courage. But the way the building had caved in, there was no way to get his sister out unless he came first. Konchesky tried to explain this, but the child was too panicked to understand.

"You come first, and I'll pull her through," Konchesky pleaded. Fire lapped at the children's legs. Soon, there'd be no way out for either child.

And behind the refrigerator was the hiss of leaking gas.

"Come on," Konchesky screamed. "We've gotta get you out of there!"

At last the boy began to climb up. First his head and then an arm poked through the hole. Konchesky grabbed tight, yanked him out and threw him over his shoulder into Fortney's waiting arms. He didn't dare turn his head and risk losing sight of the girl, who now crawled toward him. Her head was just visible. He reached for her—and a new hail of loose debris fell from above, covering them both.

As Brown came from the front, Tritchler picked his way carefully over the rubble from the rear of the house. Smoke and flames blurred his visibility. Several yards away, he saw what could have been a nest in the shattered pile. It was not—it was a child's hair.

Immediately he began leaping across mounds of brick and broken lumber. He was almost there, almost ... Then *whoompf!*—a ball of fire shot up from below. It blew Tritchler backward, torching the flesh of his arm and face.

At the back of the house, Mikalik and Fortney furiously threw off the fallen debris, reaching Konchesky and the girl, who had made her way to the top of the opening.

Flames licked higher, spurting and spitting right behind. With no time left, Konchesky grabbed the girl's hair, pulled her the rest of the way out and hollered, "Everybody, run!"

He got no more than ten feet from the hole when a muffled explosion knocked him to his knees.

Looking back, he saw flames 20 feet high where they'd been a moment before.

Neighbors and passersby crowded the yard and sidewalk. Exhausted but elated, Konchesky brought the girl to her brother. Yet for some reason, the boy was still screaming "my sister, my sister!" and still trying to run back to the fire.

What was the child talking about? "I've got your sister right here," the confused rescuer insisted.

"No," the sobbing boy cried. "My other sister."

Konchesky's heart sank. The flames engulfed the area. No way could the third child still be alive. He suddenly felt very old and tired.

Then he heard a voice call out. It was Gene Tritchler walking toward him through the crowd of onlookers. "We got them all."

❖   ❖   ❖

In shock, sobbing uncontrollably, Theresa Halbritter stood in a neighbor's yard, certain her children were dead. Then she looked up and saw all three coming toward her—her nine-year-old twins, Rachel and Robert, who had been buried next to the refrigerator, and six-year-old Shannon. She reached for them, enveloped them in her arms.

Paramedics whisked her and the children to the emergency room of a nearby medical center. Halbritter and the twins escaped with only first- and second-degree burns. Shannon, in addition to burns and scrapes, had a broken foot.

That night and the following morning, the five rescuers went to the hospital to see how the kids were doing. Greeted as heroes, they said no, they were just glad they happened to be at that intersection—the right place, at the right time.

Scout's Honor

A middle-aged man braves bugs, leaky tents and a mess hall with 300 screaming kids to see if he finally has the makings of a Boy Scout.

———

BY **JOE KITA**
FROM **MEN'S HEALTH**

Originally published in October 2018

"**A**re you all right?" the lifeguard screams. "Do you need help?" I've swallowed a lot of lake water and can't answer. Gasping for breath, I glimpse my fellow Scouts lining the dock.

We're at Camp Minsi in Pennsylvania's Pocono Mountains, trying to earn our swimming merit badge. What they can't vocalize I can see in their wide eyes: The old guy might die!

But I manage to catch my breath and paddle to the ladder without needing rescue. I climb up, embarrassed and exhausted. One boy looks up at me with a puzzled expression and asks, "What are you doing here?"

Good question. Forty-five years ago, after earning the rank of Bear in Cub Pack 47, I quit Scouting—I stank at tying knots.

However, when a man reaches middle age, funny things happen. The work-life climb is no longer well-defined and becomes more about finding a sturdy rung and hanging on. Those buds you once shared so many good times with turn into Buds you share mostly with yourself.

And if you ever happened to come across the Scout Law, you might realize that you haven't been as "trustworthy, loyal, helpful, friendly, courteous, kind, obedient, cheerful, thrifty, brave, clean and reverent" as planned. Indeed, what grown-up wouldn't benefit from a week at summer camp in Wi-Fi-free woods with plenty of time to whittle down life's priorities? Who wouldn't enjoy sitting around a campfire eating cherry cobbler bubbled in a Dutch oven and laughing until his stomach hurt?

So in an inspired moment, I approached the Boy Scouts of America and asked whether there was any way I could take up where I'd left off so long ago. Was it too late for me to become an Eagle Scout? Yes, they said. The cutoff age for Eagle is 18, and I'm seven presidents beyond that. But I could attempt to become the world's first Bald Eagle Scout. I already had the "bald" part down. "Eagle" would take some work.

❖　❖　❖

It's 6:30 a.m. on July 14, the first full day of summer camp, but

already our troop's 17-year-old senior patrol leader is whacking my tent flap and yelling "Wake up!" as reveille rat-a-tats in the distant woods. Perhaps because of the bugling and the ache in my back from spending the night in a tent, it feels like the dawn of war.

I dutifully don my uniform shirt and neckerchief, report for morning inspection and camp flag raising, and then join my troop as we trudge to breakfast at the central dining hall.

Three times a day, nearly 300 ravenous boys descend upon this hall in an attempt to stoke their raging metabolisms. Here, in the days that follow, I will watch in horror as "Fat Joey" casually chews ketchup packets until they pop inside his mouth. I will observe another youngster consume 35 iced slushies in seven days, each containing 28 grams of sugar, some along with a shot of Pop Rocks. (No wonder he wakes up one night screaming about a snake in his tent.)

And in this same hall, I—a grown man—will be dressed down by an irate scoutmaster in knee socks for joining the line too early at the salad bar. "Please sit down!" he yells.

But on this first day, I remain pleasantly naive. Breakfast ends with everyone standing for the rousing sing-along classic "I'm Alive, Awake, Alert, Enthusiastic!" Those are the only words, and it's sung to the tune of "If You're Happy and You Know It." Each time you say "alive," you touch your ankles; "awake," your hips;

"alert," your shoulders; and for "enthusiastic," you raise both arms in the air. And you do this faster and faster for what seems like 50 verses—with 300 kids.

Pumped up on empty carbs and camp anthems, I burst through the door after dismissal into the fresh mountain air, flush with promise for a new day and a new adventure.

Unfortunately, my merit-badge classes (with the exception of my near-death experience in Swimming) turn out to be boring affairs. First Aid ends up feeling a bit like a video game as kids keep asking how to medically treat fantasy: "So what do you do if someone gets stabbed in the eye with a sword?" Then, after a succession of instructors in Orienteering, most of us are, ironically, totally lost.

The event I had been anticipating most—the postlunch "siesta"—turns out to be the busiest time at our campsite. Kids are cleaning latrines, building fires and hitting things with a large ax to screams of "Break it!"

It's refreshing to see boys being encouraged to be boys. Everyone is running around with knives or spears, and not once do I hear anyone scream "You're going to poke your eye out!" Kids roam over the thickly wooded 1,200-acre property untroubled by ticks or ragweed. Shotguns are blasted, tomahawks thrown and arrows fired—all by kids.

The Muck Hike is the purest expression of this freedom to experience dirt and danger. It's a mile-long trudge through chest-high sludge. Everyone emerges from it

> ### Kids run around with spears, and not once do I hear "You're going to poke your eye out!"

like a swamp thing. But they all have smiles on their filthy faces. In these days of free-range chickens and cattle, the Scouts are raising free-range boys!

"If we see a Scout heading toward a cliff, we'll let him step off," explains one scoutmaster, "as long as it's not a big cliff. That's how they learn."

Kids also learn through failure at this camp. One out-of-shape youngster had been eagerly anticipating learning to kayak. But he was a tight fit, and after capsizing in the lake, he had to swim his boat to shore because he couldn't climb back in. At home,

> **Sitting around a campfire with 30 kids, I realize my sense of humor hasn't matured in 40 years.**

he might have been coddled, but out here he had to deal.

I start to realize that what's awful about camp is also what's great about it: You're not insulated from nature as most kids and adults are these days. You're part of it, living in the raw, as we were meant to be. Which is memorable.

Consider: On Monday night, severe thunderstorms sweep through camp and pummel my tent. Rain drips on my forehead; everything I brought is damp. I lie awake in the middle of the night wondering why I'm here, both literally and metaphorically.

On Wednesday, after the weather clears, one of our Eagle candidates builds two tree platforms, a monkey bridge and a zip line—in less than five hours. No nails, just rope lashings.

On Thursday night, we build a campfire. I sit around it with 30 kids and realize that my sense of humor has not matured one iota in the past 40 years. Fart jokes, teacher pranks and falling over backward in your camp chair are just as gut-busting now as they were when I was in Scouts.

On Friday morning, we have pizza—for breakfast!

By Friday afternoon, the kid who drank all the slushies is out of money. To feed his sugar addiction, he resorts to accepting dares whereby he eats fishing bait for cash. He starts by swallowing a mealworm for 50 cents, then a night crawler for a buck, and finally a butterworm for $2 (but we make him hold it on his tongue for 30 seconds). He heads for the camp's trading post with a wad of dough.

Being in the woods for long periods encourages contemplation. Perhaps one reason guys my age start feeling adrift is because we have little left to moor ourselves to. We've moved around, the kids have grown, and our accomplishments aren't as clear-cut as they used to be. I mean, what exactly have I built? A garden shed? A 401(k)? My great-granddads would laugh at that.

That's why it was important to make my service project meaningful. This is the bar exam for Eagle Scout candidates. You must conceive, design, finance and ultimately build or execute some project that enhances the world around you.

Some kids clean up cemeteries or build benches at churches. But as a Bald Eagle candidate, I knew mine had to be much grander. It had to be a project that was commensurate with my life knowledge and experience.

The scenes that kept coming back to me involved the boy in the kayak and those meals in the dining hall. I realized I might be able to help these kids while addressing the national problem of child obesity in my own small way through Scouting.

So I spent 60 hours (the Scouts like when you track things) creating the plan for a summer-camp competition called Fittest Scout. Points are awarded for making smart nutritional choices (e.g.,

having oatmeal for breakfast instead of a grape slushie) and participating in various physical activities. Boys with the most points at the close of the week earn the title of Fittest Scout. The unit with the most combined individual points is the Fittest Troop. There's even a Fittest Scoutmaster category.

I'm proud to say it was a hit. The head of my local council even offered to test it at camp in the future.

❖ ❖ ❖

At the end of summer, Troop 1600 holds a Court of Honor, where Scouts are singled out for various achievements. Parents (and wives) are invited, a campfire is lit and snacks are served. This Court of Honor falls on my 30th wedding anniversary. My wife is expecting big things. I tell her to dress warmly and bring a flashlight.

As we sit on logs, the scoutmaster calls me up with the rest of the kids to receive my merit badges. Everyone applauds me, the Bald Eagle.

I miss the next meeting because after the last meeting I'm, well, grounded. I'm bummed because the troop is nominating new patrol leaders. It's an important step for the kids, being recognized by their peers. One of the scoutmasters calls me the next day. "When I asked for nominations for senior patrol leader last night, one Scout raised his hand. He wondered if he could nominate you."

Maybe I'm a better man than I thought.

Bold Brothers

When a three-vehicle collision occurs near their house, Conner and Caleb Richey rush to help—and there's a twist.

BY **ALYSSA JUNG**

Originally published in November 2015

On their last day of summer break in August 2013, brothers Conner and Caleb Richey were at home in Enterprise, Alabama, when a huge crash reverberated through the two-story house.

Caleb, 19, who was playing video games downstairs, was certain that there had been a car accident on Highway 167, about 400 yards from the house. He ran upstairs and burst into Conner's room. "We have to get outside!" Caleb told his brother.

The two boys sprinted barefoot across the front yard and down a wooded hill. They saw three vehicles—a red pickup truck, a black sedan and a black tow truck—all of which had been struck. A man who looked shocked but uninjured sat on the bumper of the tow truck, which had veered off the road and into a ditch.

Conner and Caleb got to the sedan first. Smoke wafted from its mangled front end, and the driver was pinned in place by the collapsed dashboard and steering wheel. Blood covered his face, and his left arm was badly broken. "I don't know if he's going to live, but I have to do something," Conner, then 21, remembers thinking. He took off his T-shirt and pressed it against the man's bloody head. Caleb sprinted

"It was second nature to help," says Conner Richey, left, with his brother, Caleb.

back home to grab a first aid kit. He returned, gave the kit to his brother and then borrowed an onlooker's cell phone to dial 911. Later, when emergency personnel arrived, they cut off the roof of the sedan, pulled out the trapped driver and loaded him onto a helicopter bound for a nearby trauma hospital. "You probably saved his life," paramedics told Conner.

Meanwhile, Caleb rushed over to the pickup truck. When he peered through the windshield, he was surprised to see his father, Tim, inside.

"It's Dad!" Caleb called anxiously to Conner. "This driver is Dad!"

Conner ran to Caleb's side, and the boys tried to comfort their father. "Stay with us, Dad; paramedics are here," the boys repeated. As firefighters used the Jaws of Life to cut Tim, 52, out of the pickup, Conner called their mother, Denine, who was at work at the county registrar's office. She arrived in time to ride in the ambulance with Tim. Conner drove Caleb and their sister Caroline, then 15, to Medical Center Enterprise, where doctors treated Tim for bone fractures to his

vertebrae and knee, severely bruised ribs, and a right-elbow contusion.

Tim recounted the crash to his family from his hospital bed. He had been waiting in a line of traffic to turn left into his driveway when he saw a tow truck quickly approaching in his rearview mirror. Seconds later, the wrecker, whose driver was later discovered to have been texting, slammed into the rear end of Tim's truck, sending it spinning into oncoming traffic. Tim then crashed head-on into a black sedan. As the truck flipped, "it was just sky, ground, sky, ground," Tim says.

After the accident, he wore a back brace for eight weeks and a leg brace for ten and completed two months of physical therapy. The boys received an award from the Enterprise Chamber of Commerce in September 2014.

"I'm very proud of how my sons responded," says Tim. "But I'm not surprised."

The boys say their father taught them to lend a hand. "Dad raised us to always help people in need," says Caleb. "This time that rule of thumb helped him too."

"Nine Alive!"

As the world watched, rescue crews raced to find nine men trapped in a flooded Pennsylvania coal mine.

**— **

BY **CAROLINE ABELS, BOB BATZ JR., MICHAEL A. FUOCO, TOM GIBB, JOHN HAYES, L. A. JOHNSON, CINDI LASH, STEVE LEVIN, JIM MCKAY, JOHNNA A. PRO, MILAN SIMONICH AND ANITA SRIKAMESWARAN**
FROM **PITTSBURGH POST GAZETTE**

Originally published in November 2002

For thousands of years, sinuous stripes of bituminous coal have lain beneath the wooded hills and valleys of Somerset County, Pennsylvania. Coal lured immigrants to the area in the 1800s and helped forge their reputation for hard work and hard living. For generations, men have earned their livelihoods—and all too often have lost their lives—in the mines' dark confines.

Three shifts of miners show up daily at one such mine, Quecreek, lunch pails in hand, to descend more than 200 feet beneath a dairy farm for their eight-hour tours of duty. On Wednesday, July 24, 2002, 18 men on the 3 p.m. to 11 p.m. swing shift gathered at its entry portal at 2:30 p.m. They split into two crews of nine, one to enter and go straight south, the other to bear left and begin chipping at the east face. The nine men heading to the east face changed into their gear: thermal underwear, flannel shirts, blue overalls, rubber steel-toed

Safety helmets and gloves hang on a rack.

boots, knee pads and helmets.

Crew chief was 43-year-old Randy Fogle, who lived with his wife and two of his children on unpaved Fogletown Road. As you might expect, a lot of Fogles live along that road. The son and grandson of miners, Fogle had been working in or around mines for most of his life. He loved mining coal—not that there wasn't stress; for years he'd suffered from chronic heartburn—and he appreciated this crew for being efficient, smart and flexible. The guys called him Boss.

At 2:45 p.m., the miners exchanged news with the departing shift. Somebody called, "Have a good one, man." Then at 3 p.m., the nine climbed onto the mantrip, a battery-powered cart, for the half-hour ride to the coal seam where they would work, 25 stories down into the cool, damp darkness.

Rush of Water

On this day, Randy Fogle teamed up with Thomas Foy, 52, and two other miners, bolting steel rods to support a new mine roof. Tom Foy was an avid hunter and NASCAR fan, with a wife and four daughters.

Robert Pugh, 50, and Dennis Hall, 49—known as Harpo because he once sported long curly hair like Harpo Marx—were shuttle-car men, taking coal out to the conveyor belt. Harry Blaine Mayhugh Jr., at age 31 the youngest, operated the scoop, a motorized vehicle with a bucket for picking up the mined coal and dumping it on the belt for transport out of the mine. Mayhugh also happened to be married to Leslie, one of Tom Foy's daughters.

For the first half of the shift, John Phillippi operated the continuous miner, a low-slung machine fronted by an 11-foot-wide cylinder with 100 steel teeth for grinding into the seam and chewing out the coal. Then Mark Popernack, a thin 41-year-old with brushed-back black hair, took over.

Popernack was working near the sixth of seven passageways cleared into the mine. Then, just before 9 p.m., two hours from the end of their shift, routine turned to mayhem. The machine chipped away at a wall that was supposed to be hundreds of feet thick. Suddenly it gave way, unleashing 50 million gallons of groundwater into Quecreek. Inaccurate maps had led the men to believe they weren't anywhere near the abandoned Saxman Mine.

"Everybody out!" screamed Foy. "We hit an old section. There's a lot of water!"

Ron Hileman and John Unger were about 100 feet away, up a crosscut. Their machinery and ear protection covered the roar of the torrent and Foy's scream. But then they saw the water.

In a second, maybe two, water that had been gushing from a hole exploded through the wall, crashing over Popernack's machine. "Harpo! Get the hell out! Get out now!" Popernack screamed to Hall, who was right behind him in an electric-powered shuttle car.

Hall heard the warning and drove away, maybe 200 feet, before the car lost power and died. Popernack managed to jump away from the machine, but the flood had created a furious orange river, cutting him off from the others.

In a space barely four feet high, and with only the light from their

Randy Fogle held a dispirited crew together through prayer. "I mean we did a lot of praying."

head lamps to guide them, the miners on the other side of the torrent began their desperate race to get out. Amid the confusion came the first move that saved lives. Foy and Fogle yelled at Harpo Hall, who was nearest the mine phone, to call the crew working the south face.

Hall hit the intercom button. Nobody answered. Finally he heard a voice. It was the mine's "outside man"— the miner stationed on the surface for emergency purposes. Hall was telling him what had happened when one of the second crew picked up. To him, Hall screamed: "Get out! Get out, damn it! You got major water!"

Word spread quickly through the second crew. "Shut everything down," someone yelled. "We're getting out of here!"

Five miners on the south face piled into their mantrip and started driving out of the tunnel, picking up

Dennis Hall, the first hero, says simply, "I had to make that phone call. I had to."

a sixth crew member along the way. Two others were just ahead in a golf cart. The ninth man was already at the opening of the section.

Water soon sloshed up over the sides of the carts, and the men had to abandon them. They escaped on foot into another passageway, but when they got to one of the entry tunnels, a swift, cold current was there.

The water, about 20 feet across, was only a little over two feet high, but for men walking crouched in a four-foot-high space, it was up to their chests. They had to wade across— or face certain death. Once across, they headed uphill, fighting their way to dry ground. It took 45 minutes to get completely out of the mine. There they notified the foreman and waved off medical treatment for themselves.

They were looking back for lights, for any sign of the other crew. There was nothing.

"We're in Trouble"

Mark Popernack screamed at the other men to save themselves. He figured he'd probably die there alone.

The eight converged at the entry

where the conveyor belt moved the mined coal out of the shaft. They prayed this was their way out. Racing down the passageway, the miners held on to the coal conveyor to keep from falling into the violent water. They ran as fast as stooped men could. But because they were hunkered down, the water, now three feet deep, was reaching their necks.

The men crawled onto the conveyor belt, stopped now that the water had cut its power. Harpo Hall tried to clamber onto it, but couldn't get there. So Fogle grabbed him by the coveralls and tossed him up. They scrambled across the coal on the conveyor, falling, bloodying their knuckles, watching the water rise.

The two youngest, John Phillippi and Blaine Mayhugh, led the struggle along the stilled conveyor for about 2,000 feet. As they looked forward, their helmet lamps illuminated their worst fear—100 feet ahead, the water was hitting the roof. The flood was about to overtake them.

The two young miners yelled at their fellow crew members to reverse course. Thomas Foy turned to his son-in-law, Mayhugh. "We're in

trouble," the veteran miner told him.

"I know, Tom," Mayhugh responded. "I'm too young to die. I'm not afraid to, but I got two little kids. This ain't no way for us to go."

With water up to their chins, the men had to crane their necks back to keep their faces above water. Every now and then they would veer off to a crosscut, but everywhere they turned there was water. Fogle used his mason's hammer to try to break through a cement-block wall to gain entrance to another passageway, possibly a way out. He pounded as hard as he could; then Phillippi and Mayhugh took over, but the water began to rise over their heads again and they had to keep moving to higher ground.

Still alone, Mark Popernack rigged a hose under his armpits as a harness, wondering if he could tape hooks to his hands and somehow get across the raging river, clinging to the roof bolts to steady himself. He was desperate. Suddenly he saw a light. It was from Phillippi's helmet lamp across the water from him. "Get me over with you guys," Popernack shouted.

"I can't," Fogle told him. "The water's too fast. We'll have to wait for it to slow down." Eventually it did slow, just enough for Fogle to steer a scoop into the 20-foot-wide torrent.

"Randy, be careful," Hall called. "The water takes it, it's gone."

With the scoop's bucket raised above the rushing water, Fogle yelled "Jump!" Popernack leapt into the bucket. Fogle eased the scoop backward, and the nine miners again stood together.

The Rescue Begins

Dave Rebuck, owner of Black Wolf Coal Co., which mines Quecreek, was getting ready for bed Wednesday night when his wife handed him the phone. It was the mine's outside guy. Something had gone wrong. A breached wall. A flooding mine. Men possibly trapped.

Rebuck called state and federal officials, setting in motion an army of emergency workers. Mining engineers headed for Quecreek to start a rescue mission. At 9:53 p.m., Somerset County's 911 center got a call requesting an ambulance at the mine.

The job of telephoning families fell to State Police Corporal Robert Barnes Jr. He was brief and business-like. An incident had happened in the mine, he said. We'd like your family to come to the Sipesville firehouse, where we will tell you more. He wanted the families sequestered in the firehouse because he knew police would restrict access, sparing relatives from demands by the media. He also thought families could draw strength from one another.

Joseph Beer, pastor of Mount Laurel United Church of Christ, arrived at the firehouse first. He stood alone in the century-old building until the families began to troop in. They seemed shell-shocked, but questions abounded. Answers were harder to come by.

In those first desperate hours, none of the experts could speak to the most critical question—whether the men had survived the onrushing waters and found a sanctuary in the mine. As hours stretched into days, many in the firehouse would lose their composure and lash out in frustration. Susan Unger, wife of

John Unger, never did. She has multiple sclerosis and needed a walker to move about the room, but she radiated optimism. "I know they're going to come out," she told the others. Her resolve set a tone. They had to believe.

Mine operator Dave Rebuck set up a command center 200 yards from the mine portal, where there was room to spread out maps showing the 60,000-square-foot labyrinth. After using common sense to narrow down the location, they relied on global positioning satellites to find the spot where they believed the miners would go.

John Urosek, a mine ventilation expert, said an air pocket ought to exist in the mine. He suggested they pump compressed air through a bore hole to expand the air pocket and prevent the water from rising. It was an untested idea—and there were skeptics—but some thought it was worth a try.

First they'd drill a line to get communication equipment down there. The compressed air used in drilling, perhaps 100 degrees, might also offset some effects of the cold water, estimated to be 55 degrees. Rescuers feared the men were hunched in water to their chests, a circumstance that could bring on hypothermia.

Along with getting heat and oxygen to the men, rescuers would bore other holes to pump water out of the mine. Black Wolf workers began waking up anybody with a pump and a drill.

The critical job of drilling the

The miners worried that their underground nightmare was hardest on their families.

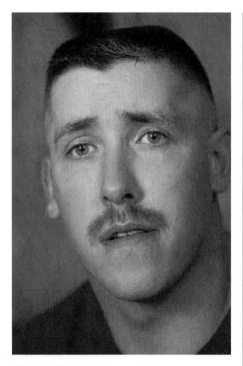

Blaine Mayhugh faced his own mortality: "We thought they gave up on us."

the pipe. Could it be? Were these clangs at 5:06 a.m. a signal that all nine were alive?

Hopes soared. Maybe, just maybe, they had all nine guys. Volunteer firefighters sealed the hole around the air compressor pipe with rubber rescue air bags. Then the drill operator cranked up his rig's air compressor.

Next, rescuers came up with an idea for using a "super drill" to create an escape tunnel for the miners. With a 1,500-pound bit, the drill could smash through the stubborn earth and create a chute wide enough to bring the men up. But it would take several hours just to haul the drill to Somerset County. And most of the rescuers had never even seen one before.

air hole began about 2:50 a.m. Thursday, six hours after the breach. The three-member drill team cracked through the mine shaft over two hours later—a blistering clip for obliterating 240 feet of topsoil and rock.

After inserting the air pipe into the mine, rescue workers tapped on the metal. Minutes passed. Then they received nine strong bangs on

Preparing for the Worst

Throughout the early morning hours, the trapped miners tried using cement blocks to dam off the water from their 18-by-70-foot air pocket. It was hard, frantic work and they were breathing low-oxygen air, known as black damp. "Is it just me?" Mayhugh said. "I can't breathe." Everyone was struggling.

But their spirits soared as the six-inch drill cut into the entry near the conveyor belt. The roar of compressed air hurt their ears. But they could put up with the discomfort; the pipe meant rescuers knew where they were.

Despite the warmth and air from above, the foul-smelling water rose foot by foot, eventually covering the air hole. They rapped on the rock ceiling instead—nine taps every ten minutes—hoping someone using specialized listening equipment could hear them.

By noon Thursday, the miners had built cement-block walls, but the water overtook them, forcing the men to retreat to the highest ground, about 300 feet from the air hole, and watch as the water continued to rise.

Randy Fogle gave it to them straight: In another hour, he estimated, all of them would be dead. There was quiet. There were tears. There were silent prayers.

Mayhugh asked if anyone had a pen, and wrote a note on cardboard to his wife and kids, telling them he loved them. He put the note in a white plastic bucket and offered the pen to the others. Each man wrote his goodbyes to loved ones. When nine notes had been placed inside the bucket, the lid was snapped on, and the bucket lashed to a boulder so it would be found.

Foy then grabbed a $\frac{3}{16}$-inch plastic-coated steel cable. He looped it onto their belts, saying that if they were to die, they would do so as a team, as a family.

Popernack and Unger weren't ready yet to tie in. They wanted to wait until the water was closer. Hall wanted no part of it at all, disdaining the thought of listening to his friends choking and drowning. He figured that when the water was about to cover him, he'd simply take a last breath and dive.

Their spirits, bodies and minds exhausted, the men settled in on an 18-by-30-foot patch of earth to await their fate. An hour passed. They were still alive. Where was the water? Perhaps it had stopped its relentless advance …

No longer resigned to the inevitability of death, they followed Fogle's orders and reverted to rescue mode. They continued to pound on the roof and turned off their helmet lamps to conserve power. Every ten minutes, one or two of them switched on their lamps to check the water level.

The dark was one enemy, the temperature quite another. To fight the cold, the men, now thoroughly drenched, covered themselves with canvas they found lying nearby. They sat back-to-back for warmth or lay on the ground, sandwiching teammates who shook with chills. Crew chief Randy Fogle remained upbeat. When one of the men would say, "We're going to die," Fogle was defiant.

"No!" he said. "We're getting out of here somehow, some way!"

His resolve steeled the crew. But when Fogle began coughing, throwing up and complaining of chest pains, they began to despair. He said it was only the fumes from the compressed air aggravating his heartburn. The other miners weren't so sure.

For long stretches, the men lay quietly in the darkness, whispering prayers to themselves. When they talked, they discussed what they'd do when they got out: attend a family reunion, one said, or enjoy their favorite foods—porterhouse steak, ribs. Popernack asked his crewmates what they would choose if they could—tobacco, beer or hot chocolate. Hot chocolate won.

They had been staring in the dark for so long that Pugh started to believe he could see his feet in the pitch blackness. Then Hileman said he could see his feet too. The others told them they were crazy. "I can even see a sky with stars, and a little town with houses and trees," Pugh said.

Sometime later, Harpo Hall's lunch pail was discovered floating about 100 feet from them. They found a corned beef sandwich, still dry, and a bottle of Pepsi. Every man took a bite of the sandwich except for Mayhugh, who figured one bite wasn't enough to end his craving for food, and Unger, who was afraid he'd vomit it up from nerves.

Things Fall Apart

The super drill arrived in pieces under police escort, sirens blaring. Assembled quickly, it was clawing through the earth by 7 p.m. on Thursday.

At that point, Mark Schweiker,

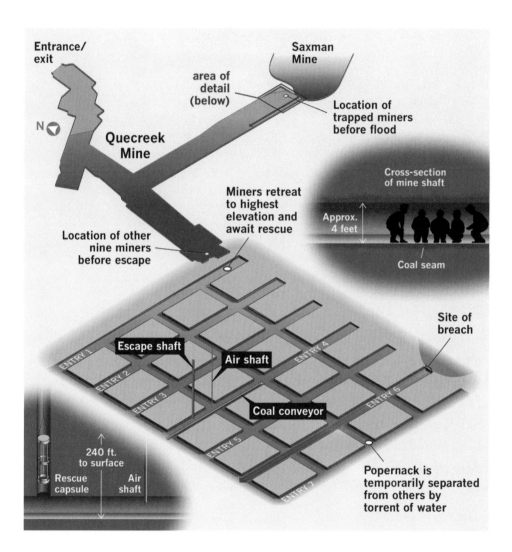

Entrance/exit

Saxman Mine

area of detail (below)

Location of trapped miners before flood

N

Quecreek Mine

Cross-section of mine shaft

Miners retreat to highest elevation and await rescue

Approx. 4 feet

Coal seam

Location of other nine miners before escape

Site of breach

Escape shaft

Air shaft

ENTRY 1
ENTRY 2
ENTRY 3
ENTRY 4
ENTRY 5
ENTRY 6
ENTRY 7

Coal conveyor

240 ft. to surface

Rescue capsule

Air shaft

Popernack is temporarily separated from others by torrent of water

governor of Pennsylvania, had arrived, and he projected that a life-saving tunnel could be dug by 3 or 4 a.m. the next day. After that, it might take another three or four hours to remove the drill and lower a rescue

basket through the 30-inch-wide hole.

There was still a lot that could go wrong. If the big drill bit punched through the roof too quickly, the pressurized air in the mine might rush upward, allowing water to fill the air

The rescue effort is derailed for 18 hours as crews labor to extract a broken 1,500-pound drill bit.

pocket and overwhelm the miners. To prevent a pressure drop, engineers fashioned an air lock to place on top of the escape hole—a 40-foot-long, three-foot-diameter tube with a sliding bottom door. It would keep air from leaking as the escape capsule was lowered to the miners.

Meanwhile, no tapping had been detected since 11:30 a.m. Thursday. Rescuers were hoping the men were still alive, still tapping. With the sounds of drills, pumps and people shouting, their signals could easily have been masked by the cacophony of surface noise.

Hope was focused on the super

drill breaking through to the miners quickly. Before the sun came up, the governor announced, "We should be good to go. We're going to get our guys out of there."

But disaster loomed.

About 1:50 a.m. Friday, as millions across the country prayed for the miners, the bit on the super drill broke. It was 105 feet in the ground, and would have to be fished out before drilling could resume. Work on the escape tunnel stopped cold.

Mary Unger, 87, whose son, John, was among the trapped miners, said what many were thinking. "It's awful, the waiting. It seems like things just keep going wrong."

The miners trapped below could hear the drilling getting nearer, steadying their hopes. Then suddenly it stopped. *Dear God,* Hall thought, *please don't let them think we're dead and give up on us.*

"They might have plugged up," Fogle said. "They might have broken a bit." Soon, he reassured his men, the drilling would start up again.

As one crew worked to fish the super drill out and get the rig started again, a second drill, erected 75 feet from the first, began punching through the earth. But it, too, would eventually break down.

Realizing they needed a specially made "fishing tool" to extract the broken bit, the drilling crews turned to Star Iron Works in Big Run, Pennsylvania. Engineering prints of the drill were faxed to Big Run; 95 machinists and welders pulled out all the stops.

"When they call and tell you a National Guard helicopter will be waiting to pick it up when you're done, you get a sense of urgency," said the plant manager. A job that would normally have taken three or four days was finished in four hours.

About 4 p.m. on Friday, the custom-made tool grabbed hold of the 1,500-pound bit and yanked it from the hole. After an 18-hour shutdown, the rescue tunnel was back in business. Hope had been restored, and the firehouse resounded with cheers.

"All Nine Here"

The drill finally punched through to the trapped miners' dank quarters late Saturday night. The escape shaft was in place.

Down below, the men had been taking turns every 10 or 15 minutes to check the area where they heard drilling sounds. Saturday at 10:15 p.m., Hileman and Foy made the trek. Their lamps were just about out of juice when they found the drill opening.

The other miners were lying down when Hileman came bounding back. "We found the hole!" he screamed. "Everyone get down there!"

No one needed a second invitation. They bolted toward the entry and began to yell: "Get us out! Help us! Please get us out."

Aboveground, rescue workers took a pressure reading and got a zero, indicating the pressure below was normal; they wouldn't need the air lock. Then they heard tapping. They couldn't contain themselves. There were high-fives, nine for nine. They lowered a probe, with a speaker and microphone, into the air pipe. A child's Glow Stick was attached.

After the probe had descended 75 feet, a rescuer began saying, "Can you hear me?"

Then, unmistakably, he heard, "We can hear you." It was miner John Phillippi at the other end, speaking into the slender microphone. To the rescuer, hearing the voice was like hearing God answer a prayer.

"Are you the trapped miners?"
"Yes, we are."
"Are you OK?"
"We're OK, except our boss is having chest pains."
"How many are you?"
"We're all nine here," came the reply.

The rescuer raised nine fingers. Word spread, and celebrations broke out. Dave Rebuck and one of his employees jumped into a police car and rushed to the Sipesville firehouse, where they met up with Mark Schweiker. Their faces telegraphed the news. All nine were alive, all in good shape.

The hall exploded in cheers, applause, shouts of "Praise the Lord!"

Miner John Unger's son, Stephen, had never seen people so emotional. Denise Foy, wife of Tom Foy, tried not to show how she was feeling. Every time she'd cried before, her daughters had cried too—especially Leslie, Mayhugh's wife. When the good news came, Denise just grabbed her daughter and squeezed.

Dave Rebuck sent his own message to Dennis Hall. "Hey, you're a hero," he said. "Your phone call saved those nine other guys." Hall, who for 77 hours hadn't known the fate of the other crew, cried when he heard the news.

Then it was time to send down the yellow steel-mesh rescue basket—a 9-foot-high capsule with lantern lights attached at the bottom. On its first trip, it carried lights, candy bars, blankets, raincoats, drinking water and chewing tobacco to squelch any cravings.

Up top, another miner joked with the trapped nine. Their families had been told they were alive, he said, and "most of them are happy about it."

Randy Fogle, who had experienced chest pains, would be first into the 22-inch-diameter rescue basket. He surfaced at 12:50 a.m. As with those to follow, the whites of his eyes shone from a face black with coal dust.

Mayhugh was second. As groundwater poured down on him from the shaft, he'd had enough. "Get me the hell up, and I mean now! Let's go!" he shouted. About three feet from the surface, he could see the bright lights, hear the applause and cheering. His heart raced; finally he broke down.

Tom Foy was next to go up. Unger, Phillippi, Hileman, Hall and Pugh followed. Mark Popernack, at 2:44 a.m., was the last man out.

Back to Normal

A doctor checked the men over. Their clothes were cut off, and special detergents used to wash away the oil from the compressor and the coal dust. Nurses started IV lines to deliver fluids, and the men

A rescue worker listens with a microphone cable for the voices of the trapped miners.

were sent to two area hospitals. The miners were smiling, alert and talking. They were also shivering. Fingers, feet and lower legs were purple and mottled from immersion.

At the hospitals, the men were reunited with their families. Denise Foy said that when she finally got to see her husband, Tom, "He just grabbed my hand and kissed me."

Six miners went home from the hospital on Sunday. Fogle and Foy were kept another day for further heart monitoring. For Fogle, it was a false alarm, brought on by gastric distress. John Unger, who

Theirs is a brotherhood strengthened by extraordinary circumstances.

complained of right shoulder pain, spent six hours in a hyperbaric chamber to allow any nitrogen gas to dissipate harmlessly.

Because the world was anxious to hear how the miners had fared during their 77 hours underground, several press conferences were arranged. "I came today to thank everybody out there," John Unger said at one, expressing a shared feeling among the men.

They had agreed on one more thing—that the muddy white bucket with their notes to loved ones would never be opened.

Even with the swirl of attention, the miners kept a sense of normalcy. At 12:55 p.m. Sunday, Governor Schweiker walked into Tom Foy's hospital room.

"Can we make this quick?" Foy asked. "My NASCAR race is going to start in five minutes."

My Greatest Olympic Prize

The celebrated athlete recalls how he almost missed out on his famous achievement—and the unlikely friend who helped him push through.

—

BY **JESSE OWENS WITH PAUL NEIMARK**

Originally published in October 1960

t was the summer of 1936. The Olympic Games were being held in Berlin. Because Adolf Hitler childishly insisted that his performers were members of a "master race," nationalistic feelings were at an all-time high.

I wasn't too worried about all this. I'd trained, sweated and disciplined myself for six years, with the Games in mind. While I was going over on the boat, all I could think about was taking home one or two of those gold medals. I had my eye especially on the running broad jump. A year before, as a sophomore at Ohio State University, I'd set the world's record of 26 feet 8¼ inches. Everyone kind of expected me to win that Olympic event hands down.

I was in for a surprise. When the time came for the broad-jump trials, I was startled to see a tall boy hitting the pit at almost 26 feet on his practice leaps! He turned out to be a German named Luz Long. I was told that Hitler had kept him under wraps, evidently hoping to win the jump with him.

I guessed that if Long won, it *would* add some new support to the Nazis' Aryan-superiority theory. After all, I am a Negro. A little hot under the collar about Hitler's ways, I determined to go out there and really show *Der Führer* and his master race who was superior and who wasn't.

An angry athlete is an athlete who will make mistakes, as any coach will tell you. I was no exception. On the first of my three qualifying jumps, I leaped from several inches beyond the take-off board for a foul. On the second jump, I fouled even worse. "Did I come 3,000 miles for this?" I thought bitterly. "To foul out of the trials and make a fool of myself?"

Walking a few yards from the pit, I kicked disgustedly at the dirt. Suddenly I felt a hand on my shoulder. I turned to look into the friendly blue eyes of the tall German broad jumper. He had easily qualified for the finals on his first attempt. He offered me a firm handshake.

"Jesse Owens, I'm Luz Long. I don't think we've met." He spoke English well, though with a German twist to it.

"Glad to meet you," I said. Then, trying to hide my nervousness, I added, "How are you?"

"I'm fine. The question is: How are you?"

"What do you mean?" I asked.

"Something must be *eating* you," he said—proud the way foreigners are when they've mastered a bit of American slang. "You should be able to qualify with your eyes closed."

"Believe me, I know it," I told him—and it felt good to say that to someone.

For the next few minutes we talked together. I didn't tell Long what was "eating" me, but he seemed to understand my anger, and he took pains to reassure me. Although he'd been schooled in the Nazi youth movement, he didn't believe in the Aryan-supremacy business any more than I did. We laughed over the fact that he really looked the part, though. An inch taller than I, he had a lean, muscular frame, clear blue eyes, blond hair and a strikingly handsome, chiseled face. Finally, seeing that I had calmed down somewhat, he pointed to the take-off board.

"Look," he said. "Why don't you draw a line a few inches in back of the board and aim at making your take-off from there? You'll be sure not to foul, and you certainly ought to jump far enough to qualify. What does it matter if you're not first in the trials? Tomorrow is what counts."

Suddenly all the tension seemed to ebb out of my body as the truth of what he said hit me. Confidently, I drew a line a full foot in back of the board and proceeded to jump from there. I qualified with almost a foot to spare.

That night I walked over to Luz Long's room in the Olympic village to thank him. I knew that if it hadn't been for him I probably wouldn't be jumping in the finals the following day. We sat in his quarters and talked for two hours—about track and field, ourselves, the world situation, a dozen other things.

When I finally got up to leave, we both knew that a real friendship had been formed. Luz would go out to the field the next day trying to beat me if he could. But I knew that he wanted me to do *my best*—even if that meant my winning.

As it turned out, Luz broke his own past record. In doing so, he pushed me on to a peak performance. I remember that at the instant I landed from my final jump—the one that set the Olympic record of 26 feet 5^5/$_{16}$ inches—he was at my side, congratulating me. Despite the fact that Hitler glared at us from the stands not a hundred yards away, Luz shook my hand hard—and it wasn't a fake "smile with a broken heart" sort of grip, either.

You can melt down all the gold medals and cups I have, and they wouldn't be a plating on the 24-karat friendship I felt for Luz Long at that moment. I realized then, too, that Luz was the epitome of what Pierre de Coubertin, founder of the modern Olympic Games, must have had in mind when he said, "The important thing in the Olympic Games is not winning but taking part. The essential thing in life is not conquering but fighting well."

English (According to the World)

Contributors to social networking site Reddit share hilarious interpretations of common English phrases.

——

FROM **REDDIT.COM**

Originally published in November 2014

My husband is Russian. He once told me, "That train has sailed." He also frequently gets the "jeeby-creepies."

—HOBBITFEET

A recent conversation with my French husband:

Husband: I almost dropped a plate, but I caught it with my arm-knee!

Me: Your what?

Husband: My arm-knee.

Me: You mean your elbow?

Husband: Yeah.

—TARANTUSAURUSREX

I'm Arab American. In Arabic, "download" and "put down" share the same word. A while back, my cousin came to stay with me. Every time he wanted me to drop him off somewhere, he would say, "Download me here." I never corrected him. It was awesome.

—JACKSRDTT

I had a German friend who tried to tell me that I left my gloves in the car: "VikingDan, you left your hand shoes in the car." I have never referred to them as gloves since.

—VIKINGDAN

I work with a few Russians, and I always laugh when they say stuff like:
"Vere ess Voice Helmet?"
"You mean a headset?"
"YES! YES! VOICE HELMET!"

—REFINEDDESIGN

It reminds me of when an ESL friend of mine referred to an air horn as "spray scream."

—CLOWN_PRINCE_OF_WEB

My Icelandic friend called dimples "smile holes."

—FIVEFOURTWO

My favorite comment: "My Dutch neighbor called the merry-go-round a horse tornado."

—V1000

My foreign friend calls a washing machine a "washine." I want that to be a real word.

—HAPPIEST_TREE_FRIEND

My German friend gets mad when he hears the phrase "back and forth." He says, "Why would you go back first! It's forth and back!"

—KLATHMON

I had a German high school teacher who was trying to rewind a tape in class and blurted out, "WHERE IS THE FAST BACKWARDS BUTTON?!"

—MYCARTEL

My Italian tour guide forgot the word for "veal" while translating a menu. Instead, she offered us "son of beef."

—ROALD_HEAD_DAHL

Sometimes, people who don't speak English fluently have a poetic way of describing things. When I was in Vietnam, this guy asked if he could practice his English. After a while, I told him I had cancer when I was younger. He said, "When I hear the words you speak, I feel sadness in my heart."

—GRANPASMEDICINE

The Dog Who Became the Dog Whisperer

Can dogs learn from their misfortune?
Here's one who just might have.

―

BY **ALISA BOWMAN**

Originally published in March 2015

As animal control officers pounded on the door to the small, one-story home in Knoxville, Tennessee, invisible fumes wafted up their noses, down their throats and into their lungs. It was ammonia, the suffocating byproduct of waste and decay.

No one answered. The officers muscled the door open. Blocking them was excrement, half a foot thick. Through the small crack, the officers could see filth, a couch covered in cardboard, and a television. *Cheers* was on.

Light streamed into the dark space, illuminating the eyes of countless dogs. The dogs rushed toward the officers. They were frenzied, crawling on top of one another, growling, snapping and fighting for freedom. The officers yanked the door, trying to close the gap, but dogs squeezed through. Two pushed past the officers and raced off. Officers tackled two more and secured them. They pushed the others back in.

Toefu (near left, with Juno) has helped a number of emotionally distressed rescue dogs.

The owners were home. That was obvious. The officers continued to pound on the door and shout through the crack. The fumes were overpowering and unbearable.

Finally, an elderly woman came to the door. She stepped outside and stood on the lawn, looking shocked and embarrassed as she watched officers don protective suits and breathing apparatuses to enter the home. One by one, the dogs were noosed with poles and dragged out of the house. Seeing sunlight for the first time, the dogs squinted and pulled back. They were emaciated, some with just hide over bones.

As each dog was brought out, it was numbered.

One ... Two ... Ten ...

Morning gave way to afternoon. *Forty ... Fifty ...*

Darkness began to fall. *Sixty ... Seventy-five.*

The elderly woman and her brother, who lived with her, were charged with aggravated animal cruelty. They were put on probation and agreed to counseling and unannounced home inspections.

The dogs were taken to Young-Williams Animal Center, where veterinarian Becky DeBolt and a team of others treated them for mange, anemia, worms and dehydration. Most had extra toes on their hind legs; some, a pronounced underbite.

These dogs sure have a short family tree, DeBolt remembers thinking.

This was especially true for dog number 16, who looked like a cross between Gomer Pyle and a vampire bat. The brown spaniel trembled, her ears back and tail tucked, as volunteers shaved her matted fur. By the time they finished, the dog was bald except for her head, her paws and the tip of her tail.

"She looked ridiculous," DeBolt says.

Three weeks later, number 16 and 48 other dogs had been nursed back to health. The rest were in such bad shape, they were put down. But important questions remained. Who would adopt a dog that couldn't stand being leashed or repeatedly threw up from fear? Could the dogs be house-trained?

Kristen Collins with dog number 16 (later renamed Toefu) soon after her rescue.

Allow themselves to be petted and cuddled? No one at Young-Williams knew the answers, so they asked the American Society for the Prevention of Cruelty to Animals (ASPCA) for help.

When ASPCA animal behaviorist Kristen Collins walked into Young-Williams, her presence set off the dogs. Their barking was deafening. She walked past run after run, eventually coming to the one occupied by dog number 16. The Gomer Pyle spaniel was asleep in a tight ball on top of a larger dog.

"She didn't even look like a dog," remembers Collins. "She looked more like an Ewok from *Star Wars*. I'd never seen such a pitiful-looking animal."

Dog number 16 lifted her head. Her eyes focused on Collins.

No, she told herself. *Don't even think about it. No.*

No turned into yes, and a few days later, Collins carried the spaniel

219

to her car for the ten-hour drive home to Illinois. She named her adopted dog Toefu, symbolic of the spaniel's extra toes.

For a year, Toefu's entire world had been walls, squalor and other dogs. She'd never even seen grass. So Collins drove Toefu, along with

> ## *Toefu continued to connect with the Chihuahua, lounging on the floor as the other dog dive-bombed her.*

Juno (the pit bull she'd adopted years earlier from a vet tech) and Wink (a border collie from a shelter), to a secluded park. Toefu fearfully plastered her body to Juno's. Slowly, she lowered her nose to the ground and inhaled the fresh scent of grass for the first time. Her entire demeanor changed—her tail shot up, and joy seemed to course through every cell of her body.

Collins helped Toefu overcome other anxieties. She was petrified of cars, so each day, Collins placed dog food closer to her car. Soon, Toefu climbed into the motionless vehicle to eat. Then she tolerated a ride around the block. Collins did the same with the other things Toefu feared—the blender, the vacuum, umbrellas, even small children.

In just a year, Toefu was behaving like a typical dog. Each morning, she woke, exploded out of her crate and wiggled her entire body with enthusiasm. Whenever Collins opened the back door, Toefu raced outside, scooped up a deflated soccer ball with her teeth and fiercely shook it back and forth as the ball made loud thwapping noises. When she wanted attention, she'd bound up to Collins, place a paw on Collins's chest and lightly tap her face with the other paw.

Phase one of Toefu's restoration was complete.

❖ ❖ ❖

A year later, in 2013, Collins moved to Madison, New Jersey, to take a challenging job overseeing the new ASPCA Behavioral Rehabilitation

Center. Shelters around the country sent her their most fearful rescue dogs. One was named Hillary.

On the floor of the center, the blue-brindled Chihuahua trembled, her eyes enormous, her brow furrowed, her mouth gaping as if she couldn't get enough air. She darted to the left of the center's vestibule. Reaching the end of her leash, she jerked back, then raced to the right, frantically trying to escape.

The Chihuahua had been rescued from hoarders who'd kept her and 19 other dogs in an outside pen, isolated from the rest of the world. The most traumatized of her pack, she was feral and showed no signs of being able to bond with humans.

For six weeks after her arrival, Hillary barked and snapped at her handlers. She cowered in the farthest corner of her run, refused to eat if people were nearby and, when someone touched her, abruptly flattened herself onto the ground as if she'd been hit with a bat.

"She was crashing and burning," says Collins. "We were stalled."

Then Collins had an idea.

She moved Hillary out of her run and into a small penned-in area in the office. Because dogs rescued from hoarders feel more comfortable when surrounded by a pack, Collins brought Toefu, Wink and Juno to work one day and left them in the office with Hillary.

Later that day, Collins checked on the dogs. Toefu bounded over, wagged her entire back end and snaked her body around Collins's legs and torso.

"How are you?" Collins sang to the dog.

Collins glanced at the back of the crate, assuming she'd see Hillary's trembling body through the slats. But the space usually occupied by the terrified dog was empty.

Her eyes shifted forward to the front of the crate. There was Hillary, peeking out, watching.

Toefu continued to wag and wiggle her body.

Hillary walked to the edge of her wire pen.

Toefu thumped her tail against the floor.

Hillary's tail began to wag.

Then, from Hillary's mouth, came a strange high-pitched yodel. It sounded as if the dog were singing.

Toefu continued to connect with Hillary, often passively lounging on the ground as the Chihuahua dive-bombed her, nipped her ears and raced over and around her body. Other times, Toefu curled up next to Hillary, wrapping her larger body around the tiny, shivering dog. At any point, Toefu could have dominated her. Instead, Toefu remained low to the ground and moved slowly, allowing Hillary the upper hand. When Hillary fled under the couch, Toefu pawed the ground but never pursued. She let Hillary come to her.

"Rehabilitation is about making decisions about when to pay attention to these dogs and when to give them space," says Collins. "The same is true during inter-actions among dogs. Toefu makes these social decisions easily, seem-ingly intuiting what these dogs need."

One day, as Collins knelt to greet Toefu, a little nose emerged from under the couch. Then a whole head. Then a whole body.

Hillary tentatively walked toward Collins. Just inches away, she stiffened, pulled her ears back and walked back toward the couch. Toefu continued to soak up Collins's attention, her tail happily thumping against the floor. Hillary did another about-face, tentatively creeping toward Collins again. Then, as before, she retreated. And that was it for the day.

A few days later, Collins was sitting on the ground with Toefu stretched out on her lap. Hillary approached Collins, but this time, she didn't pull back. Toefu reached her front legs toward Hillary, pawing her. The Chihuahua's ears perked up. She pawed Toefu back. Toefu stretched her jaw wide. Hillary did the same. The two dogs emitted guttural growling sounds. Now their heads were side by side, pushing each other back and forth, as Hillary happily emitted her high-pitched yodeling sound.

Collins's hand was just inches from Hillary. Would Hillary let her touch her? Collins slowly moved her hand closer. Hillary's body remained relaxed, her focus on Toefu.

Now closer.

Collins could feel the dog's fur against the back of her hand. The dogs pressed their heads together, pushing each other from side to side and back and forth.

Collins slowly edged her hand up Hillary's back. The dogs continued to growl and paw each other.

Collins slid her hand under Hillary's collar and scratched. Hillary abruptly stopped. She looked confused. Then "she got this dreamy, squinty, this-feels-so-good look in her eyes," Collins says. "It was magical, and it would not have been possible without Toefu."

Partly because of where Toefu came from and partly despite it, her gentle but persistent manner and intuitive understanding have helped not just Hillary but other dogs that have come to the ASPCA rehab center.

"People say that dogs live in the present," says Collins. "But they also make associations, and some of Toefu's earliest associations came from living in crowded conditions

Toefu's early experiences taught her to pay attention to other dogs' body language.

with some 75 other dogs. She had a very large family, and she knew a lot about them. Had she not learned to artfully read their body language, she might not have survived, and she might not be the dog whisperer that she is today."

Who Wanted Aaron Dead?

Clues led Detective Jim Michaud to a shocking suspect in the case of the midnight slaying of a teenager in his bedroom.

—

BY **FRED ROSEN**

Originally published in June 1997

round 1:30 a.m. on October 3, 1994, two teenage boys huddled in the cold outside a small ranch house in Eugene, Oregon. The older youth, an 18-year-old with a goatee and mustache, tapped on a window. No one answered.

"He's asleep," the boy whispered to his 17-year-old accomplice. The two were members of the 74 Hoover Crips, a gang that had recently surfaced in this peaceful university community.

The clean-cut younger kid nodded and helped lift the garage door. They slipped in.

In the rear of the garage, the goateed boy pushed at the door of a makeshift bedroom. In bed lay a muscular teenager. Steadying a revolver in both hands, the younger kid fired a bullet into the back of the slumbering boy's head. Then the two gang members fled.

❖ ❖ ❖

Even after the gunmen confessed, Detective Jim Michaud knew there was more to the case.

The house where Aaron Iturra was shot while he slept.

An hour later, the telephone woke Jim Michaud. The 41-year-old detective dressed quickly and donned his shoulder holster.

A short time later Michaud pulled up in front of a house flanked by police vehicles. The tall, rangy member of Eugene's Violent Crimes Unit walked through the garage and into the bedroom. There was a puddle of blood where the boy had been lying.

"What have we got?" Michaud asked his partner. "Teenager shot," replied Les Rainey, a stocky detective with dark brown eyes. "Name's Aaron Iturra. He's not expected to make it. His mother's in the kitchen, pretty upset."

Janyce Iturra, 42, was sitting in shocked silence with her four other children. Michaud spoke to her softly. "Do you know anyone who would want Aaron dead?"

"No," she said. "Everyone loves him." Later, after questioning others,

Michaud discovered that Aaron had been involved in an anti-gang movement in the community. Maybe this was a reprisal killing.

At about the time Michaud was talking with Janyce Iturra, the goateed 18-year-old stood on the banks of the Willamette River. He threw the revolver into the rushing white water, walked to a waiting pickup and drove away into the engulfing darkness.

Michaud was contacted by a police specialist in gang activity. He suggested getting in touch with Mary Thompson, who was tapped into the gang community. "If anything's gone down, she'll know about it," he said.

When organized gangs first came to Eugene in 1991, Thompson's son, Beau Flynn, was one of the first to join the 74 Hoover Crips. Then only 13, he was soon involved in crime and served time in a juvenile facility.

At first there was public apathy about Eugene's gangs. But then Thompson stepped forward. A stocky woman in her late 30s, she told parents, "If it could happen to my family, it could happen to

yours." Soon she was speaking at anti-gang seminars in high schools and youth centers.

As Thompson's visibility increased, she helped form a gang-prevention task force. "We need a hundred people like this," a high-ranking officer said. Thompson took her campaign to radio and TV, and she was featured in the local newspaper.

One day in early 1994 Thompson called Janyce Iturra. "I'm going into schools to counsel against joining gangs," Thompson said, "and I'm looking for the kind of kid others will listen to. I'd like Aaron to join me." A striking six foot five and 230 pounds, Aaron had flirted with gangs but had ultimately rejected the gang life himself. Still, no one messed with him.

Janyce eagerly endorsed Thompson's campaign, as did Aaron. Eventually he became one of Thompson's best spokesmen, and Thompson and Janyce became friends.

"How lucky you are to have a strong son like Aaron," Mary said one night, and added that she would love to have Aaron be a role model and a protector for her son. Janyce talked it over with Aaron. He felt honored to help Thompson by keeping Flynn "clean."

Later, Les Rainey and other police officers visited Thompson to see if she had any helpful information. She did. The day before, Thompson said, a Portland gang member named Sonny had come to her house looking for Aaron. Thompson said she felt sure that Sonny was behind the killing.

Rainey returned to headquarters, where Michaud called Portland police. They had no record of a gang member named Sonny matching Thompson's description.

Rainey wondered if fear might be preventing Thompson from telling all she knew. Michaud, meanwhile, started rummaging through files of old cases. Something was tickling his memory.

Over the next couple of days, Michaud, Rainey and other detectives interviewed about a dozen teenagers who were acquaintances of Thompson's. None could provide evidence about the murder, but two names kept coming up: "Crazy Joe" Brown and Jim Elstad. Brown was described as having a goatee and mustache. Elstad was said to look like a prep-school kid. It seemed that both boys hung out at Thompson's house. On October 6, Rainey and Detective Ric Raynor, a gang specialist, questioned Thompson.

"About three weeks ago," Thompson began, looking distraught, "Beau and Aaron were arrested." She said that some kids, including Aaron and Flynn, had gotten into a fight with another boy. A knife was pulled, and someone had "scratched" the boy's stomach. Aaron later told police that he had seen a knife in Flynn's hand, and agreed to testify against Flynn.

Thompson then related how two boys had started talking of shooting Aaron.

"Jim Elstad?" Rainey interrupted.

"And Joe Brown," Thompson continued. "I told them, 'I don't want to hear it.'"

"In the middle of the night on October third," she continued, "there's a knock at my door. Brown and Elstad are standing there. They

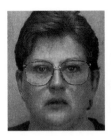   

From left: "Anti-gang activist" Mary Thompson; her son, Beau Flynn; and gang members "Crazy Joe" Brown and Jim Elstad.

said they had just shot Aaron."

Thompson said she'd been too afraid to share the information earlier: "I figured if those kids could go do that, they could do me. They could do Beau."

Elstad and Brown were arrested and interrogated. The more the boys talked, the more they implicated themselves. Finally the boys came clean, and Brown took police to the Willamette River, where they recovered the gun. A month later Brown and Elstad pleaded guilty to murder and were sentenced to prison. Police officials were relieved that they'd solved the murder. But in the mind of Michaud, the case was not closed.

On the morning of November 17, Janyce Iturra attended a hearing where Elstad was remanded from the juvenile to the adult justice system. That afternoon she was home when there was a knock at the door, and Mary Thompson barged right in.

"I saw you on TV," Thompson said. "I came to tell you how proud I am of you." Thompson threw her arms around Janyce and gave her a hug of support.

Michaud couldn't shake the Iturra case from his mind. The trigger men were behind bars, but rank-and-file gang members rarely freelance murders. Someone else, he suspected, had ordered the killing.

He thought back to the day that a vague memory had sent him flipping through his files. He had unearthed notes from an encounter two years earlier. A friend who owned a sign-

and-awning business suspected an employee of embezzling. Michaud had investigated.

His friend's receptionist was Mary Thompson. She seemed average enough, but her résumé had lied about her education. Also, Thompson listed a stint as "field investigator" for the Josephine County Sheriff's Office near Eugene. Michaud made some calls and discovered that she had actually been a drug informant.

When Michaud spoke with Thompson, she said she might have inadvertently taken some of the money and forgotten to give it back.

Preferring not to press charges, Michaud's friend fired her and the case was closed.

Now Michaud felt uneasy. Thompson was a good liar, and she had a motive in protecting her son. Could the anti-gang activist have stooped to crime to save Flynn's skin?

Some of the police saw little merit in Michaud's suspicions. They viewed Thompson as a valuable ally. But his superiors allowed him to get court permission to wiretap her home.

On January 13 the police set up a listening post in downtown Eugene, which Michaud, Rainey and others manned around the clock.

The next day Thompson was heard talking to an associate of the 74 Hoover Crips about Elstad's testimony. "They know I know more than what I'm saying," Thompson said.

"Same with me," the associate replied, "but there's no way they can prove it."

Three days later, on January 17, Beau Flynn called a 74 Hoover Crips member and clearly began to discuss a car theft. "Is Nate gonna do it with me?" he asked. When the gang member said he probably would, Flynn said, "We'll be strapped."

Listening in, Michaud stiffened. *Strapped* was a gang term for carrying a weapon. Flynn, who his mother claimed was "clean," was planning to use a revolver to commit some burglaries. He was to pick up the gun at South Eugene High School from a 14-year-old girl associated with the gang. Michaud alerted fellow officers.

That morning, the associate got into a blue Chevy with Flynn and handed him a revolver. After a high-speed chase, Flynn was caught.

He was later convicted of conspiracy to commit burglary and sentenced to 61 months in prison.

On January 21 the wiretap picked up a dial tone and an answering machine. Then Thompson's voice came over the line: "Yo—it's the brainwashing, murderous bitch. Give me a call."

Michaud became convinced that Thompson's own mouth would soon convict her.

Subsequent phone calls revealed the full extent of her activities. At one point, an associate named Steve told Thompson that police had seized a couple of guns from a friend. "None of them were anybody we loved, was they?" Thompson replied. Michaud knew she was referring to guns that members of the gang had carried.

On January 29, speaking of a suspected snitch to Flynn in prison, Thompson muttered, "We're gonna rip him." That meant hurt him badly. To Michaud, these conversations were proof of a startling truth: Mary Thompson was not just an anti-gang activist who had crossed the line once to rescue her son. She was neck-deep in gang crime herself.

The entire town had been deceived.

Thompson, it turned out, was the gang's leader. The wiretaps revealed her direct involvement in gang activity. Incredibly, her public stance against gangs was merely a facade to cover her recruitment of members. Michaud realized it was time to move on Thompson.

On June 4, 1996, Thompson was put on trial for the murder of Aaron Iturra. One associate confessed that the night Aaron was shot, she called his house to make sure he was home, then notified Thompson, who gave the go-ahead for the killing.

The jury found Mary Thompson guilty of aggravated murder. At the sentencing, the judge let Janyce Iturra make a statement. She stood before the court, angrily describing the defendant's "web of deceit." Then she turned directly to Thompson. "Aaron was your friend. You might as well have pulled the trigger."

The judge sentenced Thompson to life in prison without parole, plus 10½ years. With her incarceration, the power of the 74 Hoover Crips in Eugene was finally broken.

I'd Rather Have a Man Handy than a Handy Man

A wife's tribute to a husband whose craft surpasses his craftsmanship.

———

BY **JOYCE LUBOLD**
FROM **CONTEMPORARY**

Originally published in June 1968

Any house people live in is continually in the process of falling apart. Knobs pull off, faucets leak, lamps short-circuit, paint peels. Women are bothered by these things, and they want them fixed. Right away. But women know how long it takes to get a repairman to come to the house, so they turn to the next best thing—the man already in the house. Which is either a very good idea or a very bad idea, depending on the kind of man they've got.

There are some men to whom household chores are a pure delight. Faucets stop leaking at their touch; partitions go up in the unfinished attic as if by magic. A man like this *never* misplaces a tool, *always* cleans his paintbrush, and whistles while he works. His wife and children don't see much of him because he's usually doing a chore, but they can bear his whistling, and that's a comfort.

Then there is the other kind of man, the one who is *not* handy. For him, household chores are one long nail-bending, board-splitting, tool-losing nightmare. He can turn a dripping faucet into a major plumbing disaster, a blown fuse into a neighborhood blackout. He *never* whistles while he works; the sounds he does make are completely unsuitable for his family's ears.

Most wives persist in the delusion that there is somehow more *man* in a handy man. Nothing could be further from the truth! There's no need for a man to festoon himself with hacksaws and electrician's tape to prove his masculinity. In fact, if the wife of the unhandy man will encourage him to put down his tools and turn to all the other ways he knows of getting the job done, she will thrill to see him transformed, before her very eyes, from an ineffectual fumbler into a shrewd strategist.

Blessed though I am with such a man, I admit that I was slow to recognize his qualities, and met his initial display of genius with dismay. We were moving, with the help of a friend, into our first apartment. I asked my husband to put up the hanging rack for the pots and pans. When I came panting in the kitchen door, he stood, screwdriver in hand, the rack still uninstalled.

"Darn screw won't go in," he said amiably, demonstrating his problem.

"But you're turning it the wrong way!" I whispered, embarrassed that our friend might overhear.

"She tells me I'm doing this wrong," my husband called cheerfully as the friend toiled in with another load of boxes. "How are you supposed to do it?" The other man, a natural-born handy type, was fascinated.

"You really don't *know*?"

"Of course he knows," I said.

"No, I can't figure it out. Darn thing won't go in ..."

"Look," our friend explained. "When you want to tighten it, you go *this* way. See?"

"Say!" my husband said admiringly. "Does that work on all of them?"

"Sure. See how the other end goes in?"

"That's a real handy thing to know," my husband said. And it certainly *has* been handy for him. Since that day, scores of friends, acquaintances and casual passersby have taught him the same lesson. They enjoy doing it. He enjoys watching them do it. My man is a natural-born leader of natural-born handy men.

One day, we got a flat tire. I expected my husband to go into the Man-Being-Masterful-Changing-a-Tire act. I rehearsed mentally my "Darling-You're-Wonderful" speech. But my husband changed the script.

In less time than it would take another man to open the trunk and find he'd left the jack at home, *my* man flagged a passing car and spoke to the driver. Then he and I enjoyed the peace of the countryside—it was a *lovely* day—until the mechanic he'd sent for arrived and, in a matter of moments, switched the tires. We drove on, three dollars poorer, but with dispositions and self-respect intact. "That toggle bolt was reamed out," my husband said offhandedly. "Can't mess with a thing like that."

"Darling—aren't you—wonderful?" I said hesitatingly. After all, he wasn't playing the role I'd expected, and I wasn't sure how to react. But, a little farther on, we came upon another stranded car. A man covered with dirt and despair struggled with the flat tire while his wife handed him tools he didn't need and advice he didn't want. Some signal passed between these two unhandy men, because my husband pulled into the next gas station to send a mechanic back. "Poor guy probably had toggle-bolt trouble too," he said. "There's a lot of it going around." And then he grinned the cheerful grin of a man who is sure of himself, and doesn't have to change tires to prove it.

"Oh, Darling, Aren't You Wonderful!" I said—and I've been saying it ever since. For I have found that there is little my husband can't get done without actually having to do it himself. Where a handy man uses glue, my man uses guile; for power tools he substitutes persuasion; and his inventive imagination is an inspiration to us all.

It's hard to decide which of his methods is most thrilling to watch. One is to solve household problems by appearing to fulfill somebody else's need. For instance, we enjoy our summer evenings on a patio built entirely by city friends who thanked us, tearfully, for letting them get their hands into real dirt again.

But I think perhaps his greatness is most apparent on those occasions when professional help must be coaxed to the house. During a cold

snap, our furnace sighed noisily and stopped. When my threats failed to interest the repairman, I turned to my husband in despair. "He says he can't come till next week."

Quietly my husband reached for the phone. "Pretty busy time of year for you, isn't it?" he said sympathetically to the repairman. "Actually, I don't think it's worth fixing this time. Going to have to install a new one. I'll call Tomkins. He's not a patch on you boys for fixing, but he has a couple of furnaces in stock ..." The voice on the other end spoke urgently, and my husband shrugged. "You're welcome to come look at it if you want ... This afternoon? ... All right." Fifteen minutes after the repairman came, with folders of new furnaces in his hand, he had left, carrying my husband's sincere thanks and a bewildered look on his face. The furnace was roaring merrily again—and we spent the afternoon engrossed in some of the pleasant things there are to do around a house besides fixing it.

The fact is, as I think most wives would agree, it's really nicer to have a man handy than to have a handy man always busy doing endless chores.

Hard-Driving Sisterhood

*This rally tests drivers' skills
and builds lasting friendships.*

—

BY **LIA GRAINGER**

Originally published in 2017 in Reader's Digest International Edition

The women dance with abandon under a star-filled sky, the desert forgotten. After eight grueling days driving Morocco's sun-scarred landscape, these 316 women have completed the Rallye Aïcha des Gazelles du Maroc—an all-terrain, all-female automobile competition in the Sahara Desert.

The women are from 15 countries, but tonight they are as one, some dancing on colorful Moroccan carpets covering the golden sand, others gathered in clusters around candle-lit lanterns.

Julie Dufour and Geneviève MacEachern, a pair of Canadians, are among the revelers. At home in Gatineau, Quebec, Julie is a 41-year-old lawyer and mom. Geneviève, a 49-year-old mother of two, is an insurance claims analyst in Halifax, Nova Scotia. Tonight, though, they are Team 187, Julie the driver and Geneviève the navigator.

In the mid-'90s, Geneviève read about the Rallye and fell in love with the idea of being at the mercy

**For many of the women, the rally
in the Sahara Desert is the hardest
thing they've ever done.**

of the desert with nothing but her vehicle, her teammate and her wits to guide her. In 2007, she asked her friend Julie to join her. The rally would cost them around 40,000 Canadian dollars, and while many teams are sponsored, Julie and Geneviève spent a decade raising money to participate.

Now, dancing among new friends, they agree that finding their way across the desert together is the hardest thing they've ever done.

"I feel like superwoman!" exclaims Geneviève, throwing her arms around a grinning Julie. "Like I can do anything!"

Every spring since 1990, women from around the world have descended on the Moroccan Sahara Desert in trucks, four-by-fours, quads and buggies to compete in the world's original women-only off-road rally. French founder Dominique Serra, a travel agent, was frustrated by the lack of opportunities for women in the macho world of motor sports. She dreamed of a race for women based on navigational skill and all-terrain driving expertise instead of speed.

In 2017 the rally started on March 23. The competitors—called Gazelles—receive coordinates for checkpoints: two sets each morning and the rest at the second check-point of the day. Armed only with compasses, navigational plotters and race-issued topographical maps (no cell phones, binoculars or GPS allowed), each team—driver and navigator, sometimes alternating roles—must reach designated check-points taking the most direct route possible. The rally winner is the team that checks in at the most checkpoints driving the least number of kilometers to the rally's finish.

Many of the Europeans brought their own vehicles. But Julie and Geneviève rented their truck from a Moroccan car rental company and would have to pay for any major damage that their insurance wouldn't cover.

The patch of the Sahara where the competition occurs—about 400 kilometers (250 miles) south of Marrakech—is beautiful. But for the Gazelles, the 2,500 km (1,553-mile) course heading west-northwest can be unforgiving. There are dunes 100 meters (330 feet) high, rolling slopes covered in tire-piercing black rocks, and endless sand flats that will suck a vehicle to a stop in the 35-degree Celsius (95 F) midday sun.

As team driver, Julie had completed off-road training in Canada. But a sand pit in Quebec is not the Sahara desert, and each day of the rally brought its own challenge. Now, as she waited at the starting line at 6 a.m. on Day Three of the race, Julie nervously adjusted her helmet. The day's course would take them by the small southeastern village of Merzouga and a series of tall dunes, a challenge for all the drivers.

Within two hours they reached the foot of a peak near the town and began their climb. It rose so precipitously it blocked the morning sun. As the truck climbed the steep slope, Julie found herself pumped up with adrenaline: Other Gazelles had already got stuck near the peak, and Team 187 intended to blow right past them.

Just below the peak, Julie hit the gas to make the truck leap into

Looking for the best route, Julie and Geneviève confer with another team.

the air and over the top. Too much power and the Toyota would crash on landing. For a moment, all she could see was clear blue sky, then the truck landed hard—too hard?— on the other side of the peak. Julie slammed on the brakes and the women turned to each other, wide-eyed: They had done it.

"Woooo!" yelled Geneviève. Julie flashed back a wordless grin.

As the thermometer climbed toward 40 degrees Celsius (104 F), the hot sand became softer and more treacherous. Julie began to lose her nerve on the ascents. And, as the morning's adrenaline died down and the heat started to set in, so did her fatigue.

While they took a short break, Geneviève spotted a vehicle stuck in a nearby valley. Although teams could call a mechanic for help, they would be penalized, and the women were encouraged to help each other. They drove over and helped out the two French women, Team 122. They began traveling with them and were soon joined by another team, also from France. The group spent the rest of the day digging one another out when they got stuck and scouting the best possible routes.

After 12 long, hot hours, Team 187 reached its sixth checkpoint out of a total of seven, and decided to call it a day. Here a local Moroccan noted their arrival time and signed the daily race sheet that each team handed in at the night's bivouac.

Hundreds of colored domes rose out of the desert. They were the one-person sleeping tents, clustered at one side on the bivouac area, while on the other was a line of trailers that served as race staff headquarters. In between was the

dining tent, a 500-square-meter (5,380-square-foot) vinyl structure lined with carpets and filled with enough tables and chairs to seat the entire camp.

A short distance away was the mechanics area. There, a tanker trunk fed fuel into a mobile pumping

A checkpoint for the 2015 Rallye in Morocco's western Sahara desert.

station that would distribute 80,000 liters (21,000 gallons) over the eight-day race. The vast complex, covering 180,000 square meters (44 acres), would be torn down and rebuilt four times during the race.

By 11 p.m. the sleeping area was a sea of glowing headlamps.

Showered and fed, Julie and Geneviève crawled into their tents to catch a few hours of sleep before the 4 a.m. wake-up call.

Two days later, on Day Five, Geneviève surveyed the distant horizon through a sighting

A member of France's Toyota team digs their vehicle out of the sand during the 2015 Rallye.

compass that allowed her to see the terrain and simultaneously take a reading of its coordinates. She looked down at the 1950s military map that all racers received. There was a dark, rocky mountain that was easy to pick out, and Geneviève used it to find north. Then, using a ruler and compass, she decided that the shortest route to the next checkpoint was a mountain pass directly ahead. Julie agreed, and they began the rocky ascent.

At the summit they halted at several very large boulders blocking the way. The women got out. Julie examined the height of the boulders and the clearance of the truck's undercarriage.

"I think we can do it," she said.

Julie gently accelerated and the tires gripped the rock until the cab seemed to point almost straight up in the air. Geneviève held her breath. The truck began to level out as they reached the top, but then, on the way down, a large rock lodged in the undercarriage of the vehicle. Unable to move, they sat perched on top of the rock, on top of a mountain pass, with nothing but desert rolling out in every direction. The wheels were touching the ground but weren't able to gain enough traction to push the vehicle forward.

To Geneviève it seemed that calling for help might be the only option. "Let's wait just a little bit," said Julie. Just then, Team 410's Land Rover Dakar buggy rumbled up the slope and came to a stop behind them.

"We're too light to pull you," said the French driver. "Try piling some stones under all your wheels."

Geneviève and Julie began hauling flat stones into place, sweating in the midday sun. Suddenly they heard another motor, and Team 166, another French duo, pulled into view. Within minutes the French team dragged the Canadians' vehicle slowly backward onto solid ground.

Free at last, Julie and Geneviève headed in search of their next checkpoint. They found it on the pebble-covered plain called Hassi

Bou Haiara, the checkpoint's red flag and attendee nearly hidden in the desert brush.

When they arrived at the bivouac it was late, and other racers were already eating dinner. Geneviève headed to rally control to report their day's mileage and checkpoints. Leaving the office, she noticed some papers pinned to a wall. The rankings!

Geneviève and Julie's goal was to simply finish the race, but when Geneviève saw their names in 14th place among the 112 rookie teams, she was floored.

At dinner, she couldn't hold it in. "We're in 14th place," she whispered.

"No way!" said Julie, trying to hide a smile.

On Day Six, the wind started blowing early. All morning, Geneviève couldn't see ten feet in front of the vehicle. She strained her eyes in search of any topographical feature through the blowing sand— a riverbed, a mountain—anything. They crept forward until, suddenly, just as the wind dropped and the swirling sand abated, Julie stopped. They were at the edge of a wide, dry riverbed that stretched out a kilometer in front of them.

"The *oued*!" exclaimed Julie, using the Moroccan word for river.

The great Oued Draa marked the end of Morocco, and the distant shore, Algeria. Geneviève exhaled with relief and looked back at the map. With the Algerian border as a reference, she found north.

> ## The course is 2,500 kilometers of high sand dunes, tire-piercing black rocks, endless sand flats and sun.

"I know where we are!" she said, and plotted the way to the remaining two checkpoints of the day.

It was one of two nights competitors were required to sleep in the desert, away from the bivouac. Setting up their tents, Geneviève was struck by the silence. The wind had disappeared. In the desert there were no chirping birds, no trees, no rustling leaves.

Day Seven flew by, and then it was the final day of the race, Day Eight, March 30. Geneviève plotted their route over low grassy dunes and rocky plains. Before they knew it, it was noon.

"We should be approaching another oued soon," said Geneviève.

Suddenly there it was, right in front of them—a 20-meter-deep (65-foot) riverbed 100 meters (330 feet) wide, the rocky edge dropping about ten meters in a steep plunge and then another ten meters in a more gradual slope.

Julie got out to check how steep the drop was and to examine the rocks they would face on their path downward. "You think we can take that?" asked Geneviève.

"It looks OK from here," said Julie.

But as Julie crept forward, the truck's front right wheel suddenly dropped into a crevice running diagonally to the slope—a crevice they hadn't been able to see. When the vehicle tilted to the right, the front right wheel and the back left wheel were in the air, spinning uselessly. Geneviève's heartbeat quickened. It felt as if the Toyota was about to roll onto its right side.

"I need to think for a second," said Julie. She closed her eyes and visualized the mechanics of the truck. Their front right wheel had nothing to grip onto within the crevice, and therefore it couldn't pull the vehicle forward.

Julie pressed the button that locked the differential, essentially "locking" the rear wheels on an axle together, as if on a common shaft. This would mean both rear wheels would turn in unison, despite the left one dangling in the air with nothing to push against. Julie slowly applied gas. The right rear wheel gripped and slowly the truck inched forward, out of the crevice and back onto flat ground.

They had overcome their last major obstacle, and as they drove on, the bivouac—the final finish line— came into view. Yet as Geneviève looked at Julie, there was only one thing she could think to say: "I wish we could keep on going."

The tears running down Julie's dusty cheeks told Geneviève she felt the same way. They were working in perfect sync, a true team.

When they crossed the finish line the two women whooped with joy as their race mates cheered. For Julie and Geneviève, a decade-long journey had reached its emotional conclusion.

Team 187 ended up finishing 35th overall, and ranked 17th among first-time participants. The final prizes would be handed out at a gala in the seaside town of Essaouira two days later, but the real celebration came that last night in the desert.

Surrounded by women with hearts as full as theirs, Geneviève and Julie danced late into the night. It didn't matter if a woman was 65 or 22, if she spoke English, French or Japanese. Tonight, before they returned home to continue their lives as lawyers, mothers, teachers or doctors, they were all gazelles. They were women who raced in the desert.

They Remembered the *Birkenhead*

The legacy of a long-ago disaster continues to save lives at sea.

—

BY **KEITH MONROE**

Originally published in September 1954

n times of terrible danger at sea, Englishmen aboard ship are likely to say quietly to one another: "Remember the *Birkenhead*!" They know the story of heroism when that famous troopship met disaster in 1852, and it steadies them when panic is at their throats. Sometimes it has helped them die like gentlemen, and often it has steeled them to self-control that saved their lives.

Recently the memory of it brought hundreds of passengers safely through a close call with death, in one of the greatest sea rescues in history. Just before 7 a.m. on March 28, 1954, the British troopship *Empire Windrush* was plowing through the Mediterranean 50 miles off the coast of Algeria. Passengers up early to watch the sunrise suddenly felt the deck shudder and jump. Threads of black smoke began weaving up through the splinters. An ominous rumble came from the heart of the ship.

A seaman stumbled onto deck from a hatchway below. He had no hair or eyebrows, his face was black, and one cheek was laid open. "Fire!" he shouted. "Boiler-room explosion!"

He died a few minutes later. Three other crew members who had been in the boiler room were already dead. The fire that started there was spreading hungrily, and in a few minutes the midsection of the ship was a furnace.

Officers and crew worked fast and smoothly. They tried first to find a way of stopping or containing the fire. Captain William Wilson soon realized the blaze was beyond control. "Smoke was pouring all over the ship and flames were shooting out," he told British Admiralty officials afterward. "I gave orders to abandon ship."

Everyone aboard could see that this meant probable death for many, because some of the lifeboats and many of the storage racks for life preservers were cut off by flames. The ship was crowded. It was carrying servicemen home from the Far East, on leave or for discharge. Many had their families with them. There were 1,515 people on board—including 125 women, 87 children and 17 invalids. Only 12 lifeboats with capacities of from 49 to 100 persons remained. Obviously, there wouldn't be room for everyone.

But nobody panicked, and nobody rushed the boats. Through a megaphone came the calm voice of Colonel Robert Scott, commander of the troops on board: "This is the *Birkenhead*

drill. Stand fast on deck. Wait until you are assigned a boat."

An Australian wife asked her English officer husband, "What's the *Birkenhead* drill?"

"It isn't actually a drill," he explained. "In England the word 'drill' often means merely 'discipline.' The *Birkenhead* drill is simply to stand by and not move until ordered."

He didn't tell his wife that the *Birkenhead* discipline was used only when abandoning ship and required all men to stand motionless, at whatever peril, while women and children were put in the lifeboats.

The men on the *Empire Windrush* lived up to the *Birkenhead* legend. Smoke-grimed and half-blinded crew members stayed at their posts while the soldier-passengers quietly formed ranks on deck with their officers. The lifeboat crews herded women and children into the boats. The husbands and fathers, still in ranks, took off their coats and tossed them into the boats so that the women might keep warm if rescue ships were a long time arriving.

By 7:20 the women and children and invalids were all in the lifeboats.

The fire was now at blast-furnace intensity. The glass in porthole windows was cracking like snapping whips from the heat. There still remained room in the boats for some men.

"How shall we select which men may go?" one of the officers asked Colonel Scott.

Scott quoted the old rule that the British follow in such emergencies: "Funeral order, of course—youngest first."

The officers moved down the ranks, picking out the younger soldiers and ordering them into the last lifeboats. If even one of those who remained had dashed for a boat, scores might have followed him, but none moved. Because there was no disorder, all lifeboats were lowered without capsizing, though they were packed with passengers.

When the last lifeboat was launched at 7:32, some 300 servicemen and crew members remained on deck. With typical British reserve they showed no emotion as they watched the boats pull away. Captain Wilson's uniform was in rags and his shoes were nearly burned off his feet but he roamed his ship, leading a final search to make sure no one had been left below. He then supervised crewmen as they gathered kegs, planks and anything else that would float and tossed them into the sea so the men would have something to cling to later.

Colonel Scott shouted final orders to the soldiers: "Remove outer clothing and shoes and go overside— but do not swim to a lifeboat!" With the fire at their heels the men jumped into the sea. No other ships were in sight. No one could say how long it would be before rescue arrived, if ever. An elderly deck steward, most of his hair burned off and his face blistered, continued to lash deck chairs together as makeshift floats for men in the water. When the job was finished he jumped, followed by Colonel Scott and Captain Wilson—the last to leave the ship.

The heavily loaded lifeboats stood by, a temptingly short distance away. Most of the men in the water could easily have reached one, but they obeyed orders and kept their distance, clinging to flotsam if they could find any. Some supported shipmates who could not swim. "There was not the slightest sign of panic," Wilson reported later. "The discipline was remarkable."

At 8:15 a cheer went up from the boats. A freighter had been sighted on the horizon, coming to the rescue. Three more ships appeared within a half hour. Picking up the swimmers took slow and careful work, but by 10:15 the last survivor was saved. The glowing hulk of the *Empire Windrush* sank soon after.

Not a single person was lost except the four killed by the original explosion. The *Birkenhead* drill had paid off.

It had paid off in other disasters. When the British liner *Republic* was rammed off Nantucket Island on a black night in 1909, the men followed the *Birkenhead* tradition. Women and children were ushered into the lifeboats, then the wounded and sick, then the male passengers, and at the very last the crewmen themselves. Not one life was lost, although the ship was abandoned in total darkness with a huge swell running.

In 1913 the British freighter *Templemore* caught fire 800 miles east of the Virginia coast. Its cargo

of oil, lumber and cotton burned fast and fiercely. Yet all lifeboats were launched efficiently, and the crew was picked up without the loss of a life when a rescue ship arrived four hours later.

The men on these ships and others behaved in a tradition of discipline and courage that was established aboard the *Birkenhead* and has never been forgotten in England. The *Birkenhead* was a troopship carrying soldiers and their families. En route to South Africa it struck an uncharted rock 40 miles off Capetown at 2 a.m. Ten minutes later, while quietly desperate people were stumbling and crawling through a wilderness of smashed timber to reach the deck, the ship struck again and split in two. The forepart sank, but everyone managed to reach the stern in time.

Of the 630 people aboard, 170 were women and children. The soldiers were green recruits; the few officers were young. Three lifeboats were left, and only 60 persons could be put into each of them.

The disintegrating ship had only a few minutes to live. Anyone who didn't get a boat faced almost certain death because the waters swarmed with sharks. The stage seemed set for mass panic. Yet there was none. The commander of the troops, Colonel Sidney Seton, ordered the men mustered on deck. The hundreds of soldiers accepted their fate with composure and stood in ranks by torchlight while their children and womenfolk were placed in the three serviceable boars. As the last boat pulled away, its passengers saw the lines of red-coated soldiers still standing rigidly at attention, as if on parade. The crewmen stood with them when the water closed over their heads as the *Birkenhead* sank.

A few men struggled to the surface after the ship went down and were able to climb onto the main topsail-yard or hang onto debris. A rescue ship picked them up that afternoon. But 436 men died before help came. One was Colonel Seton, who hung on to a plank until he saw two cabin boys drowning nearby. He pushed his plank to them, and when he found that it would not support all three, he let go and sank.

Captain John Wright of the 91st Regiment, one officer who survived, reported: "The resolution of all hands far exceeded anything that I thought could be effected by the best discipline. Everyone did as directed; there was not a murmur among them. Orders were carried out as if the men were embarking instead of going to the bottom."

The *Birkenhead* story stirred England and the Empire. Monuments were erected to its men. A half century after the tragedy, Rudyard Kipling commemorated it in verse:

> To stand an' be still to the
>   Birken'ead drill
> Is a damn tough bullet to chew.

Before the *Birkenhead* disaster, when a ship was stricken it was usually "every man for himself," and the ensuing panic led to bestial stampedes; the strongest got the lifeboats, and women and children were often left to die. The tradition of "women and children first," made immortal by the famous troopship in 1852, has saved innumerable lives. In the terror of the burning *Empire Windrush*, it saved 1,511 more.

How Is He Still Alive?

The skewer that impaled Xavier Cunningham could slice into vital arteries as doctors tried to pull it out.

BY **BONNIE MUNDAY**

Originally published in February 2020

The stainless steel skewer that Xavier Cunningham found in his backyard was about a foot and a half long and the width of his pinkie. One end had four sharp prongs; the other had a single point—it was the kind of rod used to cook rotisserie chicken over a grill. It also made the perfect spear. Xavier and his friends Silas and Gavon, all ten years old, took turns seeing who could chuck it the farthest. They ditched the skewer near a neighbor's tree house, sticking the four prongs in the ground as an anchor. They then climbed up the tree house's ten-foot ladder.

But once they were in the hut they were under attack by an aggressive swarm of wasps. "I'll get my mom!" Xavier said as he descended the ladder. About halfway down, a wasp stung his left hand. Xavier swatted at it with his right, lost his balance and fell, facedown. Before breaking his fall with his arms, he felt a sting just under his left eye. *Was that a wasp?* he wondered.

In fact, it was the skewer. About six inches of it was now buried in his head. Screaming, he got up and ran to his home, some 50 feet away.

Gabrielle Miller, 39, was upstairs folding laundry in the house she shared with her husband, Shannon Miller, and their four children. Shannon had taken two of their kids to an arcade that day, while Gabrielle stayed home with Xavier and his 14-year-old sister, Chayah. She heard her son screaming and thought, *When will he grow out of this stuff?*

Xavier—called Bear by his family, after a story Shannon had told him as a toddler—always made a fuss over the smallest scratch. If one of their dogs jumped on him, he'd start screaming; he was too scared to walk Max because the dog pulled on the leash.

Gabrielle was almost down the stairs when Xavier pushed the front door open, shrieking, "Mom, Mom!"

Gabrielle tried to make sense of what she was seeing. "Who shot you?!" she said. It looked as if there was an arrow through her son's face, and a single trickle of blood ran down from it. On the back of his neck was a lump— the tip of the skewer that hadn't pierced the skin. "Chayah, go find the boys. I'm taking Bear to the hospital!"

Emergency room personnel acted quickly when Xavier walked in, giving him painkillers and sending him for X-rays. The skewer didn't appear to have hit his spine, but an X-ray can't show tissue damage.

They had to send him somewhere with more advanced imaging equipment—Children's Mercy Hospital in Kansas City, Missouri, about 40 minutes north of the family's home. To prevent Xavier from moving his head, hospital staff put a plastic cervical collar on his neck, and they wrapped his entire head in white gauze to help stabilize the skewer. The only thing left exposed besides that mud-caked metal rod was his mouth.

At Children's Mercy, doctors performed a computed tomography (CT) angiogram to see whether the skewer had pierced one of his major blood vessels. They were amazed to find that it had barely missed every vital artery when it penetrated his head. It was like the proverbial threading of a needle, only with life-and-death consequences.

But there was a wrinkle. Metal shows up on CT scans as vivid white, without defined edges. If the skewer had any kind of bend, a sharp edge, or a gap, then pulling it out now would be rolling the dice, as it could catch on an artery and rip it open.

The only other way to get a clear picture of the skewer was with

biplane angiography—a process that gives doctors a crystal clear three-dimensional view inside the vascular system. It is performed using highly specialized equipment that only some hospitals have. One of them, the University of Kansas Hospital, was just five miles away. An ER doctor got on the phone with KU to describe the case they were about to transfer.

It was now around 7:30 p.m. Xavier had been impaled for six hours.

Koji Ebersole, MD, an endovascular neurosurgeon at KU, was playing

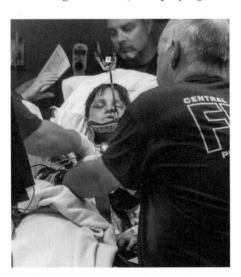

Xavier being helped at his local emergency room. On the way, he'd told his mother, "I'm dying, Mom ... I love you."

tennis when his cell phone rang. At the side of the lighted court, he took the call from another KU doctor telling him about a boy who had been impaled by a large metal skewer.

Dr. Ebersole looked at the photograph from the hospital on his phone. *Whoa,* he thought. He'd never seen anything like it. The poor boy was lying on a gurney with a huge spike sticking about nine inches out of his face. *How was this kid even alive?*

Dr. Ebersole headed home to make some calls. He knew they'd need to get the boy into the angiography suite quickly to see exactly what the skewer had damaged, or still could damage, and then remove it while carefully monitoring its exit. If it hadn't yet harmed any key vessels, it could uncork something on its way out and cause a stroke or worse.

Using the angiography suite required a team of 15 to 20 medical staff. It would be tough to get the right people together so late on a Saturday evening. But could the boy wait until morning? For now he was stable physically, but what about mentally? What if he panicked, grabbing at the skewer? Everything depended on his state of mind. Dr. Ebersole asked the doctors in the pediatric ICU, where Xavier and his family waited, to talk to them and gauge whether he was brave enough to hold on. When Dr. Ebersole heard back from the hospital at 11:30, he made his final call of the evening. "We can wait until the morning," he told a fellow doctor. "The boy is on board."

It was late now, almost midnight, and Xavier's ICU room was dim. He'd just told doctors he could stay calm a few more hours. He understood that his life depended on his not trying to pull out the skewer. He remembered a scene from the movie *Black Panther*. The hero, T'Challa, impales the villain, Killmonger, with a spear through the chest. Killmonger declares he's ready to die, pulls the spear out and collapses.

"Go to sleep, Bear," Xavier's mom told him now, holding his hand. His head was still wrapped in gauze. The four-pronged end of the skewer was still caked in mud; everyone had been afraid to try to clean it, lest it jiggle the skewer and cause injury. They could give him only painkillers, which

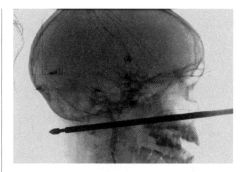

An X-ray of Xavier's skull. Doctors feared that nicking an artery while pulling out the skewer could cause a stroke.

made him sleepy, but not sedation; that could make the tongue collapse, suffocating him.

"When you wake up in the morning, this thing will be out," a nurse told him.

Xavier slept fitfully. Each time he woke up, he asked, "Is it out yet?"

"No, not yet sweetie," Gabrielle would tell him. Xavier cried softly each time he heard this.

Gabrielle, her eyes moist with tears, whispered to her son, "You're the strongest person I know."

"The biggest problem is that barbed end," Dr. Ebersole told the team assembled at 8:30 a.m. in the angiography suite. Dr. Ebersole pointed to

From left: Shannon, sisters Teah and Chayah, and Gabrielle, with Xavier and Max.

a computer screen; it revealed that the skewer had a notch in the shaft near the point. If they pulled the skewer out the way it went in, the notched tip could rip an artery open.

They discussed pushing the skewer through the back of Xavier's head to expose the notched end and cut it off before pulling the whole thing out through the front. But the rod was made of thick stainless steel, and it would take a lot of force to break that end off. The movement that this would create could tear arteries. They'd have to pull it out the way it went in—if that was even possible to do without killing him.

Xavier was wheeled to the angiography suite about 10 a.m. Meanwhile, his family and many friends were in the waiting room, and every nearby church had dedicated that Sunday to praying for the boy.

In the angiography suite, some 20 surgeons, specialists and nurses wearing blue radiation-protective gear and lead-lined glasses were waiting.

Two giant "arms," one attached to the floor and the other hanging from the ceiling, were positioned close to Xavier's head. Each arm held two X-ray devices that moved in wide arcs around his head to create three-dimensional images. The images were displayed in real time on a large flat-panel screen hanging from the ceiling at eye level for Dr. Ebersole.

Dr. Ebersole could now see the one-in-a-million trajectory the skewer had taken: It had missed his spine by about half an inch. It had missed the cerebellum, the part of the brain that controls things such as balance and speech, by the same margin.

It had punctured the carotid sheath but didn't appear to have damaged the hypoglossal nerve or the vagus nerve, which control tongue function, the swallow reflex and the voice box. Also in the carotid sheath is the jugular vein. The skewer had torn the jugular, but it appeared to have sealed itself. The skewer had missed his facial nerve, which controls facial expression and the sense of taste.

Most important, it had missed both the crucial arteries: the carotid and vertebral. In fact, it appeared to have actually nudged them out of the way without puncturing them. *I don't know how a kid can be so lucky,* thought Dr. Ebersole.

"Jeremy," he said, "put your hands on that thing, get a feel for how easily it'll move." He was speaking to chief resident Jeremy Peterson, MD, a burly 32-year-old who stood near the boy's head. It would be up to him to remove the skewer.

Dr. Peterson was nervous, but he placed a steady left hand at the base of the skewer to anchor it; his right hand grasped just above his left. He nudged it back and forth ever so slightly while Dr. Ebersole watched on the monitor in case the movement harmed a vessel. It barely moved. "It feels pretty solid," Dr. Peterson said.

"OK, let's go," said Dr. Ebersole. He'd be the eyes, watching the monitor constantly, while Dr. Peterson would have the feel of the thing as he worked on getting it out. He'd have to do it slowly, strongly, yet smoothly, mostly from his right arm, while being careful that his left hand didn't exert too much pressure—because it was literally on Xavier's eye.

The skewer was surprisingly hard to budge. It took all the strength in Dr. Peterson's right arm to move it an inch—then it stopped. "It feels stuck on something."

"OK, hands off," ordered Dr. Ebersole. Dr. Peterson carefully let go of the skewer and took a half step back, while Dr. Ebersole enhanced the view. The clearer picture showed that it was hung up on a neck ligament, not a danger. But the skewer was now so close to the vertebral artery that it was bending it.

"Jeremy, angle it a little toward you." This would move it away from that artery. Dr. Peterson did as asked. "OK, go again." It worked. Dr. Ebersole watched the tip of the skewer safely pass the vertebral artery.

"It's sliding pretty easy now," said Dr. Peterson. Yet he continued to pull it very slowly, especially as it passed the jugular—would it pull open the seal that had formed? No; the jugular had healed itself. Then, finally, the last hurdle: the carotid artery. The metal passed it smoothly too—and suddenly, the skewer was out.

It was 3 p.m. when Dr. Ebersole came into the waiting room and told Xavier's parents, "It's out. He's OK." There was a cheer from the crowd of family and friends.

"Can I hug you?" asked Gabrielle, and she did.

The only physical evidence of Xavier's unplanned adventure is a tiny bump beside his nose and some numbness on the left side of his face. And yet, things are different nowadays. Xavier often grabs the leash to take Max for walks—he's no longer scared to walk the dog alone. And when he gets a scrape or has a mishap, instead of going straight to ten on the pain scale the way he used to, he'll look at his mom calmly and say, "This hurts pretty bad."

"Is it skewer bad?" Gabrielle will ask, and Xavier will laugh.

The Day We Became Brothers

Hidden from the world, four fatherless boys learned to open up to one another.

BY **ALBERT DIBARTOLOMEO**

Originally published in June 1997

was ten years old when my father died. Eight months later my mother, believing I needed more structure and male role models, enrolled me in the Milton Hershey School in Hershey, Pennsylvania.

A knot in my stomach grew tighter as our car approached the school that February day in 1964. I told myself over and over, *Be brave. Be the man you're supposed to be now that your father is dead.* Actually, I had little idea how to be a man, except to act stoically. So I never uttered a word of protest, though every fiber of my body resisted the trip. *What was my life going to be like? How would the other boys react to me?*

When we arrived, my mother and I were given a tour of the spotless ranch-style house, which accommodated the 16 boys in my unit, with an apartment for our houseparents. My mother remained behind while I was shown the bedroom I would share with another boy.

I returned to an empty living room. "Where's my mom?" I asked.

"Oh, she left," someone said.

Left? My legs went limp. The school's counselor, I learned later, had urged my mother to slip away without saying goodbye so as to avoid a scene.

I spent the afternoon sitting in my new bedroom. When the boys returned from school at four o'clock, they came to look at me. "Boy, you're short," said one kid.

"Lee, he's not short. He's tiny."

"Let's call him Ant," Lee said.

"No, Bug is better."

"I like those extra eyes he's got," said another, pointing to my glasses. "Maybe we should call him Bug Eyes."

With that, they went about their after-school chores. After dinner, we were allowed an hour of free time until study period. I picked up a book and started reading, but my room-mate, Jim, interrupted: "There's some things you should know if you don't want to be laughed at. Somebody might ask you to go get a bucket of steam or a left-handed wrench. Your toothbrush will sometimes disappear. Oh, and you'd better keep those glasses in sight all the time."

"Thanks for the warning."

He shrugged. "You'll also probably have to fight somebody soon if you don't want to be treated like dirt."

I sat quietly for a while, absorbing what Jim had told me. Suddenly he asked, "It was your father who died, right?"

"Yes."

He looked into his book. "Nobody's going to want to hear about that."

That night I did my best not to cry. I failed.

Jim's predictions turned out to be true. I got into a fight after two boys played catch with my glasses. Angry, I rammed my head into the stomach of one and we began to slug each other.

I never mentioned my father to anyone, and no one mentioned their lost parents to me. The unspoken code that Hershey boys held was not just the denial of feeling, but the denial that our dead parents had existed at all.

One of the favorite games among the boys was tackle. A football was thrown into the air, and whoever caught it tried to run directly through the rest without being brought down. Tackle was less of a game than an excuse to deliberately smash our bodies into each other for the main purpose, I realized later, of dissipating our frustration and anger.

Late that first spring, Mr. and Mrs. Carney became our new houseparents, and loosened the reins on us. Soon, however, chores were not being done well, and some boys spoke to the Carneys rudely.

Mr. Carney's response was to hold a meeting in which the boys could air their beefs and the Carneys could express their expectations of us. To me, the Carneys were not the "enemy" but surrogate parents who genuinely cared about us. During the meeting I pointed out, "If anything, the Carneys are too nice. Some of you guys are taking advantage of that."

Cold shoulders promptly turned my way. As if to relieve me from the others, the Carneys took me that Friday evening to their weekend house, where I spent most of the time fishing.

When I returned to the unit, Jim notified me, "Everybody thinks you kissed up to the Carneys. You have a lot of guys mad at you."

Great. I had spent months trying to fit in, and in a minute I had ostracized myself. I was not surprised to find my toothbrush in the toilet the next morning.

Two months later I overheard Lee, Bruce and Jim trying to decide how to pass a long August afternoon. "Let's go down to the pond," Jim suggested.

"I say we go to the hideout," said Lee, referring to a mysterious place I had not yet seen.

"Why don't we just hike," Bruce offered, "and see where we wind up?"

"I'll go for that," Jim said.

"Me too," I added.

"Who invited you, twerp?" Lee said to me.

"Don't call me that."

"OK, Four Eyes."

Wanting to avoid another fight, I swallowed my anger.

"I'm heading that-a-way," Bruce said, motioning to the open spaces. "If anybody wants to come, fine. If not—adios." He started off, and Jim and Lee followed. I lingered briefly, then joined the group.

After crossing meadows dotted

with wildflowers, we found a thin stream. Jumping over it we soon came to a cornfield that stretched as far as we could see. "Let's go in," Lee said, and without hesitation we did.

We quickly became hidden but pushed deeper into the field. The broad leaves slashed at our faces, and the ears of corn clunked us in the head. We crossed perhaps 30 rows before we halted and sat on the ground.

"Is this the hideout?" I asked.

"Hardly," Lee said, removing cigarettes from his pants.

"I don't think you should smoke in here," Jim said.

"Me neither," Bruce added.

Lee shrugged. "All right, no sweat." This surprised me, but I soon learned there was something about the cornfield that changed our usual behavior. It was a place that melted inhibitions and tough-guy exteriors. Here, hidden from the world, we found ourselves on those roads into our interiors that we traveled only in private.

Bruce was the first to talk. "My father was a salesman," he said, "and one day a truck ran a stoplight and smashed into his car. He died right there. I was in school, and they called me home. I knew something big had happened but I never thought it was that."

"Mine died of a heart attack," Jim said. "But I hardly knew him. I was four. He was a schoolteacher."

After a pause Lee said, "My old man was a carpenter. He made me a boxcar one summer. He took me to a couple of Yankees games, and once we went to the circus. Then he got bone cancer. He was a big man, but by the time he died, he was like a string bean." Lee's eyes had become wet. He looked away into the depths of the cornfield.

The others did too. They were wearing expressions I had never seen before. No one spoke for a long time. All I heard was the rustling of the cornstalks and the cry of a distant crow.

Bruce broke our silence. "You didn't tell us about your father," he said to me.

I wasn't sure I wanted to. I had survived Hershey by remaining "strong," and I now felt reluctant to allow myself to weaken. But like them, I was eager to unburden myself of something I simply couldn't keep bottled up any longer.

"Mine had diabetes for a long time," I said haltingly, "but it was his kidneys that went bad, and that's what killed him. My mother was called away by the hospital one night. I was in bed when I heard the door open and her footsteps coming up the stairs. They sounded ... sad, so I knew before she said, 'Your father passed away.'"

We didn't talk much about how we felt when our fathers died; we could tell from our faces. Instead we talked about our fathers' lives. What they were like. Who they were. If we'd had pictures we could have shared them. But none of us had a photo, not even in our rooms, it being generally accepted that such a thing was too much of a reminder of a life more bright and normal than the one we now lived.

The talk about our fathers gave way to other, less weighty matters, and soon we were back to a lighter mood. But when we stepped out into the sunlight we did so with a common understanding—that life handed out its losses, but that we did not have to suffer them alone. For the first time we realized that we held in common not only parental loss but also the need to release the sorrow that came with it.

As we made our way home, we stopped to drink at the stream. Jim was next to me, and I watched him remove his baseball hat, splash his face and rub his wet fingers through his hair. Then instead of putting the cap back on his own head, he reached over and placed it on mine. The others gathered around, and together we jumped over the stream. And I knew as we returned to the unit that we walked as brothers.

The Wrong Man

After serving 29 years in prison for a crime he didn't commit, Ray Towler was freed by DNA evidence and the tireless efforts of a Cincinnati law professor.

BY **JACOB BAYNHAM**
FROM **CINCINNATI MAGAZINE**

Originally published in August 2011

On a Sunday in May 1981, two cousins bicycled into Cleveland's Rocky River Reservation for a picnic. Josh, 12, and 11-year-old Kate (not their real names) followed the park's winding bike trail for six miles into an area called the valley before stopping to eat. Kate talked about a place she'd found where a log had fallen across the river and you could sit and skim your toes in the cool water below. After lunch, they set out to find it—Kate leading the way, Josh pushing his bike behind. As they walked, a man came out of the trees toward them. He said he had found a deer in the woods with a broken leg. He asked if they would help him.

Josh followed him into the woods. Kate hesitated, then ran after them. After they had walked 152 feet from the bike trail—the police would measure it later— the man turned and unwrapped a revolver from the jacket under his arm. "Lie down!" he ordered. The kids froze. He grabbed Josh's arm

**"Nothing is free, not even freedom,"
says Ray Towler.**

and pushed him into a tree. Josh fell to the ground on his stomach. Then the man dragged Kate a few feet away. "What do you want me to do?" she asked.

Still holding the gun, the man untied Kate's yellow jumper. Then he sexually assaulted her. Josh kept his face buried in the dirt.

The entire "incident," as it would later be referred to in court, lasted less than 15 minutes. When the man had gone, Josh ran terrified from the woods. He found a park ranger, who took Kate to the hospital and radioed other rangers to comb the area. They found no trace of the man.

Thirteen days later, Officer Frank Ferrini pulled over a metallic green 1970 Monte Carlo after it rolled through a stop sign. The driver was a 23-year-old bearded black man named Raymond Daniel Towler. As Ferrini wrote the ticket, he checked the composite picture of Kate's rapist, drawn up from Josh's description. He asked if Towler would come in for some photographs.

Here we go, Towler said to himself. He'd heard about the park rangers hassling black people, and now, he figured, it was his turn. He politely answered the ranger's questions and agreed to the photos. He had no reason not to. A quiet, peaceable man, he lived in a small house nearby with his mother, younger sister and niece. He was a musician and an artist, and that day, he had been sitting in the park with his sketchbook.

At the station, Towler was photographed in front view and profile. When he left the camera room, he noticed his name had been written on a board, next to the word suspect. He didn't know what it meant, but he departed feeling nervous.

He had reason to worry. The snap of the shutter that day set into motion a chain of events that would irrevocably change the course of his life. Three months later—on September 9, 1981—he went on trial for raping Kate. The prosecution's case relied entirely on the word and memory of Kate and Josh as well as two witnesses who had seen a black man in the park that day. Neither of the kids had said that their assailant had a beard, yet two weeks after the rape, both picked the mug shot of a bearded Towler from an array of 11 photos.

The prosecution also admitted physical evidence—Kate's underwear, her yellow jumper, fingernail scrapings and two hairs that the ER doctor had lifted from her. A forensic scientist could find no trace of body fluids on her clothing but concluded that the hairs were "of Negro origin." That was enough for the jury to find Towler guilty of rape, two counts of felonious assault and two counts of kidnapping. After the sentencing, Assistant Prosecutor Allan Levenberg called Towler an "animal" and added, "Anyone who preys on children should be put away and the key lost."

Towler, just 24 years old, was handcuffed and led from court to start his life sentence. But the key to his freedom wasn't lost. It was imprinted in the fabric of Kate's clothes, which would sit on an evidence room shelf for almost three decades.

❖　❖　❖

Towler's first stop was the Ohio Penitentiary in Columbus, a 150-year-old facility with no hot water and broken windows that birds flew through. He was given a thin wool blanket, an inflatable pillow and two sets of clothes; he slept in a cell with four other men. The prison was crowded, and fights were frequent. Three months later, he was transferred to the maximum security Southern Ohio Correctional Facility in Lucasville, where he spent 23 hours a day in lockdown. During the one-hour recreational period when prisoners mingled outside, he saw men kill each other with

> *He never let his hopes falter as his appeals were repeatedly denied. "I've seen guys fall apart," he says.*

homemade knives over gambling debts and love triangles. Most Lucasville prisoners were serving life sentences, sometimes double or triple life. "There was no hope," Towler says. "Guys had charges stacked up so high, they couldn't make any sense."

In his first years of incarceration, Towler filed appeals and legal challenges. He applied to the governor for commutation, he wrote letters to the parole board; but he never let his hope falter as his appeals were repeatedly denied. "I've seen guys just fall apart," Towler says. "And then they go do something stupid,

The more his lawyer learned about Towler's case, the more he thought DNA science would catch up with it.

hurt somebody or hurt themselves. Give up on themselves." So he tried to find a way to face his situation dispassionately but still pursue his freedom. If the system had put him here, he thought, the system would have to get him out.

Towler mostly kept to himself through seven hard years at Lucasville, despite having to live in

at least 20 different cells with more than 50 different cell mates. His good behavior paid off; he was moved to Marion Correctional Institution, where his security level was eventually dropped to "medium" and his freedoms grew. Now he could spend his free time painting, playing guitar and keyboard, and studying. He earned two associate's degrees, in arts and business.

After his fifth year at Marion, Towler became eligible for parole for the first time. With his impeccable record, he allowed himself some hope that he would be released. The parole board not only turned him down but also declared him ineligible for another 15 years. "I think the wording was, 'Because of the seriousness of the crime, releasing you at this time would not reflect justice,'" Towler says. He knew what they really meant: "You're not going anywhere."

In 1994, he was transferred to Grafton Correctional Institution, where he would spend the next 16 years, still serving his time quietly, painting portraits and writing songs.

Towler plays bass guitar with the choir at Mount Zion Baptist Church in Oberlin, Ohio, on Easter Sunday.

In 2006, he wrote two tunes for a kids album, produced by the prison's inmates, called *Wings of Hope*. When word of his contribution got out, his photograph and the charges against him were splashed across the media again. "Sex Offender Credited for Children's Songs CD in Ohio," the headline read on Fox News. Reliving that humiliation opened fresh wounds for Towler. "That was almost worse than getting the 15 years from the parole board," he says.

When O. J. Simpson went on trial in 1995, Towler paid close attention to the use of DNA evidence and began tracking advances in forensic science. Hoping a judge would allow retrospective DNA testing for his case, he saved money for lab fees by painting more, selling pictures to guards and inmates, and sending portraits to his sister to sell on the outside. In 2001, DNA evidence freed Anthony Michael Green, also from Cleveland, who had spent 13 years in prison for a rape he didn't

Towler is the tenth wrongfully convicted person (and the longest serving in Ohio) whom the Ohio Innocence Project has helped to free.

commit. Days before he was released, Green gave Towler the phone number and address of the Innocence Project, which had helped win him his freedom.

The Innocence Project was created in 1992 by Barry Scheck and Peter Neufeld as a legal clinic at Yeshiva University in New York. Its mission was to apply the rapidly advancing field of DNA science to possible cases of wrongful conviction. Scheck and Neufeld used law students to research case histories and draft court motions under the guidance of staff attorneys who represented the inmates in court. When the New York Innocence Project exonerated several long-serving inmates—some of whom were on death row—law schools throughout the country began adopting the model. Ohio started its own project in 2003.

That year, the Ohio Senate passed a bill allowing DNA testing for convicted felons. Towler submitted the paperwork, and a judge approved his request and appointed a defense attorney named John Parker to represent him. Parker, seeking greater expertise, called Mark Godsey, the founding director of the Ohio Innocence Project (OIP).

At 43, Godsey, a professor of criminal law at the University of Cincinnati, is boyishly handsome, with a dry sense of humor and a penchant for karaoke—he knows every lyric of Sir Mix-a-Lot's "Baby Got Back." His thumbs are seldom far from his iPhone, tapping out e-mails and texts at all hours of the day, and his car is as messy as his office.

In September 2004, he and

Parker arranged for Kate's underwear, the fingernail scrapings and the two hairs to be sent to a DNA lab in New Orleans. But the lab found no trace of semen or male DNA in the underwear, and the envelopes containing the fingernail material and hairs were empty. Whether the evidence disappeared by accident, sabotage or some other means remains a mystery, but for Towler, the result was the same: He had just lost another round.

The more Godsey learned about Towler's case, the more he thought science would eventually catch up with it. "I knew that the technology was advancing," Godsey says, "so I kept the file nearby."

In 2008, Godsey arranged for the underwear to be retested. The science of DNA identification had improved, but the likelihood that it could turn up definitive new evidence was still remote. "We're talking about 30-year-old panties that had been sitting on a shelf with, at most, trace amounts of semen from the attacker," Godsey says.

Technicians at a Cincinnati lab tested Kate's underwear for free.

They did find semen in the fabric and DNA from a male that was not Raymond Towler but weren't able to locate any sperm cells. The prosecution claimed that the DNA could have resulted from contamination of the evidence— a man opening the evidence bag and sneezing, for example. "It was a dumb argument," Godsey says, "but we couldn't disprove it." The result was ruled inconclusive, and Towler remained behind bars.

Towler's adjustment to life on the outside hasn't been easy. "I still feel like a tourist," he says.

Then, within months, Godsey heard about a Texas lab that had developed a solution to draw sperm cells out of fabric. He sent the underwear there in the summer of 2009. Testing was delayed until April 2010, but the test results finally arrived by e-mail on May 3, at 6:50 p.m., when Godsey was alone in his office. He will never forget the moment he saw them. "We have now reached a point where testing can be stopped," wrote Rick Staub, the director of the forensic lab in Dallas. The DNA they analyzed from the sperm, he said, is clearly "NOT RAYMOND TOWLER."

When Towler got the news in Grafton prison, a crowd gathered around his bunk. He packed a few things to take with him—his electronic keyboard and paints— and gave away his TV, CDs, stereo and other belongings. The next day, he was in court wearing the clothes a deputy sheriff had given him— a pair of pants, a black sweater and shoes. Towler recalls his agony in the Justice Center in Cleveland, listening to Judge Eileen Gallagher go through the painstaking proceedings.

"I wanted her to hit that gavel real bad," he says. "I kept saying in my head, 'Hit the gavel now so we can leave!'"

Then the judge surprised him by stepping down from the bench and giving him a hug. It was the first affectionate touch he'd received in almost 30 years.

"Mr. Towler, it's a long day coming," she said, and then recited the traditional Irish blessing: "May the road rise to meet you, may the wind be always at your back …"

"I started smiling right there," Towler says. Then the judge slammed down her gavel, flashbulbs exploded and officials opened the door for him to leave. It was May 5, 2010, and after 28 years, 7 months and 19 days behind bars, Raymond Daniel Towler, 52, descended the courthouse steps into the fresh air of the free world.

The grin has remained a permanent fixture. "I've been smiling so much, my jaw's hurtin'," he says, "but somehow I'm just finding the energy to keep smiling."

Towler's adjustment hasn't been easy. "I still feel like a tourist," he says. He's had to relearn the intricacies of social interactions outside prison. Common courtesy has served him well so far, and he learns a lot just watching.

An executive at Medical Mutual

of Ohio in Cleveland overlooked the 29-year gap in Towler's résumé and offered him a job delivering mail in one of the company's offices. He spends his earnings on rent for his small apartment and payments for a 2010 Ford Focus. Recently he went down to an electronics store with his tax rebate and bought a television. The freedom to do something like that, whenever he wants, thrills him. "It don't take much to be happy," he says. "It's crazy how many times I say in a day, 'Man, I'm glad I'm not in prison.'"

When he's not working, Towler paints and plays the guitar for Mount Zion Baptist Church in Oberlin, Ohio. He has formed a band called Spirit and Truth with other exonerated men that has played a couple of Innocence Project fundraisers and plans to record an album. He has also returned to Grafton prison to perform for the inmates, who greeted him with a mixture of warmth, pride and desperation. Towler heard later that when news of his release was broadcast on TV at the prison, the inmates responded with celebratory whoops.

This past May, Towler received compensation money from the state, whose actuaries have determined the value of one year of freedom to be $47,000 and change. He was owed more than $1.3 million—he could also have sued for lost wages—and actually received considerably more, although he's

> **Towler relates his story with the same equanimity that helped him survive the past 29 years.**

reluctant to divulge just how much. It's nobody's business, but he also finds inquiries about how much he "won" from the state absurd: No amount is fair compensation.

"I wouldn't have done it for any amount of money. I don't know anyone with their sanity who would. Money ain't the beginning or the end. It's not what makes you live and breathe. I can't do everything I want to do right now, but I have the opportunity to. The pursuit of happiness—that's a big statement. When those old white dudes wrote that, they knew what they were talking about. That's human nature, to have a dream and go after it without having a chain on your ankle holding you back."

Among the people periodically checking in on Towler is Mark Godsey. The two have become friends; Godsey says that witnessing his release in the Cleveland courtroom that day was one of the most satisfying experiences of his life. "It's the ultimate sense of joy," he says. "There are so few who are lucky enough to get to this stage, where the evidence still exists and the DNA catches up to the case." Back in Godsey's office are boxes and boxes of case files for other OIP clients awaiting the research, court decisions or scientific advances to confirm or deny their claims of innocence.

Towler still has a beard, thicker now than when he went in and flecked with white. It sets off his broad jaw in a way that makes him look biblical, ageless, even though he is acutely aware of the passage of time: His sister, Priscilla, with whom he lived before his arrest, is now a grandmother, and his niece, Tiffany, is now a mom. His mother passed away while he was in prison. Dressed in a red polo with black stripes, Towler relates his story with the same equanimity that helped him survive the past 29 years. For this peaceful man, it's painful to look back at some of the things that happened. "But believe me, it doesn't outweigh the stuff to look forward to," he says, smiling. "Not even close."

When the Water Ran Cold

With backyard wisdom, the author's grandfather explains the secrets of aging and a life well lived.

———

BY **KITSANA DOUNGLOMCHAN**
FROM **MEDIUM.COM**

Originally published in March 2017

I ask my grandpa what it feels like to grow old. He ponders this question while we sit in his office overlooking the yard, the same yard I pulled weeds in when I was a boy.

It is late in the afternoon, but Grandpa is wearing pajama bottoms, slippers and a thick flannel shirt. His face is withered, his once-taut flesh sagging loosely from his bones. A cup of black tea rests on the wooden desk in front of him. Grandpa drank coffee most of his life but switched to tea a few years back, when coffee became too hard on his stomach.

Grandpa's mind brightens and dims like a beam of light underneath a magnifying glass on a cloudy day. But on good days, on days like this one, there's a break in the clouds and the sun shines through again.

He gazes out the office window and looks at his yard, which has gone into a state of decline in recent years. Grandpa no longer possesses the energy to maintain its once magnificent splendor. Tree branches droop over the fishpond he built, the pond's surface covered with a layer of green algae. Weeds sprout around the brick path weaving through the garden.

An empty bird feeder dangles lifelessly from a tree limb.

Grandpa and I spent many hours during my summer vacations from elementary school working in the yard. We started in the afternoon when the sun was near its zenith. Grandpa would don an Oakland Fire Department baseball cap, faded blue jeans and a white T-shirt. Back then, he was a tireless man with a burly body like a sailor.

My main job was weed patrol, because Grandpa performed the glamorous work, excavating the rich California soil for a new addition to his ever-expanding yard. He grew tomatoes on metal stakes and planted strawberries, lettuce and radishes in the ground. And when they were ripe for picking, he'd bring them inside to Grandma's kitchen so they could be prepared.

Grandpa was an artist. The yard and garden were his canvases, the flowers and plants his palette of paints. He was constantly bent over on all fours honing his art, the knees of his jeans stained brown.

At the end of the day, in the early evening, the air would become crisp and cool. Before calling it quits, Grandpa and I would wash up and get a drink of water at the hose on the side of the house. Grandpa would give the T-handle on the spigot a turn or two. The limp hose would stiffen, and then he'd cup his hand underneath the hose, the water pooling tranquilly in his palm. He'd lift his hand to his mouth and drink, quenching his thirst with each sup.

I tried imitating him but could never clench my fingers tight enough, and the water would slip through the slits of my fingers and dribble wastefully to the ground.

But before going inside, we'd fill up the bird feeder next to the pond. I'd go to the garage and find the seed bag, a blend of sunflowers, cracked corn and millet. We'd walk into the garden, sauntering along the brick path to where the bird feeder hung from the tree. Grandpa would remove the top of the feeder—a wooden rooftop—and lift me by my armpits. Then I'd pour the seed into the feeder, my shoes dangling near his thighs.

Grandpa takes a sip of his black tea, still pondering my question on aging. And without ever taking his eyes from the window, he asks me a question. "Have you ever been in a hot shower when the water ran cold?"

I tell him I have.

"That's what aging feels like," he says. "In the beginning of your life, it's like you're taking a hot shower. At first the water is too warm, but you get used to the heat and begin enjoy-

"In the beginning of life, it's like taking a hot shower. Then the temperature drops."

ing it. When you're young, you think it's going to be this way forever. Life goes on like this for a while."

Grandpa gives me a mischievous grin and leans toward me. "And if you're lucky," he whispers, just out of Grandma's earshot, "a few good-looking women will join you in the shower until you decide to settle down."

We both laugh. He leans back in his chair, looks out the window and continues on.

"But you begin to feel it somewhere between your 40s and 50s. The water temperature drops just the slightest bit. It's almost imperceptible, but you know it happened, and you know what it means. You try to pretend like you didn't feel it, but you still turn the faucet up to stay warm. But the water keeps going lukewarm. One day you realize the faucet can't go any farther, and from here on out the temperature begins to drop—you gradually feel the warmth leaving your body."

Grandpa clears his throat and pulls a stained handkerchief from his flannel shirt pocket. He blows his nose, balls up the handkerchief and puts it away.

"It's a rather helpless feeling, truth told," he continues. "The water is still pleasant, but you know it'll soon become cold and there's nothing you can do. I knew a few people who decided to leave the shower on their own terms. They knew it was never going to get warmer, so why prolong the inevitable? I was able to stay in because I contented myself recalling the showers of my youth. I lived a good life but still wish I hadn't taken my younger years for granted. It's too late now, and no matter how hard I try, I'll never get the hot water on again."

Grandpa keeps looking out the window with those eyes that have seen 91 years on this earth. Those eyes that endured the Great Depression in the '30s, those eyes that survived the Pacific Ocean in the '40s, those eyes that witnessed the birth of his three children, five grandchildren and seven great-grandchildren.

He has indeed lived a good life, I say to myself.

Later on that day, after dinner, I drive down to Home Depot and buy a bag of birdseed. I come back to the house, park in the driveway and take the bag of seed out of the car. I open the garage door and find a plastic bucket. I empty the bucket and take it out to the yard, walking alone now. The sun is setting, the twilight changing into night, but I follow the well-worn brick path leading out to the pond, pulling any weeds I spot along the way. When I come to the end of the path, I set the bucket and

seed bag down and lift the bird feeder from the tree limb. I tear a tiny hole in the bag and pour the seed into the feeder. After it's full, I replace the rooftop and hang the feeder back on the tree limb.

I leave the yard. I dump the bucket of weeds in the trash and set the bag of seed inside the garage. I go inside, excited to tell Grandpa about what I've done. But the living room is already dark. I then notice the glow of the television bouncing off the walls and see Grandpa reclined all the way back in his easy chair. A blanket is draped across his legs; his eyelids are closed.

I sit down in the chair next to him. His hands are interlaced across his stomach like a Buddhist statue, his chest rising and falling ever so faintly. I think about waking him up but decide not to disturb his sleep, a sleep that will soon last forever.

I hope he is dreaming the dreams of his youth, remembering the warmth of days gone by, the days before the water ran cold.

Credits and Acknowledgments

"The Best Investment I Ever Made" by A. J. Cronin, *Reader's Digest*, March 1951

"A Mountain of Trouble" by Kenneth Miller, *Reader's Digest*, October 2016
Photographs courtesy David Finlayson

"Let Me Explain …" by Cornelia Otis Skinner, *Reader's Digest*, August 1963
Illustration by *Reader's Digest*

"The Storybook Barber" by Andy Simmons, *Reader's Digest*, December 2016
Photograph by Saverio Truglia

"Our Horse of a Different Color" by Penny Porter, *Reader's Digest*, September 1995

"The Searcher" by Joe Rhodes, *Reader's Digest*, September 2008
Photographs by Tim Tadder

"'Six Hundred Bucks! And Nothing to It!'" by John G. Hubbell, *Reader's Digest*, May 1982

"What I Learned at the Shoe Store" by William M. Hendryx, *Reader's Digest*, November 1993
Photograph copyright Chris Ware/Getty Images

"Lost in the Pacific Woods" by Tom Hallman Jr., *Reader's Digest*, November 2018
Photographs on page 52 and 60 copyright Joseph Shom/Shutterstock; page 55 courtesy Jean Greer; page 56 by Peter Oumanski; page 59 courtesy Rick Prentics/Washington Explorer Search and Rescue Kitsap

"'I Can Quit Whenever I Want'" by Per Ola and Emily D'Aulaire, *Reader's Digest*, June 1997
Photographs by Robert Sebree

"Bear Tracks in the Bathtub" by Irving Petite from *The Christian Science Monitor* (September 7, 1960) copyright 1960 by The Christian Science Pub. Society; *Reader's Digest*, October 1960
Photograph copyright Danita Delimont/Shutterstock

"Miracle of the Flower Boxes" by Peggy Mann, *Reader's Digest*, July 1973
Photograph copyright lightphoto/Getty Images

"The Family That Robbed Banks" by Skip Hollandsworth from *Texas Monthly* (June 2014), copyright 2014 by Texas Monthly, *Reader's Digest*, November 2014
Photograph by Johnny Miller; framed photos courtesy Sheriff's Office, Fort Bend County, Texas

"High-Wire Act" by Juliana LaBianca, *Reader's Digest*, April 2017
Photograph on page 93 by Matt Nager; page 94 courtesy Mickey Wilson

"The Lady Who Lived Through Winter" by Joan Mills, *Reader's Digest*, April 1974
Photograph copyright Martin Wikar/EyeEm/Getty Images

"Blowout at 17,000 Feet" by Peter Browne, *Reader's Digest*, February 1991
Illustration by Paul Jennis